COMMUNITARIAN POLITICS IN ASIA

With the collapse of European socialism in the late 1980s, ascendancy of the liberal capitalist democracy and individual self-interest became prevalent in the West. In contrast, many polities in Asia, both by tradition and choice, have explicitly adopted communitarianism as a national ideology, for example Confucianism in Korea, Hong Kong and Japan, Islam in Malaysia and the *Pancasila* in Indonesia. Here, communitarianism arguably informs public policies and political practices and the concept of the 'social' in terms of responsibilities and collective welfare is preserved.

Communitarian Politics in Asia examines instances in Southeast and East Asian countries where communitarianism is both articulated as national ideology and embedded as the ethos of social life and assesses the relative merits of a set of practices in their respective local political context. The book not only augments existing international debate on liberalism and communitarianism but also provides empirical examples of communitarian political practices that will substantiate and/or refute conceptual points, such as redistributive justice and costs to individuals, in this ongoing debate.

Chua Beng Huat is Professor of Sociology at the National University of Singapore.

POLITICS IN ASIA SERIES
Formerly edited by Michael Leifer
London School of Economics

ASEAN AND THE SECURITY OF SOUTH-EAST ASIA
Michael Leifer

CHINA'S POLICY TOWARDS TERRITORIAL DISPUTES
The case of the South China Sea islands
Chi-kin Lo

INDIA AND SOUTHEAST ASIA
Indian perceptions and policies
Mohammed Ayoob

GORBACHEV AND SOUTHEAST ASIA
Leszek Buszynski

INDONESIAN POLITICS UNDER SUHARTO
Order, development and pressure for change
Michael R.J. Vatikiotis

THE STATE AND ETHNIC POLITICS IN SOUTHEAST ASIA
David Brown

THE POLITICS OF NATION BUILDING AND CITIZENSHIP IN SINGAPORE
Michael Hill and Lian Kwen Fee

POLITICS IN INDONESIA
Democracy, Islam and the ideology of tolerance
Douglas E. Ramage

COMMUNITARIAN IDEOLOGY AND DEMOCRACY IN SINGAPORE
Chua Beng Huat

THE CHALLENGE OF DEMOCRACY IN NEPAL
Louise Brown

JAPAN'S ASIA POLICY
Wolf Mendl

THE INTERNATIONAL POLITICS OF THE ASIA-PACIFIC, 1945–1995
Michael Yahuda

POLITICAL CHANGE IN SOUTHEAST ASIA
Trimming the Banyan Tree
Michael R. J. Vatikiotis

HONG KONG
China's challenge
Michael Yahuda

KOREA VERSUS KOREA
A case of contested legitimacy
B. K. Gills

TAIWAN AND CHINESE NATIONALISM
National identity and status in international society
Christopher Hughes

MANAGING POLITICAL CHANGE IN SINGAPORE
The elected presidency
Kevin Y.L. Tan and Lam Peng Er

ISLAM IN MALAYSIAN FOREIGN POLICY
Shanti Nair

POLITICAL CHANGE IN THAILAND
Democracy and participation
Kevin Hewison

THE POLITICS OF NGOS IN SOUTHEAST ASIA
Participation and protest in the Philippines
Gerard Clarke

MALAYSIAN POLITICS UNDER MAHATHIR
R.S. Milne and Diane K. Mauzy

INDONESIA AND CHINA
The politics of a troubled relationship
Rizal Sukma

ARMING THE TWO KOREAS
State, capital and military power
Taik-young Hamm

ENGAGING CHINA
The management of an emerging power
Edited by Alastair Iain Johnston and Robert S. Ross

SINGAPORE'S FOREIGN POLICY
Coping with vulnerability
Michael Leifer

PHILIPPINE POLITICS AND SOCIETY IN THE TWENTIETH CENTURY
Colonial legacies, post-colonial trajectories
Eva-Lotta E. Hedman and John T. Sidel

CONSTRUCTING A SECURITY COMMUNITY IN SOUTHEAST ASIA
ASEAN and the problem of regional order
Amitav Acharya

MONARCHY IN SOUTH-EAST ASIA
The faces of tradition in transition
Roger Kershaw

KOREA AFTER THE CRASH
The politics of economic recovery
Brian Bridges

THE FUTURE OF NORTH KOREA
Edited by Tsuneo Akaha

THE INTERNATIONAL RELATIONS OF JAPAN AND SOUTHEAST ASIA
Forging a new regionalism
Sueo Sudo

POWER AND CHANGE IN CENTRAL ASIA
Edited by Sally N. Cummings

THE POLITICS OF HUMAN RIGHTS IN SOUTHEAST ASIA
Philip Eldridge

POLITICAL BUSINESS IN EAST ASIA
Edited by Edmund Terence Gomez

SINGAPORE POLITICS UNDER THE PEOPLE'S ACTION PARTY
Diane K. Mauzy and R. S. Milne

MEDIA AND POLITICS IN PACIFIC ASIA
Duncan McCargo

JAPANESE GOVERNANCE
Beyond Japan Inc
Edited by Jennifer Amyx and Peter Drysdale

CHINA AND THE INTERNET
Politics of the digital leap forward
Edited by Christopher R. Hughes and Gudrun Wacker

CHALLENGING AUTHORITARIANISM IN SOUTHEAST ASIA
Comparing Indonesia and Malaysia
Edited by Ariel Heryanto and Sumit K. Mandal

COOPERATIVE SECURITY AND THE BALANCE OF POWER IN ASEAN AND THE ARF
Ralf Emmers

ISLAM IN INDONESIAN FOREIGN POLICY
Rizal Sukma

MEDIA, WAR AND TERRORISM
Responses from the Middle East and Asia
Edited by Peter Van der Veer and Shoma Munshi

CHINA, ARMS CONTROL AND NONPROLIFERATION
Wendy Frieman

COMMUNITARIAN POLITICS IN ASIA
Edited by Chua Beng Huat

EAST TIMOR, AUSTRALIA AND REGIONAL ORDER
Intervention and its aftermath in Southeast Asia
James Cotton

DOMESTIC POLITICS, INTERNATIONAL BARGAINING AND CHINA'S TERRITORIAL DISPUTES
Chien-peng Chung

COMMUNITARIAN POLITICS IN ASIA

Edited by Chua Beng Huat

Routledge
Taylor & Francis Group
LONDON AND NEW YORK

First published 2004 by RoutledgeCurzon

Published 2016 by Routledge
2 Park Square, Milton Park, Abingdon, Oxon OX14 4RN
711 Third Avenue, New York, NY 10017, USA

Routledge is an imprint of the Taylor & Francis Group, an informa business

Typeset in Sabon by LaserScript Ltd, Mitcham, Surrey

British Library Cataloguing in Publication Data
A catalogue record for this book is available from the British Library

Library of Congress Cataloging in Publication Data
Communitarian politics in Asia / edited by Chua Beng Huat.
p. cm. – (Politics in Asia series)
Includes bibliographical references and index.
1. Communitarianism–Asia, Southeastern. 2. Communitarianism–East Asia. 3. Asia, Southeastern–Politics and government. 4. East Asia–Politics and government. I. Chua, Beng Huat. II. Series.
HM758.C66 2004

306.2′0959–dc22

2003020761

ISBN 13: 978-0-415-48030-7 (pbk)

CONTENTS

CONTRIBUTORS

Daniel A. Bell teaches political theory at the City University of Hong Kong. His recent publications include *East Meets West: Human Rights and Democracy in East Asia* (2000) and the co-edited *Confucianism for the Modern World* (2003).

Ho Mun Chan is Associate Professor in the Department of Public and Social Administration, City University of Hong Kong. His research interests include comparative social and political philosophy, applied ethics and public policy, and philosophy of science and technology.

Chang Kyung-Sup is Professor of Sociology at Seoul National University. He is currently working on 'compressed modernity' in South Korea.

Chua Beng Huat is Professor of Sociology at the National University of Singapore. On communitarianism he has published, *Communitarian Ideology and Democracy in Singapore* (Routledge, 1995).

Vedi R. Hadiz is Assistant Professor in the Department of Sociology, National University of Singapore. His most recent book is *Reorganising Power in Indonesia: The Politics of Oligarchy in an Age of Markets* (Routledge, 2004).

Robert W. Hefner is Professor of Anthropology and Director of the Program on Islam and Civil Society at Boston University's Institute on Religion and World Affairs.

Tatsuo Inoue is Professor at the Graduate School of Law and Politics, University of Tokyo and publishes extensively in the field of legal and political philosophy.

Anthony Woodiwiss is a professor in the Sociology Department of City University, London. He has written books on social theory and human rights, including *Globalisation, Human Rights and Labour Law in Pacific Asia* (1998) and *Making Human Rights Work Globally* (2003).

ACKNOWLEDGEMENTS

The chapters in this book were first presented at the International Conference on Communitarianism and the Practice of Politics, held in Singapore on 27–28 September 2001. The conference would not have been possible without the generous financial support from Friedrich Naumann Stiftung, Goethe-Institut Inter Nationes Singapore and Faculty of Arts and Social Science, National University of Singapore. The generosity of these institutions and their respective directors – Mr Uwe Johannen, Dr Heinrich Blömeke, Dean and Professor Lily Kong – is greatly appreciated.

In addition to the chapters published in this collection, other presentations were made by German scholars to provide comparative perspectives to the issues discussed. Professor Michael Baurmann presented a paper entitled, 'Trust, Cooperation and Large Numbers: Free Markets and the Communitarian Challenge', and Professor Walter Reese-Schäfer presented a paper entitled, 'Communitarianism and Communitarian Activities in Germany'. The papers in this volume have all benefited from the exchanges that these two papers generated.

During the conference a panel on the theme was convened, with presentations from the Honorable Surin Pitsuwan, MP and Former Minister of Foreign Affairs, Thailand and Jürgen Morlok, Chairman of the Board of Trustees, Friedrich Naumann Stiftung. That they were willing and able to attend the conference added valuable insights into the discussions, from the practical political and administrative realm.

The conference was held almost immediately after the world-changing event of the destruction of the World Trade Center in New York City on 11 September 2001. The specter of terrorism was still fresh in everyone's mind. The participants showed their commitment to a shared intellectual concern and boarded the then much-dreaded aeroplanes to journey to Singapore, a location in the midst of the world's largest Islamic community. Of equal significance was the fact that their loved ones allowed them to get on the aeroplanes at all. Without both the intellectual commitment of the writers and the emotional support they received from members of their families, the conference would not have come to pass and this book would not be in print. To all of them, I am truly grateful.

1

COMMUNITARIAN POLITICS IN ASIA

Chua Beng Huat

The 'quest' for community, the anxiety that motivates communitarianism as an ideology, is not new in the intellectual West. It was a preoccupation of major thinkers of the nineteenth century. Its re-emergence in the early 1970s among academic political philosophers in the West was provoked, according to Bell in this volume, by the publication of John Rawls's, *A Theory of Justice* (1971). By the mid-1980s, David Miller notes, there is plenty of communitarianism around and 'it was becoming common to speak of communitarianism as an ideological rival to liberalism' (2000: 87). As Miller's comment implies, there is by now an extensive literature on communitarianism that defies any review and summary, without doing excessive violence to the nuances of the different arguments and positions. Consequently, only a brief review of the points that will set the context of the present volume will be undertaken here.

Against liberalism

Taking Rawls's text as the 'paradigm statement of contemporary liberal theory', Mulhall and Swift (1992) have used it as the foil to lay out the various 'communitarian' critiques of liberalism. A central condition to Rawls's theory of justice is 'people's freedom to make their choices, and to change their minds, not whatever it is that they choose' or alternatively put, what matters 'is not so much that people make good choices as that they are free to make their own choices'; that is, choices are or should be made without consideration of 'which ways of life are better than others' (Mulhall and Swift 1992: 6). This fundamental conceptualization of an asocial individual, unconstrained by the society and culture within which one exists, but endowed with the freedom to define, at will, what is 'good' for oneself, immediately opens itself to objections from many angles. The first objection concerns the ontological status of such an individual: 'Who is the shadowy "person" that exists independently of, and able freely to choose, the ends that give her meaning and value?' (Mulhall and Swift 1992: 10). As no one is ontologically so disposed, Bell argues in this volume, 'that it makes no sense to begin the political enterprise by abstracting from the interpretive dimensions of human beliefs, practices and institutions'. The concept of the individual is so highly abstracted from one's actual social milieu that it is without any character. For Gray, such an 'individual' is but a cipher, 'without history or ethnicity, denuded of the special attachments that in the real human world give us the particular identities we have' (1995: 5).

In the objections to the liberal conception of the individual lies the seed of what has come to be called 'communitarian' critique of liberalism. Bell, in his chapter, summarizes the central point of the critique thus: 'effective social criticism must derive from and resonate with the habits and traditions of actual people living in specific times and places'. In sum, individuals are embedded and bound by the cultural practices of the community in which they reside and which constitute them as who they are, realized in and through the reproduction of their everyday life; at its most sociological extreme, the individual may be said to be 'parasitic on society for the very way she thinks, including the way that she thinks of herself as an individual' (Mulhall and Swift 1992: 14). Therefore, any conceptualization of social and political life should begin with the concrete ontology of the community and of the embedded individual – life in and as a community – rather than the eraser of the former and the disembodiment of the latter. It is this emphasis on the concept of a community-embedded 'self' that had enables the discursive grouping of the critiques and critics of 'Rawlsian' liberalism to be grouped as 'communitarians' rather than any self-proclamation of a common position; indeed, as Mulhall and Swift point out, unlike liberalism, 'communitarianism' is hardly a 'self-conscious tradition' (1992: xvii).

With the insistence of community-embeddedness of individuals, communitarian critique has the effect of countering the ambition, if not pretension of liberalism towards universalism. As it would logically lead to stressing of differences between particular societies and cultures, each with its own justifiable and coherent set of practices, including its own conceptions of what is just. However, this was not to be. Hewed from Western philosophical traditions, these philosophical critics had been reluctant to surrender their own deep-seated liberalism and their own desire, as descendents of the Enlightenment, to seek universality for Western liberalism and humanism. This is, perhaps, partly why the philosophical critics, unlike sociologists and political scientists and other professionals, have been reluctant to declare themselves communitarians.[1] Their liberalism comes through in their adherence to the liberal ideal of an 'egalitarian political morality', whose 'bottom line in political morality is the claims of individualism and that these are spelt out in terms of the demands of justice and rights' (Gray 1995: 2). This abstract issue of individual rights and freedoms has been translated into the concrete problem of 'exit' from one's community: an individual should have the right of exit if the community to which he/she belongs is extracting a cost of membership beyond his/her willingness to bear. In such instances, Kymlicka (1995) has argued, the liberal outsider should have the duty, if not the right, to intervene in societies where individual members are not granted the right of exit.

One of the consequences of the emphasis on rights and freedoms of individuals is that, as Gray puts it bluntly, 'The community invoked by these writers is not one that anyone has ever live in, an historic human settlement with its distinctive exclusivities, hierarchies and bigotries, but an ideal community, in its way as much of a cipher of the disembodied Kantian self as the communitarians delight in deflating' (1995: 7). As discussed in the next section, contrary to Gray's assertions, American communitarians have consistently defended liberalism in the US as entirely compatible with communitarianism. However, the success of this defense is equivocal. Put more firmly, the lack of familiarity with concrete instances of what may be called 'communitarianism in practice' on the part of the philosophers has led Bell, in his chapter, to lament that 'it must be conceded that 1980s' communitarian theorists were less than successful at putting forward attractive visions of non-liberal societies'; the example Bell has in mind are Walzer's (1983) use of the Indian caste system and McIntyre's (1981) evocation of 'Aristotelian ideal of the intimate, reciprocating local community bound by shared ends, where people simply assume and fulfill socially given roles'. To cap this discussion of the communitarian reaction and critique against liberalism in Western philosophy, it would appear that the debate has been conducted at a 'great distance from political life' (Gray 1995: 7).

Political context of the 1980s

The entry of communitarianism as alternative to liberalism into popular and substantive political debates in the mid-1980s coincided historically with the collapse of actual experimentation with socialism in the ex-Soviet Union and Eastern Europe. The collapse has, as one of its effects, the shutting down of discursive-ideological spaces for communism, socialism and even social democracy. It left European and American intellectuals despondent, without a counter-discourse against globalizing liberal capitalism. To their ideological champions, liberal democracy and market capitalism – increasingly referred to as 'neo-liberalism' in contemporary academic and popular parlance – was about to realize its dream of universality. Fukuyama (1992) confidently propounded that the triumph of the West over Soviet Russia in the Cold War heralds the 'end of ideology' as liberal democracy and market capitalism will no longer face any future contest, effectively leading to 'the end of history'.

Beyond the philosophical debates, the triumph of neo-liberalism has its visible effects in the everyday social life. The subtleties and nuances of philosophical debates are displaced by popular versions of liberalism that equate individual freedoms and rights with unreflective and unabashed claims of preference, rights and privileges of self-interest. At the societal level, the conceptual and substantive slide of liberalism into 'libertarianism' requires scant intellectual work. For example, during the week when Canada legalized same-sex marriage, an explanation for its coming to pass is so reported in a local newspaper:

> The push for minority rights in politics, the professions and the social packing order evolved into the convictions that no one should be constrained by someone else's moral or religious views, and then morphed into the view that individual rights triumph all.
>
> People now say 'Private life is private life. We don't want other people interfering. If we're not hurting anyone, what's the problem? Why are you in my face?' It's a collective growing up.
>
> (*Toronto Star*, 22 June 2003, quoting an academic social historian)

One could argue that what we are witnessing, in the above reportage, is the social realization of the unencumbered individualism of liberalism. The apparent excesses of popular liberalism, which is not without its philosophical and political defense and defenders, in turn unleashed in others, the deep apprehension of a world in which the idea of the 'social' – which is, of course, simultaneously an expression of the cultural – is destroyed. The perceived and real need to preserve the social, to recover the 'community', found its expression through the idea of communitarianism. The idea gathered under its banner, individuals from the ideological 'left, right and center' (Miller 2000) who desire the reshaping of public institutions accordingly.[2] Among them were the self-proclaimed 'new communitarians' in the United States who, in contrast to the philosopher-critics who disavowed the 'communitarian' label, readily placed their names on a public manifesto, *The Responsive Community Platform: Rights and Responsibilities* (Etzioni 1998: xxv–xxxix). Concurrently, in the early 1990s, they founded a new journal, *The Responsive Community*, to propagate their intellectual and political project.

Armed with a very generic definition of 'communitarianism' as 'of, pertaining to, or characteristic of a community' (Etzioni 1998: ix), the new communitarians intend on 'taking communitarian ideas from the campus to the larger society; sharing them with public and community leaders and the citizenship at large, both in the United States and abroad' (Etzioni 1998: x). From the history of its emergence and in the pages of the journal, it is apparent that their faith in liberalism remains undiminished. To their minds, the liberal ethos in the US has been misdirected, if not subverted, by the gradual but obvious slide, since the 1960s, into excessive insistence of individual rights, or group/cultural rights writ large; a slide into libertarianism.[3] Their declared mission is, therefore, to re-establish 'the balance between social forces and the person, between community and autonomy, between the common good and liberty, between individual rights and social responsibility' (Etzioni 1998: x) Its stance is to find a 'third way' between 'the pull of radical individualists from one side, and the tug of authoritarians on the other' (Etzioni 1998: xvii).

Substantively, the new communitarians are consciously 'social problem'-oriented, seeing the 'problems' as arising from either or both excessive individualism and declining social institutions and their moral authority; the latter has supposedly been subverted by 'a society that increasingly threatens to become normless, self-centered, and driven by greed, special interests, and an unabashed quest for power' (Etzioni 1998: xxvi). The institutions and social problems on which the new communitarians focus their reform efforts are, not surprisingly, the family, the education system, followed by the 'political' community and eventually, the human community, each one increasingly more abstract and more imagined. Not surprisingly, as the new communitarians move from the concrete institutions, such as family and schools, to the abstract and imagined ones, their ability to pinpoint problems and offer 'solutions' also becomes increasingly abstract, often couched only loosely by an undefined, indeed undefinable, concept of the 'common good'.

For example, on the family, the manifesto favors '*two-parents [who] are better able to discharge their child-raising duties* if only because there are more hands – and voices – available for the task' (Etzioni 1998: xxviii, emphasis original); implicitly, this declaration has its target the high divorce rates in the US. On education, the proposal is that '*all education institutions (from kindergartens to universities), recognize and take seriously the grave responsibility to provide moral education*', which should consist of '*those values that Americans share*' (Etzioni 1998: xxix, original emphasis). Again the emphasis on 'shared values' is aimed at the fragmentation of the nation by individual rights and group right claims leading to the absent of a 'political community' (Taylor 1998). Against the claims of respect for cultural groups, not exclusively ethnic communities, the question of whether the larger 'society' has the right to intervene in fostering cultural change towards the a 'common good' raises its head. The frustration that this cannot be easily achieved within the constitution of the state has been particularly frustrating, for example, in the new communitarian understanding of AIDS prevention and drug abuse.

The above examples drawn are illustrative of the concrete concerns of the new communitarians in the US. This editorial introduction to the present collection on communitarian politics in Asia is clearly not the place nor is it its purpose to evaluate the successes or failures of these new communitarians who are, in any event, engaged in long-term reforms rather than short-term results. A more comprehensive assessment of their political position is undertaken by Bell in his chapter in this collection. For now, given the contrast between their positions with the Asian instances discussed below, it would be useful to reiterate the observation that the new communitarians are committed liberals who are out to save liberalism from itself by their emphasizing the need to re-establish the centrality of 'community' at every level of public life in a liberal US. The difficulties and frustrations of this undertaking can be readily gleaned from the defiant tone of this statement:

> to acknowledge that moral equality requires respect for diversity does not mean we must yield to parochial passion, or accept distortions of moral principle. When we are told, for example, that cultural assimilation amounts to genocide, or that every difference of origin or disposition is a radical difference, we should strongly object. These are prescriptions for fragmentation. They cannot build that unity of unities we call community.
>
> (Selznick 1998: 6)

Indeed, one sympathizes with the new communitarians because the liberal language of individual rights and freedoms undeniably stands in the way of community. Furthermore, the liberal society that is the US appears to be so bereft of any institutionalized instruments for taking the responsibility for the 'social', that '[a]ny evocation of the community good as grounds for restraint in this politics tends to be viewed with suspicion' (Taylor 1998: 50). This is perhaps the grounds upon which Gray, as mentioned earlier, raises his skepticism that the idea of 'community' is no more a cipher to the communitarian thinkers who are unable or unwilling to jettison liberalism.

Asia as context

Significantly, the historical demise of the real-socialism of Soviet Union and Eastern Europe coincided with the rise of capital in East Asia and Southeast Asia. Were it not for this coincidence, liberal democracy and market individualism would have been able to realize their universalizing desires and hegemony without any antagonist. As Fukuyama puts it succinctly:

> The most significant challenge being posed to the liberal universalism of the American and French revolutions today is not coming from the communist world, whose economic failures are for everyone to see, but from those societies in Asia which combine liberal economies with

> a kind of paternalistic authoritarianism. Asia's tremendous economic success has led to a growing recognition that the success was due not simply to the successful borrowing of Western practices, but to the fact that Asian societies retain certain traditional features of their own cultures – like strong work ethic – and integrated them into a modern business environment.
>
> (1992: 238)

As Fukuyama clarifies, East and Southeast Asia have embraced global capitalism but not liberal democracy; each location preferring apparently its own 'traditional' values. The designation of these local cultural practices as 'authoritarianism', paternalistic or otherwise is a way of noticing the absence of liberal ideology in these locations. Thus East and Southeast Asia demonstrate, substantively and conceptually the de-linking of capitalism from liberal market individualism. There are no liberal traditions here.

However, the individualizing effect derived from the intrinsic logic of capitalism is another matter. Capitalism needs to transform populations into individual active competitive wage earners with individualized rewards. This process of the proletarianization of the self is an insight that is known to every wage earner in the reproduction of his/her everyday life. The individualization effect is, of course, not restricted to the workplace but has the tendency to seep and spread into other spheres of social life, most observably, but not exclusively, in the emergent culture of competitive consumerism in developed economies. Indeed, the developed capitalist nations of the West bear witness to this process in the gradual ideological transformation of liberal individualism into its excess – into libertarianism.

Not surprisingly, therefore, some Asian politicians, social scientists and public intellectuals have the same criticism of 'liberalism' as the new communitarians. To their minds, the US typifies a 'liberal' society and polity. It is a political and social system that emphasizes individual rights, where government is reduced to a minimal state whose task is merely to provide the legal framework for orderly economic and other social and individual transactions; differences between parties are settled in court, where each party makes claims on the basis of rights; there appear to be no other moral basis for social order. Within such a system, the concept of the social can only be conceptualized negatively, as an injunction against trespassing on another's rights and interests. No collective basis can be built on this negative conception. Obviously, this reductionist picture is a serious simplification of the actual cultural and political practices in the US, but for political ideological purposes such a 'caricature' is more useful than a complex and nuanced picture.

As late developers of capitalist economies, the ideological trajectory of liberalism in the West appears to be a lesson that emerging capitalist Asia should learn and its fate one to avoid. This ideological image of liberalism's slippage into excessive individualism has become something to resist by both leaders and populace in capitalist Asia. Thus, in contrast to the liberal new communitarians who valued individualism in itself and sought only to keep it in check by the evocation of the 'social', of community, East and Southeast Asian people have taken the presence of community in their midst as given and sought to contain, if not keep out, the 'community-corrosive' consequences of the individualizing effects of a capitalism that they embraced materially. In Asia, communitarianism is thus a counter-discourse to liberalism, not a reformist one.

Community as taken for granted

In contrast to liberal communitarians who begin with the sacrosanct individual rights and freedoms and argue against its perversion by excess, many vocal Asian politicians and intellectuals begin exactly at the opposite end, namely, the obviousness of the 'social'. From the point of view derived from everyday life, the central premise of communitarianism is intuitively unproblematic, immediately recognizable and eminently reasonable to any individual. From an ordinary point of view, the idea that one is always part of a larger social unit and, thus, obligated to orient oneself responsibly to coordinate activities with others and meet the needs of others as one meets one's own is necessarily taken for granted in the smooth functioning of flow of everyday life. In this sense, that one is part of a larger social unit is uncontroversial and without doubt.

Additionally, an individual also routinely takes for granted that one is a member of more than one such larger social unit and that the degree of involvement with these different units is dependent on the contextual immediacy of the respective units. However, as a general rule, the intensity of involvement is proportional to the degree of intimacy; the scale of involvement thus runs from family, networks of friends and colleagues, residential based neighborhood and beyond that, identification with the nation of which one is citizen, and occasionally, beyond the nation to global issues, such as environmental issues or contribution to charity organizations with global reach. In all these instances, there is a sense that one's own well being and destiny is inextricably tied to those of the other members of the units. As the levels of rights and obligations towards each of these units remain largely silent rather than explicitly codified, there are significant degrees of freedom for individual preferences in practice; only when rights and obligations are explicitly codified, such as the law, is non-adherence or violation subject to negative sanctions. Such is the intrinsically social 'nature' of everyday life for every individual.

This everyday life level of the sense of organization, of structure, of order, of community provides the emotional and material resources for the formalization of a 'sense of community' into an ideology at various levels, progressively from the most immediate and concrete to pragmatic politics to abstract principles, from the 'vernacular' to 'political' and 'philosophical' (Frazer 1999: 11). From a concrete if ill-defined sense of 'community' to 'communitarianism', the 'taken-for-granted' is transformed into a conscious articulation as an explicit 'value'. From the point of view of vernacular-communitarianism and its taken-for-granted, everyday conceptualization of 'community', the liberal insistence of an unencumbered individual is distinctively an 'unnatural' idea. Furthermore, within this ideological frame politics is always about the management of the social rather than the adjudication of conflicts between individuals. It is this vernacular communitarianism that many political leaders in East and Southeast Asia ride on and abstract it into an explicitly spelt out 'national' ideology and use it to rationalize general political governance and specific administrative polices.

However, the ideological transformation of community to communitarianism does not completely erase the 'problem' of individualization and individualism. Within the taken-for-granted attitude of everyday life, one is always aware of being part of a series of social units; equally one is aware that membership in these social units creates a feeling of constraint, of repression of one's desires. No individual is so thoroughly socialized that there is no trace of a 'residual' sense of self, of agency, that does not react to repressions by the social.[4] Furthermore, the costs extracted by membership are often difficult to bear lightly by individuals. It is here that the idea of the 'individual' with 'natural' rights and freedoms, the conceptual core of liberalism, has its appeal at all, including of course people in Asia. Consequently, to successfully inscribe a communitarian ideology unto the social body, it is not enough to draw on the everyday sense of the social, it is also necessary to explicitly contest the liberal ideology as the ideological Other. It is here that the earlier mentioned intentionally reductive conceptualization of liberalism is pressed into service.

Evidence of high rates of divorce, of single parenthood, of teenage pregnancies, of unemployment, of drug addictions, of alternative lifestyles and polymorphous sexuality, and of crimes, similar to those used by the American new communitarians, is used by some Asian politicians and public intellectuals as evidence of the downsides of 'Western' liberalism. Notice that in this move, liberalism is ideologically 'demonized' as 'Western' and its effect on Asian esteem for 'social harmony' can only be wholly negative. Different political regimes in capitalist Asia, from South Korea to Indonesia, began to seek different modes and strategies to inscribe this dichotomous conceptualization of 'Western individualism' and 'Asian communitarianism' unto their respective social body and body politics. At the most extreme, Asian politicians, with or without popular electoral legitimacy, began to impose so-called 'collective' values and attendant social policies by fiat rather than through public deliberations. This was the case with Indonesia when the now-removed President Suharto imposed the ideology of '*Pancasila*' as the highest national principles unto every level of social organization, from elementary schools to military institutions and political parties. The liberal democratic critique of Asian 'authoritarianism' has, of course, been contested by local politicians and public intellectuals.

Asian responses to liberal-capitalist critique

If triumphal liberal-capitalist discourse had fed off failed socialism in Eastern Europe, its intervention into the political spheres in 'Asia' has a different and contrasting trajectory. The Cold War, from the 1950s until the mid-1980s, motivated US and Europe to pour large amounts of capital as aid and investments into many anti-communist political regimes in Asia, often ignoring the latter's human abuses. Some of these regimes have succeeded in engendering rapid economic development and improved the material life of their respective citizens, without liberalizing the political sphere. Of these, the single-party-dominant states, with or without military backing, such as Taiwan, South Korea, Singapore and Malaysia, were as glaringly successful economically as they were ruthless in suppressing political dissent on the road to successful national capitalist growth. By the early 1990s the threat of communism was all but eliminated, although the Cold War lingers on in certain flash points in Asia such as North Korea and the cross straits issues between the People's Republic of China and Taiwan. Nevertheless, advocates of liberal-capitalism, armed with the discourse of human rights, began to lift the veils of legitimacy of many of the economically successful Asian nations and uncover the records of abuses and repressions and campaign for the institutionalization of political and civic 'freedoms' in these nations.[5]

Having successfully organized the economy and achieved more than respectable growth without democratic politics, these regimes had been reluctant to succumb to external and often domestic pressures for political liberalization. To the extent that the less than democratic social and political structures and organizations developed by the regimes had contributed significantly to the economic growth in the first place, there seemed to be few compelling reasons for change. Any deficits in political 'legitimacy' were rationalized away in terms of the impressive rates of growth itself. For example, suppression of labor rights had been rationalized as necessary to produce industrial peace, which had in turn contributed greatly to the productive capacity of all the so-called Newly Industrializing Economies (NIEs). However, the 1997 Asian regional financial crisis exposed many of the weaknesses of the economic structures that were consequences of corrupt and repressive political interventions. Subsequently, the ability of some regimes to 'trade-off' authoritarian repressions and economic growth became severely constrained, thus quickening the pace of political democratization, as in cases of South Korea and Taiwan.

Faced with criticisms of abuses and repressions, the regimes and their intellectual promoters in the Asian NIEs began to articulate, retrospectively, the ideological system that had supposedly 'underpinned' their respective societies and accounted for the economic successes. Predetermined by liberalism as its discursive Other, this retrospectively articulated 'ideological system' turned out, not surprisingly, to be the various versions of communitarianism. One of these versions is the 'Asian Values' discourse which argues that in contrast to the individualism of the West, Asian cultures have always emphasized the well-being of the 'collective' as its fundamental value and as one fundamental principle of social organization. It was claimed that the set of Asian Values – including high work ethics, education attainment, family and group orientation – could be distilled from, thus in continuity with, the major 'Asian' civilizations and traditions. This argument was promoted most vigorously by the leaders of Singapore and Malaysia, the two most successful economies in Southeast Asia. It had also tacit and sometimes explicit support from segments of the leadership and intelligentsia of the other NIEs. The argument also found cultural resonance in the populations in these nations. Reflecting this regional configuration, Confucianism and Islam were included in the 'Asian' traditions while the place of Indic-Hindu traditions was muted, if present at all.

Ironically, the 'rediscovery' of Confucianism was not initiated by East Asians themselves but by Western scholars to 'explain' the rapid rise of capitalism in East Asia from the 1960s. In the search for an explanation for this rapid rise, scholars from Western academic institutions came up with what might be called, after Weber, 'The Confucian Ethics and the Spirit of East Asian Capitalism' (Tu 1991; MacFarquar 1980). What was essentially a thesis on economic development was appropriated by some politicians and discursively transformed into a political value and an attitude towards 'collective' orientation, which in turn finessed an explanation for the supposed absence of 'popular demands' for liberal democracy. The central tenants of Confucianism may indeed be read as a progressive embedding of a relational-self in higher and higher levels of collectivity: self, family, nation, the universe under Heaven. In the case of Islam, the idea of the community of believers and each individual member's obligations and duties, including financial ones, to this community constitutes the foundation of the claim to communitarian orientation. Drawing relatively narrowly from these traditions, critique of liberal individualism was replayed, in successful capitalist Asia, in terms of the collective-oriented 'Asian values' against 'West' individualism, specifically the US-styled popular liberalism.

There was therefore a historical concurrence of the emergence of new communitarian critique in both US and Western Europe and the so-called

'Asian Values' critique in East and Southeast Asia against excessive individualism. However, in the West, where the actual political sphere is dominated by liberal democracy, the communitarian–liberal debate took place largely on the conceptual plane among academics. In East and Southeast Asia, the debate continues in the realm of actual politics of state power and is reduced to questions of 'good governance' (read: stable and benevolent if authoritarian government), 'economic growth' and 'better material life' for the once impoverished population and, as noted by Hefner in his chapter, philosophical subtleties are largely ignored. Juxtaposing 'Asian Values' against liberalism has enabled some Asian governments to defend themselves against critiques of absence of 'political' and 'civic' rights in their countries with an argument for the priority of economic and social rights that are more immediately important to people in the developing world and emergent economies; an issue taken up in greater detail in Bell's chapter.

Apart from the earlier-noted Fukuyama, there are other Western intellectuals who recognize, if only grudgingly, that some form of communitarianism is in fact at work in these Asian countries. For example Miller, in his exposition of the 'left, right and centre' communitarianisms, briefly noted 'Singapore or other places in Asia' as approximating the model of 'right communitarianism'; the set of Asian Values by which Singapore is governed has conceptual affinity with conservative values in the West (Rodan and Hewison 1996). Miller defines 'right communitarianism' as an ideological position that holds that the community is inclusive and 'a source of authority' and in identifying with a community, 'I subject myself to the customs and conventions that it embraces' (2000: 104). This 'subjugation' of the self to a community has its dark logical and substantive entailments, which the British conservative thinker, Roger Scruton, conceptualizes as the 'price of community': 'sanctity, intolerance, exclusion, and a sense that life's meaning depends upon obedience, and also on vigilance against the enemy' (quoted in Miller 2000: 14).

Scruton's exposition of the 'price of community' makes apparent that slippage from inclusiveness of community members to intolerance, exclusion and demonizing of others as enemies and from abiding by the community's conventions to blind obedience to the authority of community is an imminent possibility within communitarianism as political ideology. In practice, the possible slippage to blind obedience is enhanced by a political structure which allows the incumbent of political powers to abrogate to themselves the exclusive right to define the 'collective' interests and act on this definition as a measure of 'good government'. The slippage, in good faith or bad, institutionalizes political authoritarianism in the name of the community. For example, for Miller, the Singaporean 'right communitarian' government has slipped into 'authoritarianism', when the state imposes 'a received set of moral values on unwilling subjects' (2000:

107). He may be referring to the new national ideology, the so-called 'Shared Values' introduced in parliament, with the central theme of society before community, community before self and family as the basic unit of society; a concern taken up by Chua in his chapter.

This possible slippage into political authoritarianism in political practice is a constant source of skepticism and critique of the claims to communitarianism by some Asian political leaders, such as Mohamad Mahathir of Malaysia and Lee Kuan Yew of Singapore. Pronouncements of 'communitarian' sentiments by these politicians are read cynically as thin veils of authoritarianism, which supposedly accounts for the longevity of these individuals in the seats of absolute power, with or without procedural democracy. To the extent that no Western country has declared itself to be guided explicitly by communitarian ideology, it begs the question of whether 'right communitarians' will turn 'authoritarian', should they come into power in the US, Britain and Western Europe. If not, why not? Furthermore, if not, then, what would a 'right communitarian' government in the West look like?[6] On the other hand, a general outline of an Asian country which explicitly espouses a communitarian national ideology can be limned readily; leaving a more thorough analysis to the other chapters in this collection.

One Asian instance: Singapore

Singapore, since 1968, has been governed by a single party, the People's Action Party (PAP), without disruption. It has since then won every general election conducted every four to five years and each time won close to all the seats contested. During its ascendancy to power in the immediate years of decolonization, repressive measures were commonly used to suppress dissent and eliminate opposition: including deregistration of radical trades unions, detention without trial of allegedly communists or other 'subversive' activists, closing of newspapers and taking defamation suits and making very significant financial claims against politicians from other political parties. Amendments had been made to reinforce repressive laws that were a legacy of the British colonial regime, while disingenuously disclaiming responsibilities for initiating such laws. For example, the Internal Security Act has been amended to reinforce the power to detain anyone that the Minister of Home Affairs subjectively deemed to be subversive to the national interest. Although unsavory repressions in which the hand of the state is highly visible are now relatively rare, manipulation of legislations as both instruments of social control and instruments that favor the PAP in electioneering continues and is unlikely to change in the near future.

Under PAP absolutist regime the economy of Singapore has grown and the material life of its population improved far beyond any reasonable expectations at the point of its political self-government in 1959 and subsequent independence in 1965. The rate of growth is indeed of mythic proportion and accordingly labeled miraculous by admiring observers. For many of the developing countries and cities, Singapore has become a model of what is possible if there were political will and social determination. This economic achievement has enabled the PAP government to stand squarely without flinching, let alone retreat, in the face of criticism of authoritarianism, particularly from liberals. It stands on its economic track record and embraces a self-understanding as a 'moral' guardian of the nation's interest and claims to practice communitarian politics through its social policies.

he PAP government perceives the social body of Singapore to be especially vulnerable to Western liberal individualism precisely because the country's relative capitalist economic success has greatly expanded the material life of the entire population. On the one hand, it recognizes the cultural demand of capitalism to be competitive at every level of social organization, from individual to firm to nation. It is incessantly exhorting its population and firms to meet the intense global competition, lest the firms collapse leaving behind trails of unemployed people and bringing down the national economy. On the other, it is also deeply aware that intense competition has the tendency towards hyper-individualism and intensification of class divisions, both made far more visible by the different lifestyles that are displayed through rapidly expanding consumerism in everyday life. Such tendencies in emphasizing the competitive advantages of consumption derived from one's wealth have potential negative effects on social solidarity of every social unit, from family to society. The government believes that these tendencies can be ameliorated by continuing economic development and expansion of material life. While economic expansion may intensify inequality, it will nevertheless be a 'tide that raises all ships' and thereby enhances social solidarity. It sees a need to emphasize 'collective' well-being, without dampening the motivation of those who are successful. In this sense, there are good economic reasons for the Singapore government to adopt a 'communitarian' ideology while embracing capitalism.

However, the rhetorical basis for this communitarianism had to be grounded elsewhere, outside the competitive economic sphere.[7] In the Singaporean context, two reservoirs of cultural resources present themselves. One is the above discussed, selective reinvention of some tenets of Confucianism and other 'Asian' belief systems, as the 'Asian Values' discourse in general and reformulated, in Singapore particularly, as the national ideology, known as the Shared Values.[8] In the latter the privileging of the social over the individual is explicitly articulated: nation before community and society above self; consensus instead of contention as the basis of conflict resolution, family as the basic building block of society and, regard and community support for the individual.[9]

Emphasizing the 'social' also opened up the discursive/ideological space to a second ideological resource for the PAP. It enabled the politicians to resurrect the social democratic beginnings of the party. Fabian socialism was imported into Singapore politics and social administration by the founding generation of PAP leaders who had absorbed this ideology while they were students in British universities in the immediate post-war years. Social democratic administrative policies can be seen in the redistributive effects of massive public funding of the national public housing program, expansion of health care provisions, educational opportunities and infrastructure development.[10]

A third-generation PAP ideologue, George Yeo, argues that the 'socialism' or social democracy of the founding generation should not be forgotten or forsaken, in spite of the obvious fall in fortune of the idea of socialism in the contemporary world. Significantly, in this instance, Yeo was evoking a mid-nineteenth century meaning of communitarianism: 'a member of a community formed to put into practice communistic or socialist theories' (Etzioni 1998: ix). He elaborates: in the PAP government's 'supply-side' socialism, state subsidies are made 'to maximize the ability of all human beings', which in turn improves the economic competitiveness of the nation (*Straits Times*, 17 June 1994). Obviously, the so-called supply-side socialism is not aimed at destruction or even restructuring of capitalism but instead abides closely by the disciplinary effects of the market. Yeo further argues, 'Socialism will never die, of course, because it springs from the very nature of man as a social animal. At least, the family will always stay socialist.' Similar to the philosophical anthropology evoked by some communitarians, the idea of the social, the collective is 'naturalized' as the essential human condition. Further reduction of 'socialism' to 'familialism' brings it, however, closer to the foundational concept of a Confucian society and one of the five 'national' Shared Values, which the PAP is attempting to inscribe unto the social body.

Be it Asian Values, Confucianism or supply-side socialism, these ideological articulations are more than just historical references. They are also essentializing cultural strategies aimed at binding the population to the government via the rhetoric of nationhood. They emerged at a particular historical conjuncture when the PAP government perceived an 'invasion' of liberal individualism that allegedly could unravel not only the economy but also its hegemonic hold on power. As noted earlier, critics of the Singapore government seldom address the economic redistributions and their effects on social and material life of the majority of the population but focus on the political sphere, where the PAP is far from democratic in its practices. For example, this oblique reference to Singapore in a book on democratization in Asia:

> A few authoritarian regimes that manifest commitment to collective goals and human rights might have redeeming qualities, particularly if

> they are stable and do not require excessive force to stay in power. But that does not make them democracies. Their supporters should be free to argue the positive aspects of their rule, without ignoring or denying the negative ones, but they should not attempt to claim that they are democracies.
>
> (Diamond, Linz and Lipset 1989: xxv)

The less than democratic political practices of the PAP government have been criticized usually as authoritarian or more generously as 'illiberal' (Bell, Brown, Jayasuriya and Jones 1995), implying that it is unacceptable in a world in which liberalism is hegemonic (Wallerstein 1992). The Singapore instance thus illustrates the discursive and substantive political debate between liberal individualism, as embedded in notions of political rights of individuals as the fundamental basis of democracy and a self-consciously anti-individualistic constitution of a polity and political process, with the procedures of elections and parliament in place, if skewed in favor of the ruling party.

Communitarianism as political ideological resource

To the extent that neither the socially constitutive embedding of the individual nor the residual resisting agency of the individual can be erased ontologically in social life, the political sphere will always be one characterized by a compromise between the conflicting demands generated by these two constitutive features of social life. The ideological predisposition and preference of the ruling party is, of course, a crucial determinant of which one of the two features is emphasized. A liberal government must contend itself with social welfare issue of those who fall out of the economic net; a communitarian government must give vent to the demands for individual freedoms while supporting the shoring up of conservative values of tradition. The human sufferings extracted from dogmatism of either camp will manifest themselves in social political issues that will likely destabilize the political and social order, at the peril of the ruling party. However, the costs of liberal individualism appear to be much better veiled through the development of social welfare measures than the costs of extreme communitarianism, as in some versions of religious fundamentalism.

Furthermore, and significantly, the ruling government does not possess the exclusive ideological ownership of the concepts of community and communitarianism. Their taken-for-granted character in everyday social life makes them available as a discursive/ideological political resource for differently imagined bounded groups to organize themselves into greater social units in political contestation at different levels, from local planning interests to more imagined identity organized around ethnic, religious, national or even global interests, whose organizations collectively constitutes an inclusive notion of the civil society. In the Singapore case, gay rights groups have been applying to constitute themselves as a 'registered' society, under the name of 'People Like Us'. Their application has until now been without success; however, each time the application is turned down, the government exposes its repressive hands publicly, which constitutes a political cost to its claim to being 'democratic'.

Communitarianism as a political ideology is therefore always a contested resource that is available, if unequally, to all contesting parties. The evidential material for the construction of a community varies according to each group's ability to draw on visible or invisible markers and the degree to which the identity claims are honored by the contesting parties. Contesting groups can and will evoke or criticize the concept if they can derive political positional advantages from either of the gestures. A comprehensive analysis of communitarianism in political practices must therefore cover the range of possibilities, from manipulation of the concept by the state to impose social discipline to the use of the concept by local groups in defense of their scarce resources, for example squatter settlement rights,[11] to civil society organizations as communities without propinquity.[12] This idea of communitarianism as a discursive political resource, its evocation as the template of political and social rationality of concrete actions and their effects are what motivates this collection of essays.

The essays

This collection of essays is led by a discussion that sets the stage for this volume's intervention in the ongoing debate between liberalism and communitarianism. Bell's chapter surveys the debate in the US and Britain, which has moved from abstract philosophical debate, in the 1980s, to two different political discussions: issues of human rights in post-communist and post-colonial countries and the moral basis of institutional reforms at the home front. In the first case, intellectuals in Asia drawing on their own contexts and traditions have contested the universalistic tendency of the liberal interpretation of human rights. In the latter case, Bell argues that American reform-oriented liberal communitarianism can derive useful lessons from the actual practices in Asian society, especially when communitarian commitment to one sphere of social life may contradict or jeopardize the communitarian interest of other spheres.

The potential contradictions of overlapping communitarian interests in different spheres of social life are conceptualized by Inoue in terms of the different 'ordering principles' of the three spheres of social life, the state, the market and the community. Each of these ordering principles extracts certain costs from individuals and the society itself: excessive state control constraints individual creativity and freedom, excessively free market neglects those who could not make the grade in a competitive marketplace and excessive cohesion of community deprives the larger society of its ability to change for the benefit of the greater good, in addition to extracting too high a cost from individual members. For Inoue, each of these spheres therefore engenders its own mode of 'tyranny'; hence, he addresses them as a 'triad of social orders' with a 'triad of tyrannies'. The utility of Inoue's conceptualization is examined through the effects that the strong holds that intermediate groups, such as the firm or political factions in the ruling Liberal Democratic Party, have on their members, including pathologies of its individual members and failures of larger social structuring. The next two chapters by Chang and Chua, respectively, also illustrate the ways the different social ordering principles work in different institutional contexts.

Chang's analyses of the costs that the tightly knit patriarchal 'Confucian' family in South Korea extracts from its members, particularly the women and the young, and its negative effect on the larger process of national politics also demonstrates the logical and substantive contradictions between different levels of social institutions that Inoue suggest. In the Korean case, Chang argues, strong 'familism' with its self-interests has prevented its members from fulfilling their larger civic duties, which a fully Confucian society would expect of its citizens. This withdrawal into selfish familism is a consequence of the destruction of the traditional Confucian social institutions by the development of modern capitalist economies. In Chang's words:

> Much of this cultural and ideological heritage [of Confucian familism] has survived into the contemporary era, while its embodying social, political, and economic systems were almost entirely demolished under the turmoil and disruptions of the Japanese invasion and colonial rule, the U.S. military occupation, the Korean War, and the post-war social disintegration.

The question that arises is, of course, could Confucianism be reinscribed into the social and political body of Korea in a global capitalist world of modern nation-states?

If there were a larger Confucian tradition that permeated Korea at one time, Singapore as an ex-British colony had no such tradition. The latterday Confucianism attributed to its population by the Senior Minister Lee Kuan Yew is in a strict sense a 'reinvention'. Nevertheless, the strong familial relations that Chang found in Korea can also be used to characterize contemporary Chinese families in Singapore. The picture in Singapore is, however, complicated by the fact that there are two other visible racial groups, namely 'Malays' and 'Indians' that, together with the overwhelming majority of Chinese, constitute the citizenry as a 'multi-racial' society. The long-ruling government of the People's Action Party capitalized on this multi-racial division as a fundamental condition of governance. Arguing that racial contact points are potentially volatile and might lead to collective violence, political discussions on issues of race and its connections to religion are severely suppressed. On the other hand, many of the government policies are rationalized in terms of the need to 'manage' the racial question, such as proportionate distribution of the three groups in every public housing estate, the establishment of welfare institutions along racial lines and proportionate representation in parliament. These race-based institutions, along with other political maneuverings of the ruling regime, have severely hampered the development of democratic politics in Singapore. The result is that a single party dominant state remains in place after forty years of political independence and will be likely in place in the foreseeable future.

If the Korean polity is one in which Confucianism has been significantly eroded by modern political and economic developments and Singapore is one in which Confucianism is reinvented by political motivation, Chan in his chapter argues that the ideological underpinning of Hong Kong social policy development, during both the British colonial days and as the present Special Autonomy Region of the People's Republic of China, have been very much in tune with the public sentiments of the Hong Kong Chinese population. Furthermore, the ideological concepts are demonstrably Confucian, particularly the concept of *ren*, meaning benevolence. Of particular interest in the context of the liberal-communitarian debate, Chan demonstrates his claims through experiments which are meant to elicit the 'universal' and 'natural' disposition to liberalism, as posited by Rawls' theory of justice. Conducting the experiments with Chinese subjects from Hong Kong, Taipei and Beijing, Chan shows that the results of the experiment fail to verify Rawls's arguments. Furthermore, the Chinese conception of justice hews much closer to the Confucian 'ethics of care': the needy deserve public assistance but individuals should be responsible for their own well-being through their own diligence. Finally, the use of Chinese subjects drawn from different social strata and different urban locations in East Asia lends weight to the claim that Chinese are inclined to collective orientation, even if as an ideology this inclination has been much manipulated by self-interested politicians.

The other major ideological resource for communitarianism in, particularly, Southeast Asia is Islam, the largest religion in the region. As Hefner's chapter points out, with its emphasis on the *ummah*, the community of believers and lack of separation, even distinction, between politics and religion, all Muslim thinkers in Indonesia, and elsewhere, embrace communitarianism, even if there were disagreements regarding the substantive features of its practices. However, and unfortunately, although the idea of communitarianism is constantly invoked discursively in Indonesian politics, it is an idea more abused than used in the country. The *real politik* of the country had undergone anti-communist political upheaval during the mid-1960s, subjected to military-backed, one-man authoritarian rule of Soeharto, known as the 'New Order', a gross misnaming which would have been laughable if not for the tragic consequences of corruption and abuse of power and loss of lives. Soeharto's fall and removal from the presidency after the 1997 Asian regional financial crisis left behind a trail of ethnic and religious group violence throughout the archipelagic nation, from which the nation is just beginning to recover. The Muslim conception of an Islamic nation for Indonesia based on community of believers is as a consequence placed further back into the political agenda. Furthermore, even if it were to be realized, it would have to tread through all the political maneuvering of the different groups that use the name of Islam for their own causes and self-interests.

Alongside and in contrast to Islam, there exists in Indonesia the most explicit articulation of communitarian ideology in Southeast Asia. This is the idea of *Pancasila* – the Five Principles – a supposedly homegrown Indonesian ideological system based on partly the supposedly traditional idea of '*gotong royong*' (Ramage 1995, Bowen 1986) and other 'purportedly authentic Indonesian values of harmony, co-operation, and the family, and which eschew conflict'. During the New Order regime, Suharto had elevated the ideology to the level of the 'sole ideology' of the nation, the *Azas Tunggal*. In his chapter, Vedi Hadiz argues that while the ideology had been captured by the authoritarian state, critics of the New Order were also wont to use the same ideology against the state. He argues that 'rather than mere state ideology', *Pancasila* is 'also deeply ingrained in the collective memory as an integral part of Indonesia's National Revolution – the struggle to create a just society'. He charts the micro-history of *Pancasila*, which may be said to be, by now, much denigrated by critics. Yet, in a contemporary Indonesia characterized by contesting ideologies of statism, whether Islamic populist or secular-nationalist, and economic liberalism, Hadiz argues that 'a reassertion of the social justice tendencies within *Pancasila* would most likely result only from the revitalisation of an essentially long gone political actor – the radical Left'. Here again, the affinity of communitarianism with left politics is duly noted.

Finally, the collection returns to the challenges that communitarianism as practice in Asian locations throws up to the larger issue in contemporary global, political discourse of human rights. Conventionally, Western human rights activists tend to condemn Asian political regimes for the suppression and abuse of political and civic rights of its citizens, while the defenders of Asian regimes emphasize that given the relative economic underdevelopment, economic and social rights should have priority over political and civic rights (Mahbubani 1998: 46–56). In his chapter, Woodiwiss, who has researched extensively on labor laws in various Asian countries, shows how the two sets of rights can be, and perhaps need to be made 'translatable' under different political regimes and further the protection of individuals from abuses of state power under the different regimes. Counter to the liberal individualism that underpins the idea of political and civil rights, he argues that under the hierarchical, patrimonial regimes of many Asian, and other non-Western, societies, ideas of individual political and civic rights are not useful, and indeed empirically absent. On the other hand, claims on the 'benevolence' on the incumbents of the dominant positions in the hierarchy, such as father in families and political leaders of a state, are much more effective, since the 'right' to occupy the dominant position is premised on the idea of his acting 'in the interests of all'. However, in order to 'enforce benevolence' on the incumbent of the dominant position or, put alternatively to prevent power from being 'freely appropriated by the incumbent', the translation the two sets of rights would, according to Woodiwiss, still require the protection of democracy and the rule of law in all contemporary societies.

Conclusion

The chapters in this book collectively illustrate the range of possibilities of politics conducted in the name of community and communitarianism. Framed by Bell's opening discussion of the entry of Asian voices into existing debates on liberalism and communitarianism, each subsequent chapter examines specific instances of communitarianism as political practice in East and Southeast Asian contexts. In every instance, the politics operates on a specific set of concepts that refers back to the idea and presumed presence of overlapping 'communities' in which individual actors are embedded, from the immediate family to intermediate organizations, such as the firm or ethnic group, to the abstract nation. Rather than simplistically and ideologically praise the communitarian practices, whether alleged or real, the chapters show that the realization of the greater good at each level of community also extracts its costs. These costs range from repression of particularistic individual desires to the withdrawal or prevention of individuals embedded in particularistic community, such as the family, from participation in other, higher or lower, levels of community to wholesale repression of political rights. Some cost of belonging is not avoidable. The protection of individual members from excessive costs that result from abuses of those who are incumbent of positions of power in the different levels of community is therefore necessary. In this context, as Woodiwiss argues, representative democracy and rule of law are still the most important institutional tools available for contemporary societies.

However, whether a member of the community is willing to pay the price in exchange for collective well-being is a question that cannot be solved in principle. It has to be resolved by the individual in question, with the community in question providing the rights to exit for anyone who chooses to do so. Those who prefer to privilege community over individuals might see this 'exit' clause as the thin end of the wedge that would destroy the community, fearing a mad rush for the exit once the gate is opened. This fear has often been used to denigrate those who chose exit, indeed it has been used to deny exit altogether. To this argument one can only counsel its proponents to have more faith in what the community can beneficially provide and that such benefits are unlikely to go unnoticed by its members. This is an intermediate step to the development of fully representative democracy and the rule of law in many developing nations.

To close on a personal note: Although often chastised by holders of political offices for their relative liberalism, liberal minded Singaporeans generally remain convinced of the benefits of community in good faith, even if the costs extracted are sometimes difficult to bear with equanimity. Significantly, there are no great popular outcrys against the idea of collective well-being among the citizens, as they become increasingly better educated, better informed and more aware of the difficult balance between the realization of their individual desires and freedoms and responsibility to family, religious and racial groups and nation. If there were a common lament among these Singaporeans, it is that the holders of political power have shown less faith in the people than the people deserve and thus have been more repressive in the use of state power than it needs be in the sustaining of the spirit of multiple levels of community in the everyday life of citizens.

References

Anwar Ibrahim (1996) *The Asian Renaissance.* Singapore: Times Books International.

An-Na'im, Abdullahi A. (ed.) (1992) *Human Rights in Cross-Cultural Perspectives.* Philadelphia: University of Pennsylvania Press.

Bell, Daniel A. (1993) *Communitarianism and Its Critics.* Oxford: Clarendon Press.

Bell, Daniel A. (2000) *East Meets West: human rights and democracy in East Asia.* Princeton: Princeton University Press.

Bell, Daniel A., David Brown, Kanishka Jayasuriya and David Martin Jones (1995) *Towards Illiberal Democracy in Pacific Asia.* London and New York: Macmillan/ St Anthony's College, Oxford and St Martin's Press.

Bowen, John R. (1986) 'On the political construction of tradition: *gotong royong* in Indonesia', *Journal of Asian Studies* 45(3): 545–561.

Calhoun, Craig (1998) 'The public good as a social and cultural project', in W.W. Powell and E.S. Clemens (eds) *Private Action and the Public Good.* New Haven: Yale University Press, pp. 20–35.

Chatterjee, Partha (1998) 'Community in the East', *Economic and Political Weekly*, 7 February pp. 277–282.

Chua Beng Huat (1995) *Communitarian Ideology and Democracy in Singapore*. London: Routledge.

Chua Beng Huat (1999) '"Asian Values" discourse and the resurrection of the social', *Positions: East Asia Cultures Critiques* 7(2): 573–592.

Clammer, John (1993) 'Deconstructing values: the establishment of a national ideology and its implications for Singapore's political future', in Garry Rodan (ed.) *Singapore Changes Guard*. New York: St. Martins Press.

Diamond, Larry, Juan Linz and Seymour M. Lipset (1989) *Democracy in Developing Countries: Asia*. Boulder, Colorado: Lynne Rienner.

Etzioni, Amitai (ed.) (1998) *The Essential Communitarian Reader*. Boulder: Rowman and Littlefield Publishers.

Frazer, Elizabeth (1999) *The Problems of Communitarian Politics*. Oxford: Oxford University Press.

Fukuyama, Francis (1992) *The End of History and the Last Man*. London: Penguin.

Gellner, Ernest (1994) *Conditions of Liberty: civil society and its rivals*. New York: Allen Lane.

Gray, John (1995) *Enlightenment's Wake: politics and culture at the close of the modern age*. London and New York: Routledge.

Kamenka, Eugene (ed. 1982) *Community as a Social Ideal*. London: Edward Arnold.

Kymlicka, Will (1995) *Multicultural Citizenship*. Oxford: Oxford University Press.

MacFarquar, Roderick (1980) 'The post-Confucian challenge', *The Economist*, 9 February.

MacIntyre, Alasdair (1981) *After Virtue*. London: Duckworth.

Mahbubani, Kishore (1998) *Can Asians Think?* Singapore: Times Books International.

Miller, David (ed.) (2000) 'Communitarianism: left, right and centre' in *Citizenship and National Identity*. Cambridge: Polity Press.

Mulhall, Stephen and Swift, Adam (1992) *Liberals and Communitarians*. Oxford: Blackwell.

Ramage, Douglas (1995) *Politics in Indonesia: democracy, Islam and the ideology of tolerance*. London: Routledge.

Rawls, John (1971) *A Theory of Justice*. Cambridge, Mass: Harvard University Press.

Rawls, John (1999) *The Law of the Peoples*. Cambridge, Mass: Harvard University Press.

Rodan, Garry (1992) 'Singapore's leadership transition: erosion or refinement of authoritarian rule?', *Bulletin of Concerned Asian Scholars* 24(1): 3–17.

Rodan, Garry and Kevin Hewison (1996) 'A "clash of cultures" or the convergence of political ideology?' in Richard Robison (ed.) *Pathways to Asia: the politics of engagement*, pp. 29–55.

Sandercock, Leonie (1998) *Towards Cosmopolis: planning for multicultural cities*. Chichester, New York: John Wiley.

Selznick, Philip (1998) 'Foundations of communitarian liberalism' in A. Etzioni, (ed.) *The Essential Communitarian Reader*. Boulder: Rowman and Littlefield Publishers, pp. 3–14.

Taylor, Charles (1985) *Philosophy and the Human Sciences*. Cambridge: Cambridge University Press.

Tu, Wei-Ming (ed. 1991) *The Triadic Chord: Confucian ethics, industrial East Asia and Max Weber*. Singapore: Institute of East Asian Philosophies.

Van Ness, Peter (ed. 1999) *Debating Human Rights: critical essays from the US and Asia*. London: Routledge.

Wallerstein, Immanuel (1992) 'Liberalism and the legitimation of nation-states: an historical interpretation', *Social Justice* 19(1): 21–33.

Walzer, Michael (1983) *Spheres of Justice*. Oxford: Blackwell Publishers.

Notes

1 Many social scientists and other professionals in the US have declared themselves communitarians by signing the Responsive Communitarian Platform, initiated by the sociologist Amitai Etzioni (1998: xxv–xxxix).

2 As is usually the case, once the debate between dichotomous positions, such as liberalism versus communitarianism, unfolds for a time, voices of reconciliation begin to emerge arguing for the absence of differences (Miller 2000) or for some kind of accommodation (Rawls 1999) if not a middle ground (Anwar Ibrahim 1996).

3 For a new communitarian critique of libertarianism, see Selznick (1998).

4 This is the old saw in sociology against the 'oversocialized concept of man'.

5 There is, of course, a very large volume of material on human rights debate pertaining to Asia, see Peter van Ness (1999), An-Na'im (1992) and Bell (2000).

6 Although it does not declare itself to be a 'right communitarian' government, Daniel A. Bell has suggested in a response to this paper that the US government under President George Bush, Jr. could be considered such.

7 The material in this section was first published in Chua (1999).

8 I have traced the trajectory from Confucian ethics to communitarianism in the Singaporean national ideology in Chua (1995), especially pp. 9–39 and pp. 147–168.

9 The Shared Values as explicitly articulated national ideology is contained in a parliamentary White Paper (2 January 1992). The White Paper had been debated and adopted by the House of Parliament but not translated into a legal document or statutes, consequently its legal status remain unclear. For a critical assessment of Shared Values see Clammer (1993).

10 In addition to these well-funded public welfare services, by the government's reckoning, it has redistributed 14 billion Singapore dollars, in cash and in kind, to the citizenry in the decade of the 1990s; see the 2001 National Rally Speech of Prime Minister, Goh Chok Tong (*Straits Times* 20 August 2001).

11 There is a large volume of literature on urban settlers defence, however, in this context I have in mind, Partha Chatterjee's essay, 'Community in the East' (1998).

12 Calhoun (1998: 29) attributes the term 'community without propinquity' to Melvin Webber.

2

COMMUNITARIAN PHILOSOPHY AND EAST ASIAN POLITICS

Daniel A. Bell

Modern-day communitarianism began in the upper reaches of Anglo-American academia in the form of a critical reaction to John Rawls's landmark 1971 book *A Theory of Justice*. Drawing primarily upon the insights of Aristotle and Hegel, political philosophers such as Alasdair MacIntyre, Michael Sandel, Charles Taylor and Michael Walzer disputed Rawls' assumption that the principal task of government is to secure and distribute fairly the liberties and economic resources individuals need to lead freely chosen lives. These critics of liberal theory never did identify themselves with the 'communitarian movement' (the 'communitarian' label was pinned on them by others, usually critics),[1] much less offer a grand communitarian theory as a systematic alternative to liberalism. None the less, certain core arguments meant to contrast with liberalism's devaluation of community recur in the works of the four theorists named above,[2] and for purposes of clarity one can distinguish between claims of three sorts: 'ontological' or 'metaphysical' claims about the social nature of the self, methodological claims about the importance of tradition and social context for moral and political reasoning, and normative claims about the value of community.[3] Each strand of the debate has largely evolved from fairly abstract philosophical disputes to more concrete political concerns that may have motivated much of the communitarian critique in the first place. As a result, the debate from the self has almost entirely faded from view and it will not be discussed in this essay.[4] The other two strands of the debate, however, have been shaped in important ways by political discourse in and about East Asian politics. This essay is divided into two parts and for each part I present the main communitarian claims, followed by an argument (in each part) that philosophical concerns in the 1980s have largely given way to political disputes with an East Asian component.

Universalism versus particularism

Communitarians have sought to deflate the universal pretensions of liberal theory. The main target has been Rawls's description of the original position as an 'Archemedian point' from which the structure of a social system can be appraised, a position whose special virtue is that it allows us to regard the human condition 'from the perspective of eternity',[5] from all social and temporal points of view. Whereas Rawls seemed to present his theory of justice as universally true, communitarians argued that the standards of justice must be found in forms of life and traditions of particular societies and hence can vary from context to context. Alasdair MacIntyre and Charles Taylor argued that moral and political judgment will depend on the language of reasons and the interpretive framework within which agents view their world, hence that it makes no sense to begin the political enterprise by abstracting from the interpretive dimensions of human beliefs, practices, and institutions.[6] Michael Walzer developed the additional argument that effective social criticism must derive from and resonate with the habits and traditions of actual people living in specific times and places. Even if there is nothing problematic about a formal procedure of universalizability meant to yield a determinate set of human goods and values, 'any such set would have to be considered in terms so abstract that they would be of little use in thinking about particular distributions' (Walzer 1983: 8). In short, liberals who ask 'what is just' by abstracting from particular social contexts are doomed to philosophical incoherence and liberal theorists who adopt this method to persuade people to do the just thing are doomed to political irrelevance.

Rawls has since tried to clean up his theory of universalist presuppositions. In *Political Liberalism* (Rawls 1993), he argues in a communitarian vein that his conception of the person as impartial citizen provides the best account of liberal-democratic political culture and that his political aim is only to work out the rules for consensus in political communities where people are willing to try for consensus. In the *Law of Peoples* (Rawls 1999) he explicitly allows for the possibility that liberalism may not be exportable at all times and places, sketching a vision of a 'decent, well-ordered society' that liberal societies must tolerate in the international realm. Such a society, he argues, need not be democratic, but it must be non-aggressive towards other communities, and internally it must have a 'common good conception of justice', a 'reasonable consultation hierarchy', and it must secure basic human rights. Having said that, one still gets the sense that the liberal vision laid out in *A Theory of Justice* (Rawls 1971) is the best possible political ideal, one that all rational individuals would want if they were able to choose between the available political alternatives. There may be justifiable non-liberal regimes, but these should be regarded as 'second best' to be tolerated and perhaps respected, not idealized or emulated.

Other liberal theorists have taken a harder line against communitarian concessions, arguing that liberal theory can and should present itself as a universally valid ideal. Brian Barry, for one, opens his widely cited book *Justice as Impartiality* by boldly affirming the universality of his theory: 'I continue to believe in the possibility of putting forward a universally valid case in favor of liberal egalitarian principles' (1995: 3). Barry does recognize that a theory of justice must be anchored in substantive moral considerations, but his normative vision appears to be limited to the values and practices of liberal Western societies. He seems distinctly uninterested in learning anything worthwhile from non-Western political traditions – for example, his discussion of 'things Chinese' is confined to brief criticisms of the Cultural Revolution and the traditional practice of foot-binding. One might consider the reaction to a Chinese intellectual who puts forward a 'universal' theory of justice that draws on the Chinese political tradition for inspiration and completely ignores the history and moral argumentation in Western societies, except for brief criticisms of slavery and imperialism.

Still, it must be conceded that 1980s' communitarian theorists were less than successful at putting forward attractive visions of non-liberal societies. The communitarian case for pluralism – for the need to respect and perhaps learn from non-liberal societies that may be as good as, if not better than, the liberal societies of the West – may have been unintentionally undermined by their own use of (counter) examples. In *After Virtue*, Alasdair MacIntyre (1984) defended the Aristotelian ideal of the intimate, reciprocating local community bound by shared ends, where people simply assume and fulfill socially given roles. But this pre-modern *Gemeinschaft* conception of an all-encompassing community that members unreflectively endorse seemed distinctly ill-suited for complex and conflict-ridden large-scale industrialized societies. In *Spheres of Justice*, Walzer pointed to the Indian caste system, 'where the social meanings are integrated and hierarchical' (1983: 313) as an example of a non-liberal society that may be just according to its own standards. Not surprisingly, few readers were inspired by this example of non-liberal justice (not to mention the fact that many contemporary Indian thinkers view the caste system as an unfortunate legacy of the past that Indians should strive hard to overcome). In short, this use of ill-informed examples may have unintentionally reinforced the view that there are few if any justifiable alternatives to liberalism in modern societies. Communitarians could score some theoretical points by urging liberal thinkers to be cautious about developing 'universal' arguments founded exclusively on the moral argumentation and political experience of Western liberal societies, but few thinkers would really contemplate the possibility of non-liberal practices appropriate for the modern world so long as the alternatives to liberalism consisted of 'Golden Ages', caste societies, fascism, or 'actually-existing' communism. For the communitarian critique of liberal universalism to have any lasting credibility, thinkers need to provide compelling counter-examples to modern-day liberal-democratic regimes – and 1980s' communitarians came up short.

By the 1990s, fairly abstract methodological disputes over 'universalism versus particularism' faded from academic prominence, and the debate now centers on the theory and practice of universal human rights. This is largely due to the increased political salience of human rights since the collapse of communism in the former Soviet bloc. On the liberal 'side', the new, more political voices for liberal universalism have been represented by the likes of Francis Fukuyama (1992), who famously argued that liberal democracy's triumph over its rivals signifies the 'end of history'. This view also revived (and provoked) the 'second wave' communitarian critique of liberal universalism and the debate became much more concrete and political in orientation.

Needless to say, the brief moment of liberal euphoria that followed the collapse of communism in the Soviet bloc has given way to a sober assessment of the difficulties of implementing liberal practices outside the Western world. It is now widely recognized that brutal ethnic warfare, crippling poverty, environmental degradation, and pervasive corruption, to name some of the more obvious troubles afflicting the 'developing' world, pose serious obstacles to the successful establishment and consolidation of liberal democratic political arrangements. But these were seen as unfortunate (hopefully temporary) afflictions that may delay the 'end of history' when liberal democracy has finally triumphed over its rivals. They were not meant to pose a challenge to the *ideal* of liberal democracy. It was widely assumed that liberal democracy is something that all rational individuals *would* want if they could 'get it'.

The deeper challenge to Western liberal democracy has emerged from the East Asian region.[7] In the 1990s, the debate revolved around the notion of 'Asian Values', a term devised by several Asian officials and their supporters for the purpose of challenging Western-style civil and political freedoms. Asians, they claim, place special emphasis upon family and social harmony, with the implication that those in the 'chaotic and crumbling societies' of the West should think twice about intervening in Asia for the sake of promoting human rights and democracy. As Singapore's Lee Kuan Yew put it, Asians have 'little doubt that a society with communitarian values where the interests of society take precedence over that of the individual suits them better than the individualism of America'.[8] Such claims attracted international attention primarily because East Asian leaders seemed to be presiding over what a recent UN human development report called 'the most sustained and widespread development miracle of the twentieth century, perhaps all history'.[9] In 1997–1998, however, the East Asian miracle seemed to have collapsed. And it looks like Asian values was one casualty of the crisis.

The political factors that focused attention on the 'East Asian challenge' remain in place, however. The Korean economy, for example, has been slowly recovering and relative to the rest of the world East Asia does not look badly off. China in particular looks set to become an economic and political heavyweight with the power to seriously challenge the hegemony of Western liberal democratic values in international fora. Thus, one hears frequent calls for cross-cultural dialogue between 'the West' and 'the East' designed to understand and perhaps learn from the other 'side'. Failing to take seriously East Asian political perspectives risks widening misunderstandings and sets the stage for hostilities that could have been avoided.

From a theoretical point of view, however, it must be conceded that the official debate on Asian values has not provided much of a challenge to dominant Western political outlooks. The main problem is that the debate has been led by Asian leaders who seem to be motivated primarily by political considerations, rather than by a sincere desire to make a constructive contribution to the debate on 'universalism versus particularism'. Thus, it was easy to dismiss – rightly so, in most cases – the Asian challenge as nothing but a self-serving ploy by government leaders to justify their authoritarian rule in the face of increasing demands for democracy at home and abroad.

Still, it would be a mistake to assume that nothing of theoretical significance has emerged from East Asia. The debate on Asian values has also prompted critical intellectuals in the region to reflect on how they can locate themselves in a debate on human rights and democracy in which they had not previously played a substantial part. Neither wholly rejecting nor wholly endorsing the values and practices ordinarily realized through a liberal democratic political regime, these intellectuals are drawing on their own cultural traditions and exploring areas of commonality and difference with the West. Though often less provocative than the views of their governments – in the sense that few argue for the wholesale rejection of Western-style liberal democracy with an East Asian alternative – these unofficial East Asian viewpoints may offer more lasting contributions to the debate. Let me (briefly) note three relatively persuasive East Asian arguments for cultural particularism that contrast with traditional Western arguments for liberal universalism (see Bell 2000: 23–105):

1 Cultural factors can affect the *prioritizing* of rights, and this matters when rights conflict and it must be decided which one to sacrifice. In other words, different societies may rank rights differently, and even if they face a similar set of disagreeable circumstances they may come to different conclusions about the right that needs to be curtailed. For example, US citizens may be more willing to sacrifice a social or economic right in cases of conflict with a civil or political right: if neither the constitution nor a majority of democratically elected

representatives support universal access to health care, then the right to health care regardless of income can be curtailed. In contrast, the Chinese may be more willing to sacrifice a civil or political liberty in cases of conflict with a social or economic right: there may be wide support for restrictions on the internal movement of farmers if these are necessary to guarantee the right of subsistence. Different priorities assigned to rights can also matter when it must be decided how to spend scarce resources. For example, East Asian societies with a Confucian heritage will place great emphasis upon the value of education, and they may help to explain the large amount of spending on education compared to other societies with similar levels of economic development.

2 Cultural factors can affect the *justification* of rights. In line with the arguments of '1980s' communitarians' such as Michael Walzer, it is argued that justifications for particular practices valued by Western-style liberal democrats should not be made by relying on the abstract and unhistorical universalism that often disables Western liberal democrats. Rather, they should be made from the inside, from specific examples and argumentative strategies that East Asians themselves use in everyday moral and political debate. For example, the moral language (shared even by some local critics of authoritarianism) tends to appeal to the value of community in East Asia, and this is relevant for social critics concerned with practical effect. One such 'communitarian' argument is that democratic rights in Singapore can be justified on the grounds that they contribute to strengthening ties to such communities as the family and the nation (see next section).

3 Cultural factors can provide moral foundations for *distinctive* political practices and institutions (or at least different from those found in Western-style liberal democracies). In East Asian societies influenced by Confucianism, for example, it is widely held that children have a profound duty to care for elderly parents, a duty to be forsaken only in the most exceptional circumstances.[10] In political practice, it means that East Asian governments have an obligation to provide the social and economic conditions that facilitate the realization of this duty. Political debate tends to center on the question of whether the right to filial piety is best realized by means of a law that makes it mandatory for children to provide financial support for elderly parents – as in mainland China, Japan, and Singapore – or whether the state should rely more on indirect methods such as tax breaks and housing benefits that simply make at-home care for the elderly easier, as in Korea and Hong Kong. But the argument that there is a pressing need to secure this duty in East Asia is not a matter of political controversy.

Thinkers influenced by East Asian cultural traditions such as Confucianism have also argued for distinctive as-yet-unrealized political practices and institutions that draw on widely-held cultural values for inspiration. For example, the Korean scholar Hahm Chaihark (forthcoming) argues for the need to revive and adapt for the contemporary era the Confucian censorate, a traditional institution that played the role of monitoring the dealings of the Emperor (Bell 2000: 281–334).

In contrast to 1980s' communitarian thinkers, East Asian critics of liberal universalism have succeeded in pointing to particular non-liberal practices and institutions that may be appropriate for the contemporary world. Some of these may be appropriate only for societies with a Confucian heritage, others may also offer insights for mitigating the excesses of liberal modernity in the West. What cannot be denied is that they have carried forward the debate beyond the implausible alternatives to liberalism offered by 1980s' communitarian thinkers.

It is worth emphasizing, however, that contemporary communitarians have not been merely defending parochial attachments to particular non-liberal moralities. Far from arguing that the universalist discourse on human rights should be entirely displaced with particular, tradition-sensitive political language, they have criticized liberals for not taking universality seriously enough, for failing to do what must be done to make human rights a truly universal ideal. These communitarians – let us label them the 'cosmopolitan critics of liberal universalism' – have suggested various means of improving the philosophical coherence and political appeal of human rights.

In fact, there is little debate over the desirability of a core set of human rights,[11] such as prohibitions against slavery, genocide, murder, torture, prolonged arbitrary detention, and systematic racial discrimination. These rights have become part of international customary law, and they are not contested in the public rhetoric of the international arena. Of course many gross violations occur 'off the record', and human rights groups such as Amnesty International have the task of exposing the gap between public allegiance to rights and the sad reality of ongoing abuse. This is largely practical work, however. There is not much point writing about or deliberating about the desirability of practices that everyone condemns at the level of principle.

But political thinkers and activists around the world can and do take different sides on many pressing human rights concerns that fall outside what Walzer terms the 'minimal and universal moral code' (1987: 24; 1994). This 'gray' area of debate includes criminal law, family law, women's rights, social and economic rights, the rights of indigenous peoples, and the attempt to universalize Western-style democratic practices. The question is: how can the current 'thin' list of universal human rights be expanded to include some of these contested rights?

Charles Taylor (1999: 124–145) has put forward the following proposal. He imagines a cross-cultural dialogue between representatives of different traditions. Rather than argue for the universal validity of their views, however, he suggests that participants should allow for the possibility that their own beliefs may be mistaken. This way, participants can learn from each other's 'moral universe'. There will come a point, however, when differences cannot be reconciled. Taylor explicitly recognizes that different groups, countries, religious communities, and civilizations hold incompatible fundamental views on theology, metaphysics, and human nature. In response, Taylor argues that a 'genuine, unforced consensus' on human rights norms is possible only if we allow for disagreement on the ultimate justifications of those norms. Instead of defending contested foundational values when we encounter points of resistance (and thus condemning the values we do not like in other societies), we should try to abstract from those beliefs for the purpose of working out an 'overlapping consensus' of human rights norms. As Taylor puts it, 'we would agree on the norms while disagreeing on why they were the right norms, and we would be content to live in this consensus, undisturbed by the differences of profound underlying belief' (1999: 124).

While Taylor's proposal moves the debate on universal human rights forward, it still faces certain difficulties. For one thing, it may not be realistic to expect that people will be willing to abstract from the values they care deeply about during the course of a global dialogue on human rights. Even if people agree to abstract from culturally specific ways of justifying and implementing norms, the likely outcome is a withdrawal to a highly general, abstract realm of agreement that fails to resolve actual disputes over contested rights. For example, participants in a cross-cultural dialogue can agree on the right not to be subject to 'cruel and unusual punishment' while radically disagreeing upon what this means in practice – a committed Muslim can argue that theft can justifiably be punished by amputation of the right hand,[12] whereas a Western liberal will want to label this an example of 'cruel and unusual punishment'.

As we have seen, the debate on 'universalism versus particularism' has moved from fairly abstract methodological disputes between Anglo-American philosophers to relatively concrete international political disputes between philosophers, social scientists, government officials, and NGO activists. The distinctive communitarian contribution has cast doubt on 'universal' theories grounded exclusively in the liberal moralities of the Western world, on the grounds that cultural particularity should both make one sensitive to the possibility of justifiable areas of difference between 'the West' and 'the rest' and to the need for more cross-cultural dialogue for the purpose of improving the current 'thin' human rights regime. Various contributions from East Asia and elsewhere have given some 'meat' to these challenges to liberal universalism. In any case, let us now turn to another area of controversy between liberals and communitarians – normative disputes over the value of community – that has similarly moved from philosophy to politics.

The value of community

Communitarian thinkers in the 1980s such as Michael Sandel and Charles Taylor argued that Rawlsian liberalism rests on an overly individualistic conception of the self and neglects the value of community for human well-being. Whereas Rawls argues that we have a supreme interest in shaping, pursuing, and revising our own life-plans, he neglects the fact that our selves tend to be defined or constituted by various communal attachments (e.g., ties to the family or to a religious tradition) so close to us that they can only be set aside at great cost, if at all. Hence, politics should not be concerned solely with securing the conditions for individuals to exercise their powers of autonomous choice, as there may also be a need to sustain and promote the social attachments crucial to our sense of well-being and respect, many of which have been involuntarily picked up during the course of our upbringing.

Liberals have of course responded to these criticisms (Mulhall and Swift 1996: 170–246; Bell 1993: 24–54, 90–123) but a growing number are settling on the conclusion that communitarian critics of liberalism may have been motivated not so much by philosophical concerns as by certain pressing *political* concerns, namely, the negative social and psychological effects related to the atomistic tendencies of modern liberal societies. Whatever the soundness of liberal principles, in other words, the fact remains that many communitarians seem worried by a perception that traditional liberal institutions and practices have contributed to, or at least do not seem up to the task of dealing with, such modern phenomena as alienation from the political process, unbridled greed, loneliness, urban crime, and high divorce rates. And given the seriousness of these problems in the US, it was perhaps inevitable that a 'second wave' of 1990s' communitarians such as Amitai Etzioni and William Galston would turn to the more practical political terrain of emphasizing social responsibility and promoting policies meant to stem the erosion of communal life in an increasingly fragmented world.[13] Much of this thinking has been carried out in the flagship communitarian periodical, *The Responsive Community*, which is edited by Amitai Etzioni and includes contributions by an eclectic group of philosophers, social scientists, and public policy makers. Etzioni is also the director of a think-tank, *Institute for Communitarian Policy Studies*, which produces working papers and advises government officials in Washington.[14]

Such 'political' communitarians blame both the left and the right for our current malaise.[15] The political left is chastised not just for supporting welfare rights economically unsustainable in an era of slow growth and aging populations, but also for shifting power away from local communities and democratic institutions and towards centralized bureaucratic structures better equipped to administer the fair and equal distribution of benefits, thus leading to a growing sense of powerlessness and alienation from the political process. Moreover, the modern welfare state with its universalizing logic of rights and entitlements has undermined family and social ties in civil society by rendering superfluous obligations to communities, by actively discouraging private efforts to help others (e.g., union rules and strict regulations in Sweden prevent parents from participating voluntarily in the governance of day care centers to which they send their children), and even by providing incentives that discourage the formation of families (e.g., welfare payments are cut off in most American states if a recipient marries a working person) and encourage the break-up of families (e.g., no-fault divorce in the US is often financially rewarding for the non-custodial parent, usually the father).

Libertarian solutions favored by the political right have contributed even more directly to the erosion of social responsibilities and valued forms of communal life, particularly in the UK and the US. Far from producing beneficial communal consequences, the 'invisible hand' of unregulated free-market capitalism undermines the family (e.g., few corporations provide enough leave to parents of newborn children), disrupts local communities (e.g., following plant closings or the shifting of corporate headquarters), and corrupts the political process (e.g., since the mid-1970s special economic interests in the US have gained more power by drawing on political action committees to fund political representatives, with the consequence that representatives dependent on PAC (Political Action Committee) money for their political survival no longer represent the community at large). Moreover, the valorization of greed in the Thatcher/Reagan era justified the extension of instrumental considerations governing relationships in the marketplace into spheres previously informed by a sense of uncalculated reciprocity and civil obligation. This trend has been reinforced by increasing 'globalization', which pressures states into conforming to the dictates of the international marketplace.

More specifically in the American context, communitarian thinkers such as Mary Ann Glendon (1991) indict a new version of rights discourse that has achieved dominance of late. Whereas the assertion of rights was once confined to matters of essential human interest, a strident rights rhetoric has colonized contemporary political discourse, thus leaving little room for reasoned discussion and compromise, justifying the neglect of social responsibilities without which a society could not function, and ultimately weakening all appeals to rights by devaluing the really important ones.

To remedy this imbalance between rights and responsibilities in the US, 'political' communitarians propose a moratorium on the manufacture of new rights and changes to our 'habits of the heart' away from exclusive focus on personal fulfillment and towards concern with bolstering families, schools, neighborhoods, and national political life, changes to be supported by certain public policies. Notice that this proposal takes for granted basic civil and political liberties already in place, thus alleviating the concern that communitarians are embarking on a slippery slope to authoritarianism. Still, there may be a concern that marginalized groups demanding new rights, e.g., homosexual couples seeking the right to legally sanctioned marriage, will be paying the price for the excesses of others if the communitarian proposal to declare a moratorium on the minting of new rights is put into effect.

More serious from the standpoint of those generally sympathetic to communitarian aspirations, however, is the question of what exactly this has to do with 'community'. For one thing, Etzioni (1996) himself seeks to justify his policies with reference to need to maintain a balance between social *order* and freedom, as opposed to appealing to the importance of 'community'. But there is nothing distinctively communitarian about the preoccupation with social order; both liberals such as John Stuart Mill and Confucian conservatives affirm the need for order. And when the term 'community' is employed by political communitarians, it seems to mean anything they want it to mean. Worse, as Elizabeth Frazer (1999) has argued, it has often been used to justify hierarchical arrangements and delegitimize areas of conflict and contestation in modern societies.

Still, it is possible to make sense of the term 'community' as a normative ideal.[16] Communitarians begin by positing a need to experience our lives as bound up with the good of the communities out of which our identity has been constituted. This excludes 'contingent' attachments such as golf-club memberships that do not usually bear on one's sense of identity and well-being; the co-authors of *Habits of the Heart* (Bellah *et al.* 1985) employ the term 'lifestyle enclaves' to describe these attachments. Unlike pre-modern defenders of *Gemeinshaft*, however, it is assumed that there are *many* valued forms of communal life in the modern world. So the distinctive communitarian political project is to identify valued forms of community and to devise policies designed to protect and promote them, without sacrificing too much freedom. Typically, communitarians would invoke the following types of communities:

1 *Communities of place, or communities based on geographical location.* This is perhaps the most common meaning associated with the word 'community'. In this sense, community is linked to locality, in the physical, geographical sense of a community that is located somewhere. It can refer to a small village or a big city. A community of place also has an 'affective' component – it refers to the place one calls 'home', often the place where one is born and bred and the place where one

would like to end one's days even if home is left as an adult. At the very least, communitarians posit an interest in identifying with familiar surroundings.

In terms of political implications, it means that, for example, political authorities ought to consider the existent character of the local community when considering plans for development.[17] Other (Shuman 1999) suggestions to protect communities of place include: granting community councils veto power over building projects that fail to respect existent architectural styles; implementing laws regulating plant closures so as to protect local communities from the effects of rapid capital mobility and sudden industrial change; promoting local-ownership of corporations; and imposing restrictions on large-scale discount outlets such as Wal-Mart that threaten to displace small, fragmented, and diverse family and locally owned stores (Ehrenholt 1999).

2 *Communities of memory, or groups of strangers who share a morally significant history.*

This term – first employed by the co-authors of *Habits of the Heart* (Bellah *et al.* 1985) refers to 'imagined' communities that have a shared history going back several generations. Besides tying us to the past, such communities turn us towards the future – members strive to realize the ideals and aspirations embedded in past experiences of those communities, seeing their efforts as being, in part, contributions to a common good. They provide a source of meaning and hope in people's lives. Typical examples include the nation and language-based ethnocultural groups.

In Western liberal democracies, this typically translates into various nation-building exercises meant to nourish the bonds of commonality that tie people to their nations, such as national service and national history lessons in school textbooks. Self-described 'republicans' such as Michael Sandel (1996) place special emphasis upon the national political community and argue for measures that increase civic engagement and public-spiritedness. However, there is increased recognition of the multinational nature of contemporary states, and modern Western states must also try to make room for the political rights of minority groups. These political measures have been widely discussed in the recent literature on nationalism, citizenship, and multiculturalism (Kymlicka 1995; Macedo 2000; Tamir 1993).

3 *Psychological communities, or communities of face-to-face personal interaction governed by sentiments of trust, and altruism.*

This refers to a group of persons who participate in common activity and experience a psychological sense of 'togetherness' as shared ends are sought. Such communities, based on face-to-face interaction, are governed by sentiments of trust, cooperation, and altruism in the sense that constituent members have the good of the community in mind and

> act on behalf of the community's interest. They differ from communities of place by not being necessarily defined by locality and proximity. They differ from communities of memory in the sense that they are more 'real', they are typically based on face-to-face social interaction at one point in time and consequently tend to be restricted in size.[18] The family is the prototypical example. Other examples include small-scale work or school settings founded on trust and social cooperation.
>
> Communitarians tend to favor policies designed to protect and promote ties to the family and family-like groups. This would include such measures as encouraging marriage and increasing the difficulty of legal marriage dissolution. These policies are supported by empirical evidence that points to the psychological and social benefits of marriage (Waite 1996). Communitarians also favor political legislation that can help to restructure education in such a way that people's deepest needs in membership and participation in psychological communities are tapped at a young age. The primary school system in Japan, where students learn about group cooperation and benefits and rewards are assigned to the classroom as a whole rather than to individual students, could be a useful model.
>
> (Reid 1999)

What makes the political project of communitarianism distinctive is that it involves the promotion of all three forms of valued communal life. This leads, however, to the worry that seeking the goods of various communities may conflict in practice. Etzioni (1993), for example, argues for a whole host of pro-family measures: mothers and fathers should devote more time and energy to parenting (in view of the fact that most childcare centers do a poor job of caring for children), labor unions and employers ought to make it easier for parents to work at home, and the government should force corporations to provide six months of paid leave and another year of unpaid leave. The combined effect of these 'changes of the heart' and public policies in all likelihood would be to make 'citizens' into largely private, family-centered persons.

Yet Etzioni also argues that the American political system is corrupt to the core, concluding that only extensive involvement in public affairs by virtuous citizens can remedy the situation: 'once citizens are informed, they must make it their civic duty to *organize others* locally, regionally, and nationally to act on their understanding of what it takes to clean up public life in America' (1993: 244). But few can afford sufficient time and energy to devote themselves fully to both family life and public affairs, and favoring one ideal is most likely to erode the other. Surely it is no coincidence that 'republican' America in Jefferson's day relied on active, public-spirited male citizens largely freed from family responsibilities. Conversely, societies composed of persons leading rich and fulfilling family lives, such as contemporary Singapore, tend to be ruled by paternalistic despots who can rely on a compliant, politically apathetic populace.

Communitarians who advocate both increased commitment to public affairs and strengthened ties to the workplace (to the point that it becomes a 'psychological community') also face the problem of conflicting commitments. Michael Sandel, for example, speaks favorably of 'proud craftsmen' in the Jacksonian era and of Louis Brandeis's idea of 'industrial democracy, in which workers participated in management and shared responsibilities for running the business' (1996: 213). Identification with the workplace and industrial democracy are said to improve workers' civic capacities, but that may not be the case. In the same way that extensive involvement in family life can conflict with commitments to public life, few persons will have sufficient time and energy for extensive participation in both workplace and public affairs. Recall that the 'republican' society of ancient Athens relied on active, public-spirited males freed from the need to work (slaves did most of the drudge labor).

It is also worth noting that devotion to the workplace can undermine family life. As Tatsuo Inoue argues, Japanese-style communitarianism – strong communal identity based on the workplace, with extensive worker participation in management – sometimes leads to *karoshi* ('death from overwork') and frequently deprives workers of 'the right to sit down at the dinner table with their families' (1993: 534).[19] Just as liberals (pace Ronald Dworkin) sometimes have to choose between ideals (e.g., freedom and equality) that come into conflict with one another if a serious effort is made to realize any one of them fully, so communitarians may have to make some hard choices between valued forms of communal life.

Still, there may be some actual or potential 'win-win' scenarios, cases where promoting a particular form of communal life can promote, rather than undermine, other forms – and 'political' communitarians will of course favor change of this sort. For example, critics have objected to 'residential community associations', or 'walled communities', on the grounds that they undermine attachment to the polity at large and erode the social cohesion and trust needed to promote social justice and sustain the democratic process.[20] Might it then be possible to reform urban planning so that people can nurture strong local communities without undermining attachment to the national community, perhaps even strengthening 'broader' forms of public-spiritedness? Many practical suggestions along these lines have been raised. Architects and urban planners in the US known as the 'New Urbanists', for example, have proposed various measures to strengthen community building – affordable housing, public transport, pedestrian focused environments, and public space as an integral part of neighborhoods – that would not have the 'privatizing' consequences of 'gated communities'. The problem, as Gerald Frug points out, is that 'virtually everything they want to do is now illegal. To promote the new urbanist version of urban design, cities would have to revise municipal zoning laws and development policy from top to bottom' (1999: 152–153).[21] This points to the need for public policy recommendations explicitly designed to favor complementing forms of communal attachments.

But how much of this is relevant for East Asia? According to Etzioni, communitarian politics is only relevant for a society that suffers from an excess of 'rights thinking':

> The basic Communitarian quest for balances between individuals and groups, rights and responsibilities, and among the institutions of state, market, and civil society is a constant, ongoing enterprise. Because this quest takes place within history and within varying social contexts, however, the evaluation of what is a proper moral stance will vary according to circumstances of time and place. If we were in China today, we would argue vigorously for more individual rights; in contemporary America, we emphasize individual and social responsibilities (1993: 254–255).

But it is a mistake to view the relation between individual liberties and commitments to the common good as a zero-sum game. Just as it would be wrong to assume that communitarian goals always conflict, so one should allow for the possibility that individual rights and communitarian goals can co-exist and complement each other.[22] In Singapore, for example, it can be argued that more secure democratic rights would have the effect of strengthening commitment to the common national good.[23] The Singapore government does not hide the fact that it makes life difficult for many who aim to enter the opposition arena on the side of opposition parties: Between 1971 and 1993, according to Attorney General Chan Sek Keong, eleven opposition politicians have been made bankrupt (and hence ineligible to run in elections).[24] Whether intended or not, such actions send an 'unpatriotic' message to the community at large: 'Politics is a dangerous game for those who haven't been specially anointed by the top leadership of the ruling party, so you should stick to your own private affairs'. As Singaporean journalist Cherian George puts it, one can hardly blame people for ignoring their social and political obligations 'when they hear so many cautionary tales: Of Singaporeans whose careers came to a premature end after they voiced dissent; of critics who found themselves under investigation; of individuals who were detained without trial even though they seemed not to pose any real threat; of tapped phones and opened letters ... The moral of these stories: In Singapore, better to mind your own business, make money, and leave politics to the politicians' (*Straits Times*, 11 July 1993). Put positively, if the aim is to secure attachment to the community at large, then implementing genuinely competitive elections, including the freedom to run for the opposition without fear of retaliation[25] is an essential first step.

The Singapore case, however, points to another dimension of the 'politics of community' that brings us back to the communitarian defense of cultural particularism. Democratic reformers in Singapore typically think of democracy in terms of free and fair competitive elections – what Western analysts often label 'minimal democracy'. In Hong Kong, the situation is similar – the aspiration to 'full' democracy put forward by social critics turns out to mean (nothing more than) an elected legislature and Chief Executive. Put differently, it is quite striking that the 'republican' tradition in communitarian thought – with its vision of 'strong' democracy supported by active, public-spirited citizens who participate in political decision-making and help shape the future direction of their society though political debate – seems completely absent from political discourse in Singapore and Hong Kong, and perhaps East Asia more generally. Many East Asians are clamoring for secure democratic rights, but this doesn't translate into the demand that all citizens should be committed to politics on an ongoing basis or the view that, as David Miller puts it, 'politics is indeed a necessary part of the good life' (2000: 58). At one level, this can be explained by the fact that there are no equivalents of Aristotle and Jean-Jacques Rousseau in East Asian philosophy. It can also be argued that republican ideas fail to resonate because East Asians typically place more emphasis on other forms of communal life – the family in particular has been an important theme in Confucian ethical theory and practice (relative to Western philosophy). To the extent that different forms of communal life do conflict in practice, in short, it may be the case that different cultures will draw the line in different places.

But this is not to suggest that each community draws the line in its own way, and there is no more room for moral debate or social critique. While there may be a strong case for endorsing 'the way things are done' if shared understandings conform to the views shared by both defenders and critics of the political *status quo*[26] more often than not social critics will find fault with the communitarian excesses in this or that society. For example, Chang Kyung-Sup argues that Korean 'familism' harms individuals and poses a serious stumbling block to the establishment of a democratic polity in Korea.[27] In this context, it may well be counter-productive to place too much emphasis on the moral qualities of family life.[28] But other societies – relatively individualistic societies suffering from the undesirable social consequences of divorce and single-parent families or communitarian societies that justify sacrificing families in the interests of the workplace – may need to rejuvenate family life and they may well look to Korean 'familism' for ideas. In other words, what seems like a communitarian 'excess' in one society can be a source of inspiration for another. There may be much to learn from the different varieties of communitarian politics in East Asia.

References

An-Na'im, Abdullahi (1992) 'Toward a Cross-Cultural Approach to Defining International Standards of Human Rights: The Meaning of Cruel, Inhuman, or Degrading Treatment or Punishment', in Abdullahi An-Na'im (ed.) *Human Rights in Cross-Cultural Perspectives: A Quest for Consensus*. Philadelphia: University of Pennsylvania Press, pp. 19–43.

Avineri, Schlomo and Avner de-Shalit (eds) (1992) *Communitarianism and Individualism*. Oxford: Clarendon Press.

Barry, Brian (1995) *Justice as Impartiality*. Oxford: Clarendon Press.

Bauer, Joanne R. and Daniel A. Bell (eds) (1999) *The East Asian Challenge for Human Rights*. New York: Cambridge University Press.

Bell, Daniel A. (1993) *Communitarianism and Its Critics*. Oxford: Clarendon Press.

Bell, Daniel A. (1995), 'Residential Community Associations: Community or Disunity', *The Responsive Community*, 5(4): 25–36.

Bell, Daniel A. (1995a) 'A Communitarian Critique of Authoritarianism', *Society*, July/August, pp. 38–43.

Bell, Daniel A. (1997) 'Communitarianism' in Patricia H. Werhane and R. Edward Freeman (eds) *The Blackwell Encyclopedic Dictionary of Business Ethics*. Malden: Blackwell, pp. 126–127.

Bell, Daniel A. (2000) *East Meets West: Human Rights and Democracy in East Asia*. Princeton: Princeton University Press.

Bellah, Robert *et al.* (1985) *Habits of the Heart*. Berkeley: University of California Press.

Benhabib, Seyla (1992) *Situating the Self: Gender, Community and Postmodernism in Contemporary Ethics*. Cambridge: Polity Press.

Berten, Andre, Pablo Da Silveira, Pablo and Herve Pourtois (eds) (1997) *Liberaux et Communautariens*. Paris: PUF.

Caney, Simon (1992) 'Liberalism and Communitarianism: A Misconceived Debate', *Political Studies*, June, pp. 273–290.

Chua Beng-Huat (1995) *Communitarian Ideology and Democracy in Singapore*. London: Routledge.

D'Antonio, Michael (1994) 'The High-Rise Village: Public Housing Creates a Community in Harlem'. Washington: The Communitarian Network.

Ehrenhalt, Alan (1999) 'Community and the Corner Store: Retrieving Human-Scale Commerce', *The Responsive Community*, 9(4): 30–39.

Etzioni, Amitai (1993) *The Spirit of Community*. New York: Crown Publishers.

Etzioni, Amitai (ed.) (1995) *New Communitarian Thinking*. Charlottesville: University of Virginia Press.

Etzioni, Amitai (ed.) (1995a) *Rights and the Common Good: The Communitarian Perspective*. New York: St. Martin's Press.

Etzioni, Amitai (1996) *The New Golden Rule*. New York: Basic Books.

Etzioni, Amitai (ed.) (1998) *The Essential Communitarian Reader*. Lanham: Rowman & Littlefield.

Etzioni, Amitai (2001) *The Monochrome Society*. Princeton: Princeton University Press.

Frazer, Elizabeth (1999) *The Problems of Communitarian Politics*. Oxford: Oxford University Press.
Frug, Gerald E. (1999) *City Making: Building Communities Without Building Walls*. Princeton: Princeton University Press.
Fukuyama, Francis (1992) *The End of History and the Last Man*. New York: Free Press.
Galston, William (1991) *Liberal Purposes*. Cambridge: Cambridge University Press.
Glendon, Mary Ann (1991) *Rights Talk: The Impoverishment of Political Discourse*. New York: The Free Press.
Gutmann, Amy (ed.) (1992) *Multiculturalism and 'The Politics of Recognition'*. Princeton: Princeton University Press.
Hahm, Chaibong (2003) 'Family versus the Individual: The Politics of Marriage Laws in Korea', in Daniel A. Bell and Hahm Chaibong (eds) *Confucianism for the Modern World*. New York: Cambridge University Press, pp. 334–360.
Hahm, Chaihark (2003) 'Constitutionalism, Confucian Civic Virtue, and Ritual Propriety' in Daniel A. Bell and Hahm Chaibong (eds) *Confucianism for the Modern World*. New York: Cambridge University Press, pp. 31–53.
Helgesen, Geir (2003) 'The Case for Moral Education' in Daniel A. Bell and Hahm Chaibong (eds) *Confucianism for the Modern World*. New York: Cambridge University Press, pp. 161–180.
Inoue, Tatsuo (1993) 'The Poverty of Rights-Blind Communality: Looking Through the Window of Japan', *Brigham Young University Law Review*, January.
Jacobs, Jane (1965) *The Death and Life of American Cities*. New York: Random House.
Kymlicka, Will (1995) *Multicultural Citizenship*. Oxford: Clarendon Press.
Macedo, Stephen (2000) *Diversity and Distrust*. Cambridge, Mass.: Harvard University Press.
MacIntyre, Alasdair (1978) *Against the Self-Images of the Age*. Notre Dame: University of Notre Dame Press.
MacIntyre, Alasdair (1984) *After Virtue*, 2nd edn, Notre-Dame: University of Notre-Dame Press.
MacIntyre, Alasdair (1988) *Whose Justice? Which Rationality*? Notre Dame: Notre Dame Press.
McKenzie, Evan (1994) *Privatopia*. New Haven: Yale University Press.
Mason, Andrew (2000) *Community, Solidarity and Belonging: Levels of Community and their Normative Significance*. Cambridge: Cambridge University Press
Milbank, Dana (2001) 'Is Bush a Communitarian?', *The Responsive Community*, 11(2): 4–7.
Miller, David (2000) *Citizenship and National Identity*. Cambridge: Polity Press.
Mulhall, Stephen and Swift, Adam (1996), *Liberals and Communitarians*, 2nd edn, Oxford: Blackwell.
Rasmussen, David (ed.) (1990) *Universalism* vs. *Communitarianism*. Cambridge, Mass.: MIT Press.
Rawls, John (1971) *A Theory of Justice*. Cambridge, Mass.: Harvard University Press.
Rawls, John (1993) *Political Liberalism*. New York: Columbia University Press.
Rawls, John (1999) The Law of Peoples; with The Idea of Public Reason Revisited. Cambridge, Mass.: Harvard University Press.

Reid, T.R. (1999) *Confucius Lives Next Door.* New York: Random House.

Rosenblum, Nancy (1998) *Membership and Morals.* Princeton: Princeton University Press.

Sandel, Michael (1996) *Democracy's Discontent.* Cambridge, Mass.: Harvard University Press.

Sandel, Michael (1998) *Liberalism and the Limits of Justice.* Cambridge: Cambridge University Press.

Shuman, Michael H. (1999) 'Community Corporations: Engines for a New Place-Based Economics', *The Responsive Community,* 9(3): 48–57.

Tam, Henry (1998) *Communitarianism: A New Agenda for Politics and Citizenship.* Basingstoke: Macmillan.

Tamir, Yael (1993) *Liberal Nationalism.* Princeton: Princeton University Press.

Taylor, Charles (1985) *Philosophy and the Human Sciences: Philosophical Papers 2.* Cambridge: Cambridge University Press.

Taylor, Charles (1999) 'Conditions of an Unforced Consensus on Human Rights', in Joanne R. Bauer and Daniel A. Bell (eds) *The East Asian Challenge for Human Rights.* New York: Cambridge University Press, pp. 124–145.

Waite, Linda (1996) 'Social Science Finds: "Marriage Matters"', *Twenty-First Century Series in Communitarian Studies.* Washington: Institute for Communitarian Policy Studies.

Walzer, Michael (1983) *Spheres of Justice.* Oxford: Blackwell.

Walzer, Michael (1987) *Interpretation and Social Criticism.* Cambridge, Mass: Harvard University Press.

Walzer, Michael (1994) *Thick and Thin.* Notre-Dame, Ind.: University of Notre-Dame Press.

Young, Iris M. (1990) *Justice and the Politics of Difference.* Princeton: Princeton University Press, 1990.

Notes

1 Both Taylor and Walzer identify themselves as 'liberals' in Amy Gutmann (1992). MacIntyre says 'In spite of rumors to the contrary, I am not and never have been a communitarian' (letter to *The Responsive Community* (Summer 1991), and Sandel uses the label 'republican' rather than 'communitarian' in the second edition of *Liberalism and the Limits of Justice* (Cambridge: Cambridge University Press, 1998).

2 For relevant references, see the bibliographies in Schlomo Avineri and Avner de-Shalit (1992); Daniel Bell (1993); Andre Berten, Pablo Da Silveira, and Herve Pourtois (1997); Stephen Mulhall and Adam Swift, (1996); David Rasmussen (1990).

3 This essay draws on the threefold distinction in Bell (1993). For a similar threefold distinction, see Simon Caney (1992) but for an expanded fivefold classification of arguments, see Mulhall and Swift (1996).

4 For an account of this debate, see my entry 'Communitarianism' in the on-line *Stanford Encyclopedia of Philosophy.* This entry also covers the other two main strands of the debate, and I would like to thank the editors for permission to draw on this material.

5 This is the language Rawls employs on the last page of the first edition of *A Theory of Justice.*

6 See, e.g., Charles Taylor (1985), ch.1; Alasdair MacIntyre (1978), chs 18–22; and MacIntyre (1988), ch.1; and the discussion in Benhabib (1992), pp. 23–38, 89 n4.

7 This section draws on the introduction to my book (Bell 2000). Another challenge to Western-style liberal-democracy has of course been mounted by Islamic civilization, though Islamic countries have not been as economically and politically successful (compared to East Asia) and therefore fail to pose as significant a challenges the claims of Western liberal-democrats that only capitalism and liberal democracy can cope with the requirements of modernity.

8 Quoted in the *International Herald Tribune*, 9–10 November 1991.

9 Quoted in Barbara Crossette, 'UN Survey Finds Rich-Poor Gap Widening', *New York Times*, 15 July 1996.

10 Interestingly, this moral outlook still seems to inform the practices of Asian immigrants to other societies. According to the *New York Times* (11 July 2001), fewer than one in five whites in the US help care or provide financial support for their parents, in-laws or other relatives, compared with 28 percent of African-Americans, 34 percent of Hispanic-Americans and 42 percent of Asian-Americans. Those who provide the most care also feel the most guilt that they are not doing enough. Almost three-quarters of Asian-Americans say they should do more for their parents, compared with two-thirds of Hispanics, slightly more than half the African-Americans and fewer than half the whites.

11 Terrorist groups that justify mass killing of civilians are the obvious exception. It is interesting to note, however, that even Osama bin Laden does not go so far as to publicly proclaim responsibility for the September 11th attack, presumably on the grounds that this would undermine his base of support.

12 According to Abdullahi An-Na'im (1992: 34), however, the prerequisite conditions for the enforcement of this punishment are extremely difficult to realize in practice and are unlikely to materialize in any Muslim country in the foreseeable future.

13 For book-length treatments of communitarian politics in the US, see, Amitai Etzioni (1993, 1996, 2001) and for a book that derives largely from the UK context see Henry Tam's (1998). See also Etzioni's edited books (1995, 1995a, 1998).

14 Both Democrats and Republicans seem to be receptive to 'communitarian' political ideas. The political theorist William Galston, a co-editor of *The Responsive Community* and author of *Liberal Purposes* (1991), was President Clinton's Domestic Policy Adviser. In 2001, President Bush unveiled a four-year Communities of Character project that was developed following consultations with Etzioni (*Washington Post*, 29 July 2000; see also Milbank (2001)), but it was canceled following the September 11th terrorist attacks on the grounds that Americans had rediscovered civic virtue and therefore the initiative was no longer necessary.

15 This section draws on my entry 'Communitarianism', in *The Blackwell Encyclopedic Dictionary of Business Ethics* (Bell 1997).

16 This section draws on Bell (1993: 90–207). See also Andrew Mason (2000). Mason usefully distinguishes between different levels and kinds of communities, though one can question his argument that the ideal of global *community* is coherent in principle and useful in practice. In my view, communities are particularistic in nature and presume an inside/outside distinction, and even if this ideal is coherent it is unclear to what extent the ideal of 'community' does much work for defenders of universal liberal principles and global institutions.

17 Jane Jacobs (1965) famously documented the negative effects of razing, instead of renovating, run-down tenements that are replaced by functionally adequate but characterless low-income housing blocs.

18 Though conceptions of the family can also include an 'imagined' component – for example, the widespread practice of ancestor worship in East Asian societies with a Confucian heritage suggests that (deceased) ancestors are considered as ongoing participants in the good of the family.

19 According to Inoue's contribution in this volume, workplace communitarianism also has negative economic and political effects. But for a more positive assessment of workplace communitarianism in Japan, see Anthony Woodiwiss's contribution in this volume.

20 See Evan McKenzie (1994), Bell (1995) and for a contrasting account, see Nancy Rosenblum (1998).

21 But for an account of an actual example of diverse, mixed-income and mixed-race urban housing project that contrasts with homogenous, upper-class 'walled communities', see Michael D'Antonio (1994).

22 For a critique of Etzioni's argument, see Bell (1995a).

23 This argument is developed at length in Bell (2000: 233–276). See also Chua Beng Huat (1995), esp. ch. 9.

24 In the latest case (mid-2001), J.B. Jeyaratnam has been declared bankrupt and has had to forfeit his Parliamentary seat.

25 The Singapore state, it must be said, resorts to endlessly creative tactics to curb opposition attempts to reach out to the electorate and communicate alternative ideas and policies. The opposition Singapore Democratic Party was informed by the Singapore police that it needed to engage 13 officers for crowd control purposes for a planned national day rally on 26 August 2001, amounting to several thousand dollars. One wonders if the ruling People's Action Party needs to pay for its own security for its rallies (not to mention the question of who pays for the undercover officers at opposition rallies).

26 Consider, e.g., the widespread acceptance of constraints on criticism of the Thai King; see the discussion of the Dr Sulak Sivaraksa case in Bauer and Bell (1999: 14–15).

27 See Chang Kyung-Sup's contribution in this volume.

28 But for contrasting views on the role of the family in contemporary Korean society, see the contributions by Hahm Chaibong and Geir Helgesen in *Confucianism for the Modern World* (2003).

3

PREDICAMENT OF COMMUNALITY

Lessons from Japan

Tatsuo Inoue

Introduction

Many advocates of the so-called 'Asian Values' have confidently claimed that the 'miraculous' economic development of several Asian countries is due to their success in adapting their emerging capitalist economic systems to the communitarian values embedded in their traditional culture. The postwar Japanese political economic system that reached its peak in the 1980s was once regarded as a paradigm of communitarian reconstruction of capitalism that brings about rapid economic growth without undermining social harmony and political stability. In this system, the communitarian mode of Japanese identity-formation and conflict-resolution pervades the closely cooperative and integrative labor–management relationships, long-term dealings and group-oriented practices of business, and the informal and conciliatory way of governmental intervention in the market. Recent setbacks of Asian newly industrializing economies and the prolonged economic and political dêbâcle of Japan since the 1990s have, however, eroded popular confidence in the tenacity of the communitarian practices that were said to be constitutive of the 'Asian way' of social ordering.

Japan, under prolonged economic slowdown, has undergone a conspicuous change of collective self-perception. The elated self-confidence that used to prevail with the nation has been replaced by deep frustrations and paralyzing diffidence. In the 1990s – the so-called 'lost decade' – the Japanese government has attempted to revive national vigor via many political and administrative reforms, only to change the institutional façade leaving the covered architecture intact. As the public sense of crisis became keener, the Koizumi administration that replaced its hopelessly discredited predecessor, the Mori administration, with overwhelmingly strong popular support, in 2001, has pledged to carry out 'structural reforms without any intact sanctuaries'.

The gist of the advocated structural reforms is to establish rigorous discipline of market competition by typically neo-liberal measures such as deregulation, privatization and downsizing of the public sector, financial consolidation involving restraints on social welfare spending, 'fluidization' of employment, that is, to put it bluntly, making lay-off easier, and simplifying the legal process for liquidating failed firms. The perception that reforms along these lines are unavoidable is widely propagated, so too are vehement objections to the onslaught of neo-liberal politics. Objections are raised by those who are anxious to protect the interests of the weaker and vulnerable part of the population by the welfare state regime, which they hold to be indispensable to promote communitarian ethics of mutual care and interdependency at the national level.

This familiar confrontation of neo-liberalism and welfare state ideologies and its deregulation–protectionist dichotomy of policy choice, however, do not adequately capture the nature and roots of structural failure and the thus direction of required structural reforms of contemporary Japanese society. Contrary to the 'third-way' view favored by some Euro-American communitarian theorists that the challenge today in advanced capitalist societies is to revive intermediary communities that have been eroded both by market forces and the centralized welfare state bureaucracy, I want to make an opposite point: the Japanese predicament originates from rampant forces of intermediary communities that have been dominating both market economy and political process of the state.

My argument is informed by problems conspicuous in the context of contemporary Japan, but I hope it reveals the larger conceptual and substantive point of the entrapment of communality that is relevant to other societies. I want to situate my argument in a larger theoretical framework for comparative social pathology that shows the merits and limits of the current communitarian analysis and helps us to understand different plights of different societies.

In the following two sections I will present the triad of social orders and triad of tyrannies as a theoretical framework in which social structural problems, including those of contemporary Japan, can be located and compared with each other. Finally, I will briefly discuss how the political and economic regime of postwar Japan has been dominated and distorted by a variety of intermediary communities and what reforms are needed to correct the resultant structural failure.

The triad of social orders

The state, market and community are three distinct ordering principles of contemporary society. The state regulates social life by exerting centralized, organized force and implementing the legal system that authorizes and controls the use of this force in terms of some conception of rights and an idea of justice. Market coordinates human collaboration involving production and distribution of goods and services through rules of fair competition as well as systems of free exchange and private property, which disperse among individuals the power to decide resource allocation. Community unites individuals and reconciles their differences not only by mutual attachment and shared basis of self-identity but also through the practice of generalized reciprocity – long-term and circular balancing of favor as distinguished from contractural exchange – that maintains and is maintained by shared vulnerability and close interdependency of members of the community. Given the concurrence of these three ordering principles, the coercive apparatus of the state does not monopolize completely the effective means of social control, while market and community both have their own resources for controlling deviant behaviors and resolving disputes.

Free-market-extremists often assert that even public goods such as policing and adjudication of disputes are better supplied by private firms dealing in security and arbitration services than by the police and courts of the state. Communitarian extremists, on the other hand, emphasize that historically communities have been able to maintain their internal order by resorting to conciliation and informal sanctions such as ostracism or exclusion from the network of generalized reciprocity, without depending on the organized force of the state. Each of the two extremist perspectives has its grain of truth. Ordering principles of market and community have the merits of delimiting the need for use of physical force. Market expands the scope of individual initiatives and activates social mobility. Community assures equality of its members as effective participants in the informal mutual control process and reinforces their group-identification. Market and community therefore exercise restraints on the hierarchical stratification of those who have effective control of the organized force and those who do not.

However, these two extreme conceptions of social order go too far in claiming that market and community, respectively, can save us from the need for the state. For example, poor people may not be able to buy adequate protection service in the extreme free-market regime, and socially different individuals may be defenselessly exposed to violation of their rights in the extreme communitarian regime. On the other hand, the state that justifies its claim to sovereignty by its role of protecting all the people within its territory can and must provide shelter for all of the people. At a macro level, communities need the protection of the state against external invaders if they do not want to be forcefully colonized and absorbed into other states. Finally, market economy itself depends on the state to establish its institutional infrastructure and enforce the legal system.

The three ordering principles and their underlying values – individual liberty and social mobility in market, egalitarian solidarity and secured identity in community – are all deeply rooted human aspirations and irreducible to each other, the three cannot in practice replace each other. Consequently, they are locked in competition with each other. This means that, analytically, we have to combine the three competing ordering principles in such a way that their competition becomes complementary. The liberal ideal of separation of powers offers us an archetype of such combination. This ideal is based on the plural equilibrium model of check and balance between three differentiated and competing functions of the state power: legislation, adjudication and administration. We can extend this model from internal competition of the state power to its external competition so as to conceive check and balance between the three competing ordering principles, the state, market and community in the following way.

First, safeguards against the menace of the state's organized and centralized force are provided both by the market system of dispersing the power to decide resource allocation and distribution, and by the decentralized self-rule of a variety of communities. Second, the danger of a community exerting informal and pervasive oppression over heterogeneity of nonconformist members, thus losing its sense of responsibility and fairness to outsiders, is warded off, on the one hand, by the state's enforcing rule of law and implementing constitutional protection of human rights and, on the other hand, by the market's function of providing opportunities for those who leave their communities. Last, exploitative and destructive activities of economic powers formed in the market are curbed both by the state that provides social security through regulating, among others, monopoly, environmental disruption, and labor conditions, and by communities that supply an informal safety-net of generalized reciprocity and put social pressure upon irresponsible economic agents. This extended model of tripartite check and balance might be called the triad of social orders. It does not give us any fail-safe system for solving dilemmas of human society, but it provides a benchmark for identifying and comparing the different predicaments of different societies.

The triad of tyrannies

The fundamental problem with the triad of social orders is that there can be no assurance of persistent equilibrium. Indeed equilibrium collapses easily. The way it collapses, however, varies from society to society. Let me present three basic types of pathological dislocation of the triad of social orders that may be respectively called totalitarian, capitalist and communitarian tyrannies.

Totalitarian tyranny prevails when hypertrophied state power permeates and controls the whole of social life and thus, suffocates not only the market economy but also more or less autonomous intermediary communities, including families in extreme cases, that shelter individuals. Nazism, Stalinism and arguably Maoist Cultural Revolution are paradigmatic examples of this tyranny that modern history provides. The potential of this tyranny may be said to be inherent in the modern sovereign state. Alexis de Tocqueville thus perceived that the dark side of the French Revolution lay not in the temporary frenzy of the 'Terror' but in its acceleration of the persistent historical process of centralization initiated by the *ancien régime* of the absolutist monarchy. In this process, feudal powers or other dispersed self-governing social units were dissolved and governmental administration permeated every detail of social life including treatment of remains of the deceased. Even the US, proud of its constitutional protection of liberty, revealed its vulnerability to this tyrannical potential when it was under the sway of national hysteria in instances such as the 'Red' purge of McCarthyism.

Capitalist tyranny emerges when victors of market competition use their power of accumulated capital to dominate not only economic processes but also political processes of the state and to undermine communal forms of human life. Contemporary communitarians have warned us against the erosive effect of the market economy on communal lives, such as massive national chain stores that disrupt self-governing communities sustained by locally committed small businesses, and urged the need to regulate such market influences. Regulatory faculties of the state are also susceptible to invasion of market control. The dismayingly great extent to which effectiveness of election campaigns and political advocacy depend on donated money in contemporary industrial democracies shows that plutocracy remains a matter of grave concern.

Moreover, the subjection of the state to market, of politics to economy, is not confined to the domestic context in the contemporary world. Deregulation of international capital transfer and permeation of information technology in financial transactions have made instantaneous and massive cross-border capital flight possible. It is now more than an imagined possibility that actors of the globalized market can shop around for a political regime that offers the optimum environment for their investment. The state that burdens market actors with the greater responsibility of bearing the cost of social welfare, consumer protection and environmental protection may be 'punished' by capital flight that devastates its economy. This globalized form of market control over state can also undermine democratic self-governance because freely moving capital has no democratic accountability to the citizens of the affected state whose policy choice it constrains.

Communitarian tyranny obtains when intermediary – between state and market – communities can abuse their resources of informal control, their political leverage of organized votes and their financial patronage to paralyze the state's faculty of securing individual rights and the public interests at large and/or to obstruct fair market competition. Such tyranny has internal and external aspects. Intermediary communities are internally tyrannical when they can indulge in violating individual rights of their members by excluding the state's legal intervention and closing 'the exit' of attractive alternative life opportunities that sound market could have provided. Thus, Tocqueville who praised communal life of small American townships as a seedbed of civic virtue that invigorates democratic tradition did not fail to see that they have a tendency to generate tyranny of the majority that is comparable to internal communitarian tyranny. Intermediary communities are externally tyrannical when they can secure their collective vested interests at the sacrifice of the general public interest by controlling both the political decision-making process and market transactions. Interest-group pluralism common in contemporary industrial democracies involves danger of generating external communitarian tyranny. While potential for communitarian tyranny is found in all democratic societies to some extent, I think that contemporary Japan is conspicuous among major industrial democracies by the staggering extent to which its political and economic regime is dominated by the forces of internal and external communitarian tyranny. The problems that this tyranny causes in Japan will be identified in the next section.

The triad of tyrannies elucidated is meant as no more than ideal types. The reality of each society involves complications and ambivalence that cannot be totally and reductively subsumed in a single type of this triad. Nevertheless, each or some combination of them helps us to characterize the most pressing plight of each society. The triad of social orders and the triad of tyrannies that I have presented above show how the universalistic and contextual perspectives on societal ordering can be integrated. The ideal of the plural equilibrium of three competing ordering principles has universal validity because their underlying values represent deeply rooted and competing human aspirations that we have no other choice but to accommodate together, lest each or all of them degenerate into perversion. The fact that different societies at different times lose the equilibrium in different ways implies that appropriate diagnosis and remedy for social pathology varies with the historical context of each society. Such a simultaneously universalistic and contextual stance does not endorse value relativism instead it clarifies the relativity of social predicament.

For example, the communitarian diagnosis and remedy can illuminate and cope with the pathology of those societies where both the dynamics of free market and regulatory power of the activist welfare state compete with each other for hegemony and alternate in predominating while jointly undermining the vitality of intermediary communities. To put it another way, the communitarian perspective shows a way out for the societies under the sway of complicity-through-rivalry of the potentials of capitalist and softened totalitarian tyrannies. Contemporary American society may well be regarded as typical of them. Yet, this communitarian perspective does not adequately capture the plights of other societies. For example, post-communist countries in Eastern Europe and former USSR regions are facing more complicated and demanding challenges than the communitarian position would suggest: the task of simultaneously cultivating competitive discipline of market economy and communal solidarity for self-governing intermediary associations of civil society independent of the state. This should be the challenge for China also, although the Chinese communist government is eager to activate only the market economy and is alert to stemming the growth of independent intermediary associations. There is also important difference in social plight within the so-called 'Western' world. Germany, for instance, with its strong tradition of social democratic and corporatist management of economy proved to be too rigid to respond to recent technological revolution quickly. It is facing the difficult task of reinforcing the competitiveness of its economy without simultaneously undermining the social responsibility of economic agents and inseminating chauvinistic and xenophobic forms of communal passions among those who feel defeated and alienated in the economic competition. To oversimplify in order to highlight a point: taken together, the communitarian project is to rescue community from market and the state, and while the post-communist project is to rescue market and community from the state, the post-corporatist project in Germany is to rescue market from community and the state without degenerating the last two.

Like post-communism and post-corporatism, the predicament of contemporary Japan also defies the communitarian analysis, in that community is not the remedy but the cause of illness in the political and economic body. The challenge for Japan is to rescue the state and market from community. Let me discuss the Japanese case briefly in the last section.

The Japanese predicament

Postwar Japanese society has achieved miraculous development and transformed itself into a major economic power while maintaining a stable democratic regime. Apart from international conditions, there are two basic domestic factors that made this possible: communitarian reconstruction of capitalism called *kaishashugi* (companyism) and consensus-based structure of political decision making established by the so-called 55 *nen taisei* (the 1955 regime) that coopted various political forces under the guise of the one-party dominance of the Liberal Democratic Party (LDP). These two systems and other concomitant elements of social regimentation, such as the education system, made a great success in forging political consensus on government policies that gave priority to mobilizing national energy for high and fast economic growth. However, this success involved great social cost and sacrifice and the reasons for the success turn out to be also the cause of their own failure in engendering an overheated bubble economy and its eventual breakdown. The systems revealed their inability to cope effectively with the resultant débâcle, as they increasingly became obstacles to necessary structural reforms. Neither neo-liberal deregulationist language, prevalent among reformists, nor the protectionist language of their critics, is able to capture the core of the current Japanese predicament adequately. The problems of the current economic and political regimes of postwar Japan can be best illuminated, I will argue, in terms of communitarian tyranny both in its internal and external aspects.

In contemporary Japan, internal communitarian tyranny is found not just in the remnant traditional local communities or fanatical organizations, such as religious cults and political extremists, but also pervades modern firms where ordinary people work. To understand this, we have to have some idea of *kaishashugi* regime. This idea and its materialization have turned Japanese firms, except small businesses, into a kind of constitutive communities that engage the self-identity of all their employees. Individual interests of the employees, whether labor or management, merge not into the collective interests of the wage-earning class as a whole but also into the collective fate of their respective firm. The regime promoted 'communalization' of firms through processes that dissolve traditional labor–capital conflict, while reinforcing internal cohesion. These processes included transfer of corporate governance from external shareholders to the management representative of the employees, close communication between management and labor, long-term employment, long-term incremental promotion giving equal incentive of skill development to all the employees and mitigation of the blue–white-collar stratification.

This displacement of class-based capitalist exploitation and alienation of labor increased labor productivity immensely. For the same reason, it brought about what may be called communitarian exploitation of individual employees: excessive demand upon the employees for their personal devotion and loyalty to their firms, complicity of management and union or colleagues in repressing nonconformist individual employees, and difficulty of finding an escape in the external labor market. Consequently, individual employees rights to personal autonomy, including right to life, were and continue to be violated. They are deprived of opportunity and energy to perform their responsibility for their families and in other spheres of social life outside their firms. This is symbolized by the death and suicide of Japanese workers from overwork, disruption of their families, their political apathy, weakness of their critical resistance to their firms' organizational crimes and other anti-social activities.

The prevalence of such internal communitarian tyranny in firms has been facilitated by the passivity of the Japanese government, especially the courts, in intervening in the internal affairs of firms. Government respects the self-rule of firms as a community of employees gives the firms' interests precedence over individual rights of each employee. This tendency of the government to give communal self-rule priority over individual rights is not confined to firms but is generalized to other intermediary communities. This passivist stance of the state, including the notorious judicial passivism of its courts concerning protection of constitutional rights of individuals, allows internal tyranny to prevail in various communities in Japan.

External communitarian tyranny at the societal level has been prevalent under the regime of consensus-oriented democracy, which stresses governance through consensus formation among various political forces, each representing special interests of a certain intermediary community. The formal ending of the 1955 regime in 1993, when one-party rule of the LDP was replaced by a coalition of former opposition and new parties seceded from the LDP, did not change the structure of consensus democracy. Instead, this made it more visible. Under this consensus regime, intermediary communities that are internally cohesive enough to supply organized votes beyond a certain threshold can exert strong political veto and secure their vested interests, at the expense of the general interests of the society. On the other hand, the general public who can only supply 'floating votes' is unreliable for politicians and does not, indeed cannot, have a persistent hold over the political process. Political ineffectuality induces in the public political apathy, resulting in poor turnout at the polls, which further reinforces the political influence of the organized communities. So we have a vicious circle here.

Like politicians, bureaucrats are also dominated by organized communities. Although it is often said that bureaucrats of centralized administrative authorities dominate Japanese politics, it is far from the case. To be sure, the Japanese bureaucracy pervasively intervenes in economic and social activities, but its function is to mediate in the conflicting interests of competing groups. Even this function is often left up to the interest groups concerned to reconcile their differences. Thus, in practice, bureaucrats do not have real political power to break up the vested interests of the organized groups and carry out consistent public policy from a long-term point of view. For example, the so-called *tatewari* (vertically split) administration that generates inter-ministerial and intra-ministerial conflicts of jurisdiction reflects conflicts of interests between different organized groups, which are taken care of by different ministries and departments. The notorious *amakudari* (coming down from the heaven), the practice of appointing former government officials to high positions in private firms or other nongovernmental institutions, shows not the strength but weakness of the bureaucrats because they are thereby coopted and made dependent on the interest groups that are supposed to be controlled. Finally, organized communities that have political leverage over legislative and administrative processes use regulatory power of the state over the market economy to protect their vested interests against competitive pressures, so that their dominance permeates the market, too. Thus, we have seen, albeit in a cursory way, how contemporary Japan is dominated by the internal and external momentums of communitarian tyranny. The state's incapacity in securing discipline of public responsibility and erosion of the market discipline of fair competition are the results of this tyranny, which is a root cause of Japan's current economic and social maladies and its incompetence to cope with them effectively.

The above analysis points the way to required structural reforms. In this, neo-liberal deregulationists are misguided in assuming that the over-regulatory big government is the source of the Japanese economic problem. Actually, the government in Japan is too weak to enforce necessary public regulations for such economic processes as fair competition, environmental protection and consumer protection. Indeed, instead of deregulation, the regulatory power of the state must be reinforced in these areas. For example, as far as social welfare expenditure is concerned, Japan has been a 'small government' compared with the Western industrial democracies, including the US, because it has been able to depend on the informal safety net that firms, agricultural cooperatives, small business associations, professional associations, a local network of mutual assistance and other intermediary communities provide for their members, in return for the protection of the respective organization's vested interests. As market discipline of fair competition that is needed in Japan is bound to weaken these informal safety nets, they must be replaced by a formal and universalistic safety net of extra-market redistribution by the welfare state that is open to all, irrespective of political leverage of special interests. Such a formal safety net is more equitable than the informal ones. The current challenge of the Japanese state is to establish fair market competition and a fair welfare state simultaneously.

Protectionists, on the other hand, are wrong in failing to distinguish between the particularistic protection of vested interests of organized intermediary groups through restriction of competition and the universalistic protection of rights to decent minimum standard of living through extra-market redistribution. Recipients of the former protection regard themselves as 'the weak' or 'the marginalized'. Actually they are 'the strong' that possess the political power to impose the cost of their special privileges on the general public, which includes many who are poorer than these recipients and have their livelihood severely damaged by the cost-bearing in the form of tax or increased consumer prices. This mode of particularistic protection should be abolished whereas the universalistic protection should be reinforced.

To sum up, Japan needs reinforcement of the state and revitalization of the market to correct the defects of communitarian tyranny. However, the kind of strong state that it needs is not a Machtstaat but a Rechtsstaat that has the moral and legal muscle to enforce the universalistic principle of justice and human rights. The kind of vigorous market that it needs is not the laissez-faire jungle but the stage of fair competition where no one is allowed to gain or retain competitive advantage by unfair means and everyone is assured of decent safety net so that the defeated can try to challenge again. Overall, reinforcements of judicial remedies are needed both to protect individual rights effectively against the forces of internal communitarian tyranny and to control potential abuses of power of public regulation of a reinforced state.

Conclusion

As communitarians point out, intermediary communities can play a vital role in cultivating civic virtue, fostering voluntary cooperation and reinforcing civil society that curbs the state tyranny. That it applies to Japan also is not to be denied. The argument here is that they can play such a civic role in an appropriate and responsible way only if they are situated in an institutional framework that prevents them from going unchecked in exercising their political leverage. It is not just the state but also all the social forces including civil society associations that are governed by Lord Acton's dictum that 'Power corrupts and absolute power corrupts absolutely'.

To carry out the reforms of the state, Japan has to transform the structure of its political decision making process. For this purpose, an alternative model of democracy that can overcome the defects of consensus-oriented democracy is needed. Although there is no space for a discussion of critical democracy here, let me say a few words about it. Instead of power-sharing based on the consensus principle of contemporary Japanese politics, critical democracy is based on the majority principle to enforce democratic accountability of the political forces that dominate the collective decision making process. It deprives organized intermediary communities of the political veto that they have exerted to protect their vested interests. Simultaneously, it reinforces judicial protection of constitutional rights as a fair scheme of minority protection that checks the danger of majoritarian tyranny.

4

THE ANTI-COMMUNITARIAN FAMILY?

Everyday conditions of authoritarian politics in South Korea

Chang Kyung-Sup

Introduction

In East Asia, communitarianism as an ideology is tied invariably to Confucianism. Within the latter, the self is always relational to a larger unit and the cultivation of the self is not simply a process of individualist self-formation but deemed as the preparation for managing the family, governing the nation and bringing peace on earth. The family, not the individual, is deemed the fundamental unit of social life – that is, community life. As familial well-being is the responsibility of all its members, the family as an institution operates not only as an enabling institution that provides for its members but also as a strict disciplinary agency in constraining the lives of its members. Within this doubled function the actual working of the family and the costs it extracts from its members for its own welfare are often invisible to the ideological configuration of its place in generating communitarian spirit in the larger society.

In contemporary South Korea (Korea hereafter), Confucianism remains an abiding ideology of everyday life. The idea and substance of the family as the fundamental unit of social life of individuals still holds sway. Although alienated from institutional political processes under military dictatorship and personalized clique politics, Korean citizens have nevertheless lived politically contentious personal lives because the family functions as a crucial political arena, mechanism/institution, organization, and ideology. Since political primacy of the family is not confined to purely private relationships and encounters but extends into public political domains, the authoritarian political culture in Korean society may be said to be firmly embedded in Koreans' familism in everyday life.[1] I will examine in this essay the family-centered nature of Koreans' everyday social relationships and political encounters as a crucial obstacle to communitarian civil and political life.

The family as the arena and basis of everyday politics can be observed in such aspects as: excessive engulfing of individuals, particularly youth and women, in intra-familial relationships and processes as a cause of their indifference to communal relationships and duties; externalization of familial patriarchal authoritarianism into social organizations and political relationships; reliance on and use or abuse of familial relationships in fulfilling class interests and controlling political resistance; enforcing patriarchal standards and ideologies for the normative control or punishment of non-familial groups or individuals.

It is important to note here that all these activities are conventionally rationalized in terms of 'collective' welfare of the family, hence, a form of 'communitarianism' at its own level. Yet, historically, these sociopolitical instances of familism are engendered by the demise of the earlier Confucian communitarian order in social, political, and economic life during the turbulent twentieth century. Furthermore, as I will demonstrate in this essay, the emergence of intense familism has, as one of its effects, critically hindered the establishment of a communitarian foundation in contemporary civil life and political participation in Korea. Just as Michele Barrett and Mary McIntosh (1991) found the family-centered life of contemporary (English) people highly 'anti-social', there seems to exist a sort of anti-communitarian family in the social, political, and economic life of South Koreans, such that despite much democratization of formal institutional politics in recent years, the political quality of everyday life of ordinary South Koreans is critically curtailed by these family-based or family-centered practices.

The family-centered nature of private and public politics in Korea is not historically unprecedented. Traditional dynasties had relied on various versions of Confucianism in their use of familial norms and relationships in political control. Neither are aspects of familial political primacy unique to Korean society. Other East Asian societies such as Japan and China seem to share substantial parts of Koreans' family-centered social, economic, and political life. Indeed, in varying degrees and substance, familism has affected political, social and economic life of almost all nations. Historical antecedents aside, familial forms of social conflict and political control prevalent in contemporary Korea must also be seen as cultural reinventions created and used in its adaptation to explosive modern social transformations.

Of course, after four decades of rapid capitalist economic and consumerist expansions, there are many signs that familism is significantly weakening in Korea. Above all, the widening intergenerational differences in personal attitudes and social norms have led people to predict, often deploringly, the decline of familial values and relationships. The rapid rise of individualism among the 'new generation' – a popular suspicious branding of youth – supposedly attests to this weakening. However, such weakening does not necessarily harbor a significant possibility of revival of communitarianism in civil life and political order.

Historical contexts of familism

There is ample historical evidence that Koreans used to live in a civilization of fundamentally family-centered social, political, and economic orders. That tradition was epitomized in the so-called neo-Confucian philosophy which was brought in from China but later refined into a much more ingenuous system of thoughts by Chosun scholars. According to this philosophy, the social, political, and economic systems of the entire nation were elaborately attuned to the moral integrity and organizational stability of individual families (Choe 1991). Chosun people could be loyal and useful to the state mainly by being faithful to their families. In fact, the state itself was conceptualized as a family of which the King served as grand patriarchal father to ordinary people.

Much of this cultural and ideological heritage has survived into the contemporary era, while its embodying social, political, and economic systems were almost entirely demolished under the turmoil and disruptions of the Japanese invasion and colonial rule, the US military occupation, the Korean War, and the postwar social disintegration. This was in part because of the absence of any indigenous social revolution that would have required a total cultural regeneration of society as well as a total restructuring of social institutions and relations.[2] The postwar modernization elite did not attempt to implement any full-scale cultural engineering to change Korea's Confucian family-centered life. Instead, the modern school system, which incorporated the entire population without distinction between aristocrats and commoners, began to educate the public with social values and attitudes that substantially reflects the Confucian tradition.

More importantly, most Koreans had to depend on familial relations and resources in coping with the turbulent social, political, and economic environments. When colonial economic exploitation and political abuse of grassroots were rampant, when war denied any certainties in social relations and economic activities, and when political regimes were unstable and only authoritarian in managing civil life, most people felt that their own family was the only reliable source of protection and survival. Even when full-scale industrialization began in the early 1960s, migrant workers, urban peddlers, urban industrial entrepreneurs, and other actors of capitalist industrialism had to eke out resources and strategies for economic success from the family and other groups with familial social characteristics.

Familism in Korean society is derived, therefore, not just from its Confucian heritage of family-centered life, but more critically from the process and method by which Koreans have coped with various socio-cultural, political, and economic forces. The ideological and practical primacy of the family over the individual and society in various domains of life is thus as much a modern reinvention as a tradition. The authoritarian developmentalist regime under Park Chung Hee did not attempt to change such grassroots familism, but instead utilized it as the main institutional framework for mobilizing social and economic resources and manipulating political attitudes.

These tendencies should not be theoretically simplified as a symptom of lack of modernity or undermodernization. On the contrary, the macro-social significance of Koreans' familism requires a fundamental rethinking of the conventional thesis of cultural modernization or rationalization. The seemingly archaic familism that has forcefully driven Korean society, economy, and politics, constitutes one of the most crucial components of Koreans' modernity, although not without resultant problems and costs (Chang 1997b). It should be acknowledged that familism, among other inherited and/or reinvented cultural elements, has open 'elective affinity' with various modern social formations and changes.[3] Familism has combined with, has altered, and has been reworked by numerous projects of Koreans' modernity, among them political democratization being not the least important.

Familial political arena and empty civil society

As elsewhere, most men and women in Korea are born and raised in families, marry to form families, and get old and die in families. The sheer amount of time spent in various forms of interactions with family members makes the family the most dominant arena of social life (cf. Corr and Jamieson 1990). Thus the political quality of intra-familial interactions is a crucial determinant of the democratic or authoritarian nature of one's life. In this sense, the time-worn ideal of patriarchal authoritarian communitarianism in Korean families, whether fully realized or substantially resisted, cannot but deny a truly democratic life to average Koreans.

The cultural tradition in its most recent version of neo-Confucianism rigorously stipulates the 'proper' patterns of inter-gender, inter-generation, and inter-sibling relationships mainly in terms of hierarchy and role differentiation (Choe 1991). For instance, the 'norm of three followings' for a woman – following her father in childhood, following her husband after marriage, and following her son(s) in old age – was effectively, though not always consciously, enforced well into recent decades. Perhaps younger generations of women would dispute not only the relevance of this norm but also its actual influence on them. But the prevalent social structural conditions make them (and their parents) pursue – in fact, want to pursue – the feminine life course of obedient and dependent childhood, adolescence, marriage, and old age. Those women whose life has been disrupted from this life sequence are more likely to deplore such disruption instead of welcoming it. Of course, the affectionate union between husband and wife does not have to presuppose any hierarchical order, but the influence of the Confucian tradition of gender hierarchy and differentiation has not evaporated clearly.

Ironically, the modern (Western) family ideology also tends to reinforce women's passivity. The image of the family as an emotional union for which the domestic role of the full-time wife-mother is central (cf. Shorter 1975) has been powerfully inculcated into the mind of young women of all social strata and regions. Indeed, the image of women in the modern or Western middle-class family is in a curious harmony with that in the traditional aristocratic class (*yangban*) family in Korea. Whenever this role is attainable, in particular for an educated or affluent husband, most Korean women tend to accept it. Ironically, this phenomenon is most distinct among the most highly educated group of women (i.e., college graduates), whose employment rate is rather lower than women with less education. On the surface, this may be because they are much more likely to marry well-educated and capable husbands. More fundamentally, however, they are rarely given other meaningful choices as full members of society. Women's economic participation, if any, has been disproportionately concentrated in agricultural and menial service sectors where personal or collective efficacy is hard to achieve (Chang 1995).

One interesting consequence of women's dependent life course is the emotional friction between a man's wife and his mother. An old woman's psychological as well as material dependence on her son inevitably contradicts her daughter-in-law's wish for the affectionate conjugal relationship of an independent nature. Moreover, the mother's dependence on her son in everyday life is instrumentally possible not by her home-absent son's occasional lip service but by her home-staying daughter-in-law's hard work. The traditional nature of such in-law relationship is known to be usually authoritarian. Here lies one of the most serious intergenerational conflicts in Korean society – '*gobugaldeung*' (mother-in-law vs. daughter-in-law conflict) (Han 1989: 213–228). The current generation of mothers-in-law, after having served an almost exclusive mission of caring for their own, mostly authoritarian parents-in-law in this welfare-absent society, feel much betrayed and frustrated by their daughters-in-law with 'individualist' attitudes, even as they appear to accept the changing reality by giving up their hope for being served by a co-residing son and his wife (Kong *et al.* 1990).

Learning the proper patterns of interaction according to age, gender, and generational order in the family (and society) is a daunting task for Korean children. This process is often in conflict with children's desire for autonomous interpretation of social order. Under the Confucian social order, children find themselves surrounded only by those who can demand respect and obedience from them as one-way traffic. Younger siblings, if any, are the only exception. In exchange for such respect and obedience, children are offered various material resources by parents until well into their twenties and thirties. This means that social subordination is translated into prolonged material dependence. And children's material dependence further justifies their social subordination. Recently, middle-class Koreans' accommodation of the Western notion of pure and fragile childhood that requires intensive emotional as well as physical care (cf. Sommerville 1990) has led to some weakening in the authoritarian disciplining of children. None the less, the chain reaction process between children's social subordination and material dependence is still a dominant obstacle to children's autonomous and democratic individuality.

For most children, the chain is broken through their social experiences outside the family, i.e. at schools, streets, etc. At such places, children's social subordination to other children is not compensated for materially. Moreover, they get exposed to various new types of norms and cultures concerning human relationships with which their parents are not familiar. The propensity of Korean society to bring in foreign cultures rapidly and the sheer speed of its internal social change (Chang 1999) make the intergenerational sociocultural gap ever grow bigger and bigger. However, the real problem concerning the intergenerational gap lies not with its magnitude but with parents' reliance on an authoritarian disciplinary measure to force conformity –another part of the Confucian sociopolitical culture (Kang 1994). Children respond strategically to this situation by avoiding or reducing their encounters with parents and, when encountered with parents, by instantly pretending to follow parents' will. As children would not bother to express their real self at home, many parents, when summoned to a school or a police station for their children's' misdemeanors, have a hard time understanding the seemingly obedient children's totally different attitudes and behaviors revealed to them.

Korean wives and youth may as much detest such restrictive and overstuffed social relationships within the family as their counterparts in other societies would and instead like to liberate themselves beyond home if personal and social conditions allow. However, this remains too remote a possibility.[4] First, except in a few professional activities such as teaching, arts, and music, women's participation or employment has not been warmly welcomed and respected. Women do work outside home – currently, about half of the working-age women participate in economic activities. But the work conditions, including social relationships in the work process, are particularly abrasive in sectors and occupations that are staffed mainly by women (Chung 1994; Lee 1993). Few women in such 'feminine' sectors and occupations want to pursue their current work as a life-time career. In the early phase of industrialization, women were 'socialized' into primitive farmwork to make up for men's urban migration; in the high tide of labor-intensive industrialization in the 1970s, women were the core of the sweatshop workforce; since the mid-1980s, various service sectors such as home service, menial office errand, food catering, and shop-keeping have made many jobs available for women but usually on a non-regular basis (Chang 1995).

Also, the prevailing political culture defines politics as a primarily men's issue, so that women's political activities are extremely rare and, if any, given only a symbolic meaning. Women are expected to feel satisfied by some political role in 'women's issues'. Even most of the civil social and political movements are led by male intellectuals, whereas female activists are concentrated in gender equality movements. Women's representation in major political and governmental positions remains at one of the lowest levels in the world. In a 2001 report on the Gender Empowerment Measure (GEM), the United Nations Development Plan ranked South Korea at the 61st among 64 countries surveyed.[5] The GEM reflects female representation in parliamentary, high-level administrative and managerial, and professional positions, gender inequality in income, female participation in the policy-making process, etc. Despite the noisy reform policies of the civilian political regimes since the early 1990s, the recent political situation does not significantly differ from before in women's point of view.[6]

However, women's role in the informal (and often illicit) world is significant as they are given many secretive functions to play. Wearing a sort of *social chador*, women contact friends and relatives to lend or borrow money, consult realtors for speculative real estate transactions, meet teachers to buy favoritism or arrange private lessons for their children, and even visit their husband's office superior's home to deliver gifts and curry favor. The aggregate outcomes of these '*chimabaram*' (skirt wind) activities are often stunning as illustrated by their large shares of capital formation for many big corporations, the skyrocketing of house and land prices, the colossal amount of private educational spending (even surpassing the public educational spending), etc. The political dilemma in this regard is that the societal consequences of such informal activities of women are often perceived negatively and thus reinforce women's exclusion from the mainstream formal world. In many instances, families of elite figures were found involved in these immoral and sometimes illegal activities. In the ensuing inquisition process, wives would take the entire moral and legal responsibility lest their husbands should jeopardize occupational career and social status (Byun 1994).

Second, the economic and political activities by youth, particularly teenagers, have not been socially considered appropriate. Their life course, if beyond home, has been expected (and somewhat idealized) to proceed only through schooling and, for boys, military service until they become fully mature for employment and marriage. Society and parents suggest almost no social activities as desirable for youth except the preparation for the college entrance examination (Kim and Park 1992). When they work for wages, adults would consider it either pitiful or suspicious. When they gather outside home or school, parents, teachers, and sometimes police will immediately worry about possibilities of deviance and agitation and want them to immediately disperse back into home or school. They cannot even vote in political elections until they turn 20 years old.

An interesting development along the college entrance of youth is that young college students were the most active political group against military dictatorship for three decades. Once 'liberated' into college campus from family, Korean youth showed explosive degrees of social and political activism and thereby led Korean society toward a progressive direction (Kim 1993). Security police have tried to bring the family back in by asking radical student demonstrators' parents to persuade their children out of anti-governmental or 'pro-communist' rioting. The opposite side of the coin is that many such parents, after finding out police brutality and governmental hypocrisy against their 'conscientious' children, have come to politically sympathize with their children and even form their own social movement organizations for political democratization. *Minjuhwasilcheongajogundonghyeobuihoe* (Democracy Promotion Family Movement Council) is perhaps the most important case.

Another significant trend of politicization of youth has been triggered as part of the 'internet revolution'. On-line political space cannot impose arbitrary institutional barriers to youth, who in fact are the most skilled users of the electronic arena of political communication and debate. As Korean society has become the internationally acknowledged experimentation ground for not only on-line commercialism but also on-line democracy, Korean youth have actively captured this opportunity to establish themselves as a powerful political class. This is a sort of unintended consequence of the informatization project that has been pursued by the conservative administrations mainly as an economic task. Within the family, parents have felt much frustrated at their inefficacy in monitoring and controlling their children's cyber activities. In the presidential election of 2002, internet political movements led by youth resulted in intergenerational political rivalry as generation became a most powerful determinant of political choice (Song 2003). The winner, Roh Moo-Hyun considered himself an internet president, and even asked people to send popular recommendations for new ministers via the internet. However, it has yet to be seen whether internet politics will actually reform or revolutionize institutional politics in the long run. On-line political activism has lost much of its steam after the presidential election.

All these said, it is obvious that the family in Korean society functions as the powerful mechanism for the containment and surveillance of women and youth away from the civil social space. The Korean family idealizes social non-action and effectively denies the membership in civil community to women and youth. This anti-community function is so effective that youth and housewives are simply absent in most of civil social events making civil community, when it exists, appear quite patriarchal. For youth, however, the future possibility that they may participate in student social movements at colleges or join labor unions at work presents a signal for political liberation from family into society. Furthermore, the so-called 'internet revolution' has elevated youth to the status of mainstream political players, at least for certain political issues and events. For housewives, there is no such prospect for institutionalized political liberation, whereas personalized options such as divorce and separation often result in isolation from both family and society.

Authoritarian communitarianism in family, society, and polity

The demands of authoritarian Korean society on the family are not limited to the containment and surveillance of women and youth within its walls but extend into the creation of social members with personalities and attitudes suitable for – or at least compatible with – the dominant sociopolitical culture. In this sense, the resemblance between family and society in their authoritarian organizational culture becomes a critical condition for the sustenance of the authoritarian order in society and polity. Such need was recognized at the universal level by Parsons (Parsons and Bales 1955) when he defined the family as a main institution for 'pattern maintenance'. There is a debate on the internal contradictions in Parsons' understanding of the family both as a pattern maintenance institution (for contractual, non-affectionate society) and as a socially secluded, affectionate union of a married couple and their children (Lasch 1983). In Korea, however, as authoritarian communitarianism – or authoritarian collectivism with some paternalist flavor – is a common denominator of both family and society, such a theoretical contradiction is not obvious.

Compatibility or harmony between familial and social norms of order was a core doctrine of Confucian sociopolitical order (Choe 1991). The family as the main social institution for pattern maintenance is also a Confucian proposition that has already been discussed for thousands of years. Socially and politically acceptable attitudes of individuals were supposed to be cultivated within the family. The failure to do so was considered an utmost shame to the entire family. The very system of promoting this sociopolitical function of the family, involving authoritarianism as patriarchal moral compulsion, was the key source of familial disciplining. Patriarchal authoritarianism was thus both the method and goal of familial disciplining. At the societal level, the Chosun dynasty was an officially familial state in which the king–people relationship was characterized as analogous to the father–children relationship. People were expected to defer to the king in the same way as they revered their parents. This norm had an additional effect of precluding the possibility that people's attachment to their parents (family) would weaken their loyalty to the king (state).

There was a conscious effort at reinvigorating such sociopolitical tradition in the modern era of authoritarian developmentalism. Park Chung Hee, a military general-turned-president, tried to portray himself as a moral patriarch for the whole nation in order to culturally justify his dictatorship and politically reinforce his developmentalist leadership. The philosophical code of political loyalty and filial piety (i.e., *Chunghyosa-sang*) – with a strong suggestion to serve the state (the president) just like parents – was thus reinvented in the new era and incorporated into the formal school curricular. In a country where only right-wing nationalism was allowed after progressive ideologies had been wiped out in the aftermath of the communist versus capitalist civil war, followed by the Cold War, Park's appeal to patriarchal and mercantile nationalism was not historically out-of-context. Nonetheless, it was not clear how much Koreans' extraordinarily strong filial piety was actually translated into their respect or at least endurance for the authoritarian patriarch of the state. In the long run, it was evident that more and more people, particularly the urban educated, got fed up with Park's endless dictatorship and sided with resistant politicians and intellectuals in various ways. Yet, since the mid-1990s, political instability and economic crisis came to lead many people and media into the so-called Park Chung Hee nostalgia. His patriarchal nationalist authority has been reevaluated as an indispensable virtue for the then seemingly helpless nation.

Since the 1990s, patriarchal authoritarian communitarianism has also been cultivated by those opposition politicians who criticized and resisted Park's dictatorship, such as Kim Young-Sam and Kim Dae-Jung, and by Park's political heirs, like Kim Jong-Pil and Chun Doo-Hwan. There seems to exist a sort of pseudo-familial attachment to those patriarchal politicians who, by cultivating and manipulating regionalism, have intensified extremely hostile inter-regional rivalries and bigotries. These leaders have intentionally appealed to the deep-rooted hatred and jealousy among peoples of different regions in order to portray themselves as patriarchal saviors. Other politicians, who desperately need the approval and support of these patriarchs for their election into parliamentary seats, have to show absolute loyalty and obedience to them.

Aside from national politics, patriarchal authoritarianism prevails in most of the social, political, and economic organizations including schools, political parties, business offices, factories, and even academic departments and associations. The modernization thesis of the transition from *gemeinschaft* to *gesellschaft* is not tenable as the supposedly *gesellschaft*-type organizations are constructed and operated on the basis of a core version of *gemeinschaft* organizational culture. And those young people who fail to adapt to such organizational culture are readily and sometime, openly suspected of having received improper disciplining from the family. Senior people in these organizations like to compare themselves to the elder brothers and even parents of junior people in demanding obedience and respect. 'We are the family' is the most used motto of Korean organizations. While it is often accompanied by various material benefits as a gesture of family-like generosity, its sociopolitical implications in everyday life are often dreadful.

Family-divided community: class struggle and political control

As mentioned earlier, the family-centered life of Koreans has been nurtured both by historical traditions and the social, political, and economic environments with which they cope by depending on familial relationships and resources. Under the turmoils and disruptions of colonialism, war, and dictatorship, Koreans came up with what might be called *instrumental familism*.[7] This means that Koreans' family stands as the key organizational unit and/or corporate actor for, through, and by which they pursue social, political, and economic activities. The family is supposed permanently to serve its members' survival and success in competitive and hostile society by mobilizing, sharing, and pooling all possible means and resources in it.[8]

Under instrumental familism, Koreans have engaged in vibrant inter-familial competition and conflict for sheer survival to hegemonic dominance. Peasants, industrial workers, merchants, and even major capitalists have adopted familial strategies for intra-class competition and inter-class struggle. From family farming to *chaebol* business, the real unit of class conflict and domination has been the family. In particular, the famous family-based control of ownership and management in Korean *chaebol* corporations has been seen responsible not only for their rapid success and demise but also for their inharmonious relationship with workers and small stock-holders (Cho 1991). The quick formation of a good-quality workforce for new industries since the 1960s was an aggregate outcome of the efforts by millions of peasant families which sent motivated children and siblings to cities and supported their education, occupational training, and even livelihood in the enthusiastic hope of achieving intergenerational upward social mobility (Chang 2001b). Among the urban middle and upper class – and perhaps among the entire Korean population – children's competition for college entrance examination, *ipsigyeongjaeng*, represents the main arena in which the fierce inter-familial struggle, in terms of expensive private tutoring and other means, has been staged (Kim 1992). Even their children's marriage is considered a critical mechanism for status advance or maintenance at the familial level, so that the excessive parental intervention in children's mate selection and the lavish spending on the wedding ceremony and dowries are common. For the underclass that need social welfare protection, the extremely conservative developmentalist regimes have called for their familial self-reliance under the rubric of a 'uniquely Korean, family-based welfare system' (Chung 1991).

The family is also a unit of political control and domination. As illustrated vividly by the Kim Hyun-Chul scandal during his father, Kim Young-Sam's presidency, the power of major political leaders has often been delegated to their sons and brothers, so that one's political election, appointment, or popularity actually implies the political empowerment of his whole family. When an effort is made to convert or extend economic power into political power by business elite, it is often son, brother, and/or son-in-law that is strategically selected and supported to undertake such a political mission. Of course, there exist more serious examples in many other societies. The Korean dilemma is that such apparently archaic political behaviors cruelly betray Koreans' pride in their painstaking achievement of democracy.

Family connection in elite politics is never seen as desirable or acceptable by grassroots Koreans. But they are not taken by surprise in this regard, either. Elite politics as familial conspiracy has been too frequent. But, more fundamentally, the success of children, especially sons, in political, bureaucratic, economic or professional careers is the most common 'objective of life' to an overwhelming majority of Korean adults.[9] The meaning of Koreans' everyday social life is rarely detached from the success and welfare of their family. Conversely, society will take a parent to be morally, legally, and sometimes politically responsible for the goods and wrongs of his/her family members, including grown-up ones. Most Koreans would not dispute this responsibility, in part because doing so is to be considered as an extremely cowardly and unethical act.

As the family dominates the social, economic, and political processes, there are interesting and important consequences that further complicate the situation. First, intergenerational change or succession in social, economic, and political domains has been extremely tardy at the societal level but problematically abrupt and frequent at the familial level. That is, as the hereditary succession of corporate ownership/management, media control, political appointment, and even religious leadership has been attempted widely, next generations of non-kin elite are forfeited their hope and right to acquire social, economic, political, and religious leadership careers. Problems of this familial succession have manifested in terms of not only moral and legal defects but also functional inefficiencies. Recently, many *chaebol* heirs, often in their thirties or forties without much business experience, hastily tried to impress the founders by outdoing them in the expansion of corporate sizes and domains and consequently led their business inheritance into inescapable financial troubles.

Conversely, in areas where hereditary succession is not easy or feasible, succession as a whole has been refused. Perhaps the best example may be found in professional party politics, in which many aged and detested leaders would have already retired had it been possible for their male children or siblings to inherit their power or positions. It is in this context, the slogan of *sedaegyoche*, the argument for replacing old generations with the new, itself has become one of the most forceful political ideologies. For example, in the 1997 presidential election race, Rhee In-Je, a man in his early fifties, once commanded a popular support rate of more than 30 percent almost solely on the basis of his *sedaegyoche* slogan. The winner of the 2002 presidential election, Roh Moo-Hyun was less explicit in the same slogan, but widely believed to have crucially benefited from the *sedaegyoche* mentality of young voters.

Second, in-law relationship, in particular among elite figures, has functioned as a powerful tool for political and economic activities. Children of *chaebol* families are most likely to marry children of other *chaebol* families whereas children of many high-level bureaucrats and influential politicians also marry children of *chaebol* families (Kong 1990). More specifically, the preferred marriage pattern of *chaebol* families is known to let their sons marry daughters of bureaucrats and politicians and let their daughters marry sons of other *chaebol* families. This is because corporate inheritance by a son is possible while bureaucratic or political position cannot be inherited. In this way, most of the dominant capitalists and many of the political and bureaucratic leaders get intricately interlocked through in-law relationships and help each other strategically. A grassroots version of such strategic in-law relationship used to be found when academically high achieving sons of poor peasant families, after having passed the national tests for high-level administrative, judiciary, and diplomatic positions, were lured by urban rich families to marry their daughters for enormous dowries.

Third, while relying on their own instrumental familism for strategic internal support and protection, the dominant groups intentionally induce and abuse grassroots people's instrumental familism. Grassroots families are pitted against one another concerning various social matters, so that their lateral cooperation and collective consciousness necessary for pressuring the dominant political and economic groups to take responsibility and make concessions become difficult to attain. When grassroots people are preoccupied with familial support and protection, they hardly have time to analyze the structural causes of their hardships or pursue collection actions beyond each familial boundary. Such dilemmas are particularly evident in many social policy areas including education, housing, health and environment (Chang 1997a). The ultra-conservative developmentalist regimes have refused to take any meaningful corrective and/or redistributive measures in these matters. The opportunistic competition among ordinary families has caused such self-abusive consequences as corruption of teachers, inflation of housing prices, etc.

Instrumental familism in its diverse variants has enabled Koreans to resiliently and successfully cope with the turbulent political, social, and economic conditions in the twentieth century. Simultaneously, it has been abused and distorted to maintain various unjust practices of control and domination and to preempt meaningful social associations necessary for the formation of a democratic civil society. In this context, many social movement groups and intellectuals came to launch various campaigns against the so-called '*gajokigijuui*' (familial egoism), a notably anti-social variant of instrumental familism (e.g., Byun 1994). In Korea, where familism has been a dominant ideology in society and polity, the family is explicitly seen as antithetical to democratic civil society.

Prejudice politics against non-patriarchal families

As the stable operation of authoritarian society and polity depends crucially on numerous functions of the authoritarian patriarchal family, there are various systematic efforts to valorize the patriarchal family structure and ideology and repress other types of family structures and ideologies. In social, political, and even economic activities and relationships, one's 'sound' (patriarchal) family structure and culture serve as valuable assets. Various social disadvantages to 'non-traditional' types of families, both explicit and subtle, are simply formidable, so that many of those who want to break out of the patriarchal family structure and ideology for personal reasons fail to do so. Even many legal stipulations and government policies concerning family formation and welfare presuppose such patriarchal family structure. Consequently, families led by a woman or composed of only youth and children have to suffer from various disadvantages knowingly and unknowingly.

Throughout the 1980s, the so-called New Right or neo-conservative political regimes on both sides of the Atlantic Ocean called for the recovery of 'family values' on the premise that the disruption in the family norms and structures, supposedly accelerated by redistributive welfare policies, had been the main cause of social problems including poverty, crime, and welfarism itself (Somerville 1992). In a similar period, there were similar political efforts in Korean society to re-emphasize the ideal of patriarchal, extended familism and blame the individualism of 'new generations' and, in effect, underclass, as supposedly evidenced by increasing divorces, filial disobedience and family abandonment. The economic miracle of compressed capitalist development (Chang 1999) was inevitably accompanied by various symptoms of social disintegration. As the ruling camps of the authoritarian developmentalist state and large capitalist industries had not prepared and had no serious intention of preparing any comprehensive set of redistributive and/or therapeutic social policies as counter-measures, they looked out for a convenient and familiar scapegoat to be blamed as the main cause of such social problems.[10]

Thus, families with new structures and norms, instead of conservative capitalists and authoritarian politicians, were brought in under the abusive political discourse until quite recently, i.e., until the election of relatively progressive presidents like Kim Dae-Jung and Roh Moo-Hyun. Despite the fact that Koreans were still living perhaps the most family-centered life in the world, there were only criticisms and laments on the supposed moral and structural disintegration of the family when politicians, bureaucrats, and 'civil' leaders, most of them being aged patriarchs within their own families and organizations, gathered frequently to discuss the recent social problems in a preset format of 'familial crisis'. Even mass media did not hesitate to follow suit by introducing such biased discussions noisily and frequently and reporting various social problems in the same perspective. All these tendencies strikingly resembled the neo-liberal politics of the family in the West. However, one major difference in the Korean situation was that it was a continuous, not new, conservative political move since the country had not attempted any welfarist intervention previously.

Such conservative politics of the family impeded any progressive political or administrative initiatives to relieve the difficulties of families without a father or both parents concerning education, culture, deviance, crime, poverty and housing. However, even more serious burden and stress on those families and individuals broken out of the patriarchal family structure were generated by the prejudice, both conscious and unconscious, of other ordinary people in everyday life. In job and school interviews, personal encounters, and many other occasions, young persons are often asked by adults, 'what does your father do?' Such question is premised on the widespread habit of socially positioning young persons' identity according to their father's status or occupation. If their father happens to be dead or absent for other reasons, it immediately becomes an embarrassment to both parties of the conversation because life without a father readily implies an utmost hardship regardless of the young persons' actual life situation. In reality, families without a father have particular worries about children's friendship, marriage, employment, and other social relations, thinking that their children might become less preferred ones in such important events. This is the most important reason for Korean mothers to try to avoid or postpone, until their children grow up and get married, divorce even in extremely intolerable situations caused by their husbands such as repeated violence and adultery (Kong *et al.* 1990).[11]

There are, of course, pity and consideration shown by neighbors to families without a father. However, when children without fathers commit personally offensive or socially disruptive acts, neighbors and sometimes society as a whole will make issue of their defective family structure as a critical factor. It is often thought that such bad acts are made not out of the children's desperation in a difficult life situation but out of lack of discipline and morality. A lamentable example was found in the *Jijonpa* incident which shocked and horrified the entire nation by brutal killings. A few young men, whose life situation in their hometown had been miserable socially and economically, fled into cities only to experience even more hostile and abrasive treatments. Out of their total abhorrence of the whole society, they formed a crime group under the name of *Jijonpa* (utmost precious sect) and killed several randomly encountered people in extremely cruel ways. As reporters dug into their personal and familial backgrounds and found out that most of them belonged to a single-parent or no-parent family, news media immediately and loudly pointed out a possible moral and disciplinary defect of these young men from *gyeolsongajeong*, or 'deficit family' (e.g. *JungAng Ilbo*, 12 October 1994). Some of their family members protested against the media in floods of tears, saying that living without parents itself was a severe misery.

Unfortunately, academics have contributed to strengthening such popular prejudice against 'deficit families' in a systematic manner. A simple-minded positivist proposition based upon the statistical association between broken family structures and juvenile deviance and crimes has been upheld unquestioned for many years and thereby misled society and the government into a 'scientific' prejudice against the concerned youth population.[12] While such statistical relationship can be found in many other societies as well (Choi 1994), what living in a 'deficit family', especially without a father, in Korean society means emotionally, socially, and materially has not been properly interpreted in presenting research outcomes (Kong *et al.* 1995). Children of such families can commit problematic acts due to various unfair disadvantages and hardships imposed on them rather than due to any moral and disciplinary failure supposedly inherent in their families. Moreover, the possibility that a third factor, or a group of third factors, may have caused both family dissolution and its children's deviance or crime has not been taken into account. For instance, an unexpected, severe economic crisis may cause a father's death from stress or overwork on the one hand and, his children's deviant behavior out of desperation on the other hand. In this, not infrequent, situation, the children's deviance is simply an outcome of the economic crisis and has nothing to do with the broken family structure. Regardless of these possibilities, the proposition on 'the higher likelihood of deviance by children of deficit families' has been firmly ingrained into the minds of public officials and ordinary citizens and thereby induced them to treat the concerned youth in various unfavorable ways. Such unfair treatment in turn puts them in even more difficult situations and thus prompts them toward further acts of deviance – a ghastly self-fulfilling of the inattentive 'scientific' proposition.

Conclusion

The political implications of Koreans' familism need to be evaluated against the overall process of Korean democratization. In the turbulent twentieth century, Koreans arduously fought their way not only to accomplish rapid economic development but also to achieve serious political democracy. Both the Korean economy and politics used to impress peoples of Developing World countries who have been frustrated not only by elusive material progress but also by chronic political authoritarianism and corruption. In the 1990s, however, Koreans were found not as much successful in consolidating their improved economy and politics as in developing them in earlier decades. They had to confront an unprecedented economic crisis in late 1997 due to corporate overinvestment and bureaucratic mismanagement. Politics under two democracy-fighter-turned presidents (i.e., Kim Young-Sam and Kim Dae-Jung) was plagued with various undemocratic tendencies, including familism in grassroots life and elite politics.

Among others, there seem to be three major weaknesses of Korean democracy. First, there is a serious disjuncture between formal institutional politics and civil political activism – Koreans' two precious political achievements. They have arduously won, on the one hand, procedural democratic order after almost three decades of abusive authoritarian rule and, on the other hand, politically vigorous civil society pressing for various democratic rights. However, professional political parties under the firm personal control of patriarchal bosses have failed to incorporate civil activism into representative politics. Second, national political democratization has not induced lively local politics. Instead, the endemic interregional rivalry, which had been abused for political manipulation not only by military rulers (like Park Chung-Hee and Chun Doo-Hwan) but also by democratic leaders (like Kim Young-Sam and Kim Dae-Jung), contaminated local political energy, if any, into personalized loyalty to region-based patriarchs in national politics. Third, the micro-foundation of grassroots political participation either in formal procedural politics or civil activism is very frail. Professional parties are dominated by a Korean version of 'political class' whose birth was rather an accidental historical outcome in the immediate post-liberation period whereas civil social and political organizations are shouldered mainly by intellectuals and students. By contrast, most grassroots people are beset by familial relations and interests and usually indifferent to both formal procedural politics and civil political activism. Even when they attempt to participate in political matters, their judgment and action are often dictated by the powerful ideology of familism and thus deviate from a genuine communitarian cause.

Democratic life requires individuals to actively interpret and reinterpret various rules and values imposed on them in everyday social, economic, and political life before they begin to enter social relationships and perform social roles on the basis of such rules and values. The family, especially in Korea, critically influences such democratization of everyday life by determining the modes of social existence and reasoning of ordinary citizens and elite alike. By and large, familism as observed in Korean society tends to hamper autonomous and responsible social interactions and associations of individuals in everyday life as well as in elite politics. By all accounts, the prevalent familial forms of social conflict and political control in Koreans' everyday life pose a serious stumbling block to the establishment of democratic polity and society with a sound communitarian basis. This subtle but firmly rooted social predicament will be responsible for undemocratic relationships and encounters for a substantial period no matter how successfully the recent project of formal democratization proceeds in South Korea. The political effectiveness of even vibrant civil society and routinized procedural politics can be seriously undercut by the obstinate attachment to familial values and interests by both political elite and grassroots.

References

Barrett, Michele and Mary McIntosh (1991) *The Anti-Social Family*, 2nd edn, London: Verso.

Byun Hwa-Sun (1994) 'Family Toward Communitarian Life' (in Korean). *Open Society and Family*, Proceedings of the 'International Year of the Family' Seminar, the Korean Women's Development Institute and UNESCO Korea Commission, pp. 133–167.

Chang, Kyung-Sup (1995) 'Gender and Abortive Capitalist Social Transformation: Semi-Proletarianization of South Korean Women', *International Journal of Comparative Sociology* 36(1/2): 61–81.

Chang, Kyung-Sup (1997a) 'The Neo-Confucian Right and Family Politics in South Korea: The Nuclear Family as an Ideological Construct', *Economy and Society* 26(1): 22–42.

Chang, Kyung-Sup (1997b) 'Modernity through the Family: Familial Foundations of Korean Society', *International Review of Sociology* 7(1): 51–63.

Chang, Kyung-Sup (1999) 'Compressed Modernity and Its Discontents: South Korean Society in Transition', *Economy and Society* 28(1): 30–55.

Chang, Kyung-Sup (2001a) 'Compressed Modernity and Korean Family: Accidental Pluralism in Family Ideology', *Journal of Asian-Pacific Studies* 2001(September): 31–39.

Chang, Kyung-Sup (2001b) 'The Social Investment Family in Crisis: Private Family, Public Education, and Globalization in South Korea', Paper presented at the first Asia-Pacific forum on 'Glocal and Intergenerationally Responsible Public Philosophies', Kyoto International Conference Hall, 1 September 2001.

Chang Kyung-Sup, Jang Kui-Yoeun and Yee Jaeyeol (2002) 'Cold War, Compressed Modernity, and Labor Politics: Dislocated Political Society and Democratic Labor Party in South Korea' (in Korean), *Journal of International Studies* 24: 151–191.

Cho Dong-Sung (1991) *A Study of Korean Chaebol* (in Korean). Seoul: Maeil Economic Daily.

Choe Hong Kee (1991) 'Confucianism and the Family' (in Korean), *Journal of the Korean Family Studies Association* 3: 207–227.

Choi In-Seop (1994) 'Crime and Family' (in Korean). Korean Family Studies Association, ed., *Modern Family and Society*, pp. 232–256. Seoul: Gyoyukgwahaksa.

Choi Jae-Seok (1982) *A Study of the Modern Family* (in Korean). Seoul: Iljisa.

Chung Duck-Jo (1991) 'Korean Family Welfare Policy' (in Korean). *Korean Family Welfare Policy and Elderly Problem*, Seminar Proceedings, the Korea Family Welfare Policy Institute, pp. 5–42.

Chung Il-Seon (1994) 'Gender and Economic Activities' (in Korean). Society for the Study of Our Society, ed., *Gender and Modern Society*, pp. 106–151. Taegu: Parannara.

Corr, Helen and Lynn Jamieson. (1990) *Politics of Everyday Life: Continuity and Change in Work and Family.* New York: St. Martin's.

Geertz, Clifford (1973) *The Interpretation of Cultures.* New York: Basic Books.

Han Nam-Je (1989) *A Study of the Modern Korean Family* (in Korean). Seoul: Iljisa.

Internet Hankyoreh. JungAng Daily.

Kang Dae-Geun (1994) 'Youth as Master of the Future and Family' (in Korean). *Open Society and Family*, Proceedings of the 'International Year of the Family' seminar, the Korean Women's Development Institute and UNESCO Korea Commission, pp. 41–67.

Kim Do-Jong (1993) 'The Current Situation and Problems of Student Movement Studies: With a Focus on the Korean Student Movement' (in Korean). Kim Do-Jong, ed., *Student Movement in the World.* Seoul: Him, pp. 37–67.

Kim Jae-Eun (1992) 'Beyond Familial Egoism' (in Korean). *College Entrance Examination and Family*, Proceedings of the First Symposium of the Society for the Study of Family and Culture, pp. 61–67.

Kim Mun-Jo and Park Young-Jin (1992) 'I Am Not Myself: Study Pressure Felt by Students Themselves' (in Korean). *College Entrance Examination and Family*, Proceedings of the First Symposium of the Society for the Study of Family and Culture, pp. 14–23.

Kong Jeong-Ja (1990) 'The Marriage Patterns of Chaebol Families' (in Korean). Women's Society for the Study of Korean Society, ed., *A Study of the Korean Family.* Seoul: Kkachi, pp. 37–59.

Kong Se-Kwon *et al.* (1990) *The Changing Family Functions and Role Relations in Korea* (in Korean). Seoul: Korea Institute for Health and Social Affairs.

Kong Se-Kwon *et al.* (1992) *The Family Formation and Fertility Behavior in the Republic of Korea* (in Korean). Seoul: Korea Institute for Health and Social Affairs.

Kong Se-Kwon *et al.* (1995). *Characteristics of Family Deficit Types and Approaches to Family Policy* (in Korean). Seoul: Korea Institute for Health and Social Affairs.

Lasch, Christopher (1977) *Haven in a Heartless World: The Family Besieged*. New York: Basic Books.

Lasch, Christopher (1983) 'The Family as a Haven in a Heartless World', in Arlene Skolnick and Jerome Skolnick, eds, *Family in Transition*, pp. 102–113, Boston: Little, Brown and Company.

Lee Jeong-Ok (1993) 'Labor: Toward Gender-Equitable Labor Structure' (in Korean) in Lee Yeong-Ja *et al.*, eds, *Sociology of Gender Equality*, pp. 202–267. Seoul: Hanul Academy.

Parsons, Talcott and Robert Bales (1955) *Family, Socialization and Interaction Process*. New York: Free Press.

Shim Young-Hee (1992) *Women's Social Participation and Sexual Violence* (in Korean). Seoul: Nanam.

Shorter, Edward (1975) *The Making of the Modern Family*. New York: Basic Books.

Somerville, Jennifer (1992) 'The New Right and Family Politics', *Economy and Society* 21(2): 93–128.

Sommerville, C. John (1990) *The Rise and Fall of Childhood*. New York: Vintage.

Song Ho-Keun (1995) 'Social Democratization in Korea: Conclusion' (in Korean). *Korean Sociological Review* 2: 198–204.

Song Ho-Keun (2003) *South Korea, What Is Happening?: Generation, the Aesthetics of Conflict and Harmony* (in Korean). Seoul: Samsung Economic Research Institute.

Song Seon-Hui (1993) 'Women and Politics' (in Korean) in Kim Dong-Il, ed., *Sociology of Gender*, pp. 197–232. Seoul: Muneumsa.

Yi Soon-Hyung (1994) *Political Socialization: Social Cognition and Practical Participation* (in Korean). Seoul: Seoul National University Press.

Notes

1 In sociological literature on family-centered private life and social order, both familism and familialism are used interchangeably. Since I have used familism in my earlier writings, it is also used here.

2 Two potential social revolutions from below – i.e., the Donghak Peasant War in the late nineteenth century and the socialist movement in the immediate post-colonial period – were defeated mainly by Japanese and American military intervention respectively. Such defeats resulted in the complete disorganization of grassroots civil (communal) society beyond kinship.

3 The open elective affinity between Developing World indigenous cultural elements and modern social formations and changes of *developmental contents* was pointed out by Clifford Geertz (1973) as 'internal conversion'.

4 For comprehensive discussion on the familial constraints on the social and political participation of women and youth in Korea, see Shim (1992) and Yi (1994).

5 (http://www.hani.co.kr/section001001000/2001/07/001001000200107162052001.html).

6 By contrast, the Gender Development Index (GDI), which reflects women's literacy, schooling, and life expectancy among others, ranked South Korea at the

29th among 146 countries surveyed. These results imply that women's high education does not enable them to become mainstream participants in the economy, government, and politics.

7 See Chang (2001a) for highly diverse familial norms and ideologies of contemporary South Koreans.

8 Some historical origins of instrumental familism may be traceable. For instance, among grassroots people, it seems to have its economic historical origin in family farming in which family relationships were pragmatically mobilized to undertake agricultural production and sidelines and meet various material consumption needs. Among the ruling circle, it was evident in the intense social and political competition among aristocratic families in which the strategic utilization of kin support often made crucial differences.

9 Another manifestation of this parental orientation is excessive son preference, which in turn is responsible for South Korea's extremely high level of sex ratio at birth. See Kong *et al.* (1992) for a detailed recent account of South Koreans' son preference.

10 Elsewhere, I discussed this conservative family politics in terms of social welfare implications (Chang 1997a).

11 An irony in this regard is that while fatherless families are often looked at suspiciously, widowed or divorced mothers are seldom likely to remarry (Choi 1982). On the surface, they simply do not think of remarriage, but in reality they cannot find any men willing to marry them because of their 'already owned' status in Korean men's mind.

12 For a detailed discussion on scholarly and administrative approaches to the relationship between family structure and juvenile delinquency and crime in Korea, see Choi (1982: 284–296).

5

COMMUNITARIANISM WITHOUT COMPETITIVE POLITICS IN SINGAPORE

Chua Beng Huat

The long-ruling, single-party-dominant government of People's Action Party (PAP) in Singapore has been denounced as illiberal, in a world where liberalism is dominant if not hegemonic (Bell *et al.* 1995). There is no doubt that the PAP government is illiberal, preferring to label itself as 'pragmatic' and 'communitarian'. The 'communitarian' claim is embedded in its 1991 ideological manifesto, the Shared Values, in which the interest of the 'nation', rewritten as the 'collective', is to be held supreme above all other interests (Chua 1995: 31–35).[1] This ideological preference is arguably an issue that can be settled between the government and the electorate who can, in principle vote out the government if it is against this illiberalness. However, this ability to replace the ruling government is largely absent in the present form of government, which in turns leads to questions on the PAP government's claim to being democratic. Admittedly, since 1959, when the PAP won its first overwhelming majority of seats in a general election, an electoral system has been always in place. This has displaced substantial amount of criticism that might have been otherwise generated, domestically and internationally. It has also 'enabled' the PAP government to claim legitimacy to govern. However, there is no denying that the electoral process has been severely altered to the incumbent government's advantage. Nor is there any denying that, using its absolute majority in parliament to pass legislation with ease, there are some anti-democratic legislations and administrative practices in place. Consequently, it is the democratic claims of the PAP regime that political criticism holds more conceptual and substantive consequences.

This chapter analyzes the claims and practices of 'communitarian' ideas in a context of absolutist parliamentary power where competitive party politics is as good as absent and the likelihood of changing government is equally unlikely. While it is true that no government can be absolutely insulated from the larger social processes at home and from global international political pressure, it is nevertheless the case that with absolute power, the practices of politics and administrations of the PAP may be said to issue directly from the government, or more strictly speaking from the Cabinet of Ministers. The occasional concessions to certain desires from the electoral ground facilitate the governing process without conceding political power. In this sense, the 'communitarian' ideology may be read as a commitment of the government rather than an ideological desire generated from the populace, among whom there may be very substantial resonance notwithstanding. The immediate task here is to provide the political context that frames the communitarian ideology.

Non-level playing field

The electoral process has been subjected to consequential interventions in the following manner:

1 The government has engaged in very severe gerrymandering as a legitimate instrument of electioneering. Constituencies with significant anti-PAP votes are likely to be erased in the immediate subsequent general election, as their geographical boundaries are redrawn, the electorate redistributed, absorbed and contained by the majority of pro-PAP voters. This is true of every general election up to the most recent one in December 2001. The practice has been so blatant, with dire consequences on other political parties, that there are now emergent voices calling for the establishment of an independent electoral commission.[2] The government, not surprisingly, has rejected such calls and argued that the constituency boundaries are delineated according to geographical shifts in population on the island, by the present electoral commission staffed by civil servants.

2 In the government's own view, the major 'innovation' it has made to the electoral system in conventionally understood democracy is the institutionalization of the Greater Representative Constituencies (GRC). A number of constituencies (up to six) are strung together to form a GRC. During general elections, each contesting political party has to field a team of candidates. The team that garners the largest number of aggregated votes wins the entire slate of seats in parliament. The initial rationale for the GRC was ostensibly an attempt to ensure that the minority races, namely Malays and Indians, are represented in all future parliaments, should the overwhelming Chinese majority decide to vote along racial lines. Consequently, each contesting team must have at least one minority member.

In principle, this arrangement is not prejudicial to any contesting parties. However, in practice, in a politically hegemonic context in which even the ruling party has difficulties in recruiting candidates for election, the GRC disadvantages the other political parties. Furthermore, the very high level of financial deposit required for each candidate to qualify to contest in an election makes it difficult for small political parties to raise sufficient funds to constitute a team to contest in a GRC. On the other hand, as part of the Member of Parliament's monthly stipend is contributed to the party, the PAP has a large war chest and would have no problem meeting the financial demands even when it fields candidates in all constituencies.[3]

3 Another innovation is the introduction of different categories of Members of Parliament, in addition to those who are duly elected in contested elections. Two categories are established. The first is the Non-Constituency Member of Parliament (NCMP). Since the mid-1980s, the PAP government recognizes the palpable desire of the electorate for opposition presence in parliament. As a concession to this, up to three defeated non-PAP contestant who garnered the most votes during the general election will be inducted into parliament as NCMPs. They have full rights of participation in parliamentary proceedings, except voting on issues of finance, constitution and votes of no-confidence. If up to three non-PAP candidates were elected to parliament, no NCMP will be inducted.

The second category of non-elected MP is the Nominated Member of Parliament (NMP). An individual with an 'outstanding' track record in his or her profession may be nominated by others as NMP, to provide independent opinions on issues facing the government. Selection is by a parliamentary committee. The number of NMPs in any parliament is determined by the elected government, depending on the number of opposition MPs elected. The initial impulse of inducting independent minded individuals has been significantly 'subverted' and the NMP positions have been transformed into a channel for interest group representation. Organizations with identifiable constituencies have begun to use it as a means of gaining representation in parliament by nominating their own members, for example there have been a labor NMP, nominee of the National Trade Union Congress, in the past few parliaments.

Both the NCMP and the NMP concepts were introduced by the PAP to ameliorate the desire of the electorate for critical and opposition voices in parliament. Of the two categories, the NMP scheme appears to have been more successful; most Singaporeans would rate the NMPs more favorably than the NCMPs. The NMPs, unencumbered by the interest of specific electorates or political party platform, can and have been taking up more principle-based issues that provide more room for debate. Not forgetting that the parliament is also a theatre for performance, the NMPs have provided more eloquent parliamentary speeches that reflect their personal professional cultivation, hence, more positive public assessments.

4 However, in spite of its relative success, the clamor for opposition and critical voices in parliament appears to be more demanding than the NMPs can satisfy. Thus, after the most recent general election in November 2001, the PAP government, having won all but two seats in a parliament of more than 80 seats, will be designating a portion of its own members to constitute a 'PAP Forum', whose function is to provide additional and presumably at times critical comments on government practices. Skepticism about how such an engineered 'opposition' would work is understandable, even among some of the PAP members themselves; although there is at this point no evidence of how it would work.

The most immediate consequence of all these alterations to the electoral process is put most straightforwardly by a civil society organization, the Roundtable, 'elections are increasingly becoming non-events because they have become less and less competitive' (*Straits Times*, 10 November 2001). We move next to identify some of the anti-democratic legislations in Singapore, which the government readily deploys as instruments of social and political control. Among the more seriously anti-democratic strictures are the following legislations:

1 The Newspaper and Printing Act (1974) imposed strict limits on the ownership of media and a restrictive definition of its role as 'supportive of government interests'. All newspapers are to be Singaporean public companies with two types of shares, ordinary shares and management shares. The latter, constituting only one percent of ownership, must be held only by Singapore citizens and Singaporean-owned corporations. Both must be approved by the government, which has the power to revoke ownership at any time. Such management shares have 200 times voting power over ordinary shares in matters of editorial policy and other matters, including the appointment or dismissal of directors and editorial staff. Not surprisingly, management shares have been allocated to government-owned holding companies and trusted individuals, including past directors of domestic intelligence service, the Internal Security Department, have been continually appointed to the management board. The summary effect of the Act was that it 'cleared up all ambiguities by legitimatizing the PAP leadership's direct control over the press, through its nominees' (Tan 1990: 6). In addition the press, with its strictly defined role operates with annually renewable licenses which can be revoked at the government's discretion. It is legislations that constrain the media in Singapore rather than the close monitoring or direct instructions from the government on the

day-to-day activities, although direct interventions by government is the commonly held belief of the public.

Over the years, the effects of the legislations can be seen in both journalistic practices and commerce in media industries. Commercially, all the national newspapers, in all the official languages, are now owned by a single company, the monopolistic Singapore Press Holdings, offering 'added convenience of centralized control as well' (Tan 1990: 7). All television stations were state-owned until late 1990s, since then cable television that carries imported channels is available and in 2001, Singapore Press Holdings began to set up its own entertainment television stations. As for journalistic practices, regardless of what individual journalists may feel and do, the press can be generally described as pro-government, if not exactly 'docile', particularly in view of the fact that the history of the press was strewn with direct acts of repression in the 1970s and 'selected members of the editorial management, [remain] frequently gripped by fears of imagined reprisals' (Tan 1990: 9).[4]

2 The Societies Act has been amended to severely restrict the freedom of association. The Act delimits 'political' activities narrowly to the purview of political parties and disallows civil society organizations from affiliation with political parties. This erases the possibilities of coalition building between oppositional social forces. It also restricts every civil society organization to activities within its declared constituency of interests and members and disallows such organizations to form coalitions in pursuit of collective interests (Rodan 1996: 100). Actual restriction on freedom of associations goes beyond these specific constraints.

The Act requires all voluntary associations to register with the Registrar of Society. Registration is, however, not automatically granted. The Registrar is empowered to deny registration with the minimum of reasons. He is also empowered to deregister an organization when the latter allegedly 'threatens' public interest, an act that renders all subsequent activities of the deregistered group illegal and thus open to criminal charges. As Tan and George (2001) argue, the Registrar's power to deny registration, on presumption that the activities of an organization seeking registration may have negative consequences on public order, contravenes the constitutional guarantee for freedom of association. To be consistent with the latter, registering should be merely a procedure of notifying the Registrar, who should have no power of denying registration, as the power overrides the rights of the individuals to association. The government has provided no reasonable response to this constitutional issue.

There is one very significant exception to the rule of no affiliation between civil organizations and political parties. The National Trade

Union Congress (NTUC) was established by the PAP government, after it had destroyed by deregistration the radical Singapore Trade Union Congress in the early 1960s. Since then, the NTUC has been in a 'symbiotic' relationship with the PAP. The Secretary-General of the NTUC is a member of the Cabinet of Ministers, usually without other portfolio, ostensibly giving workers direct input and access to government policy making. No office holders of any of the NTUC-affiliated unions are permitted to be members of any political party, except the PAP, in spite of the fact that such office holders are elected by rank and file members of their respective unions. The effects of this symbiotic relation on labor relations and the power of unions is too vast to take up here, suffice it to say that a potentially significant social force for change has been appropriated by the ruling regime for its own purposes, and this is to put it very mildly. It is also the primary reason why civil society organizations do not include the NTUC as a constituent of its community.

3 The Public Entertainment Licensing Unit (PELU), housed in the Police Department, Ministry of Home Affairs, is as the name suggests the agency that issues licenses for public entertainment. Again, the basis of denying a permit for public performance is a simple 'Police assesses that the event has the potential to lead to law and order problems'. Again, the same argument regarding constitutionality of the administrative prohibition applies. Significantly, giving of speeches in public is defined as 'public entertainment' and thus a license is required. This is arguably contrary to the principle of freedom of expression, again guaranteed by the state constitution. In practice, it restricts non PAP politicians' ability to engage the public. Indeed, the Secretary-General of the Singapore Democratic Party has decided to defy the law on constitutional rights to free speech. As a result he had been imprisoned three times since early 2000, each time for 'providing public entertainment without permit'. The most recent imprisonment also disqualifies him from contesting the next general election, to be held no latter than 2007. Apart from individual politicians, organized groups have also been denied permits for public forums, or issued restricted permits.

Again, in recognition of the persistent public complaints of the absence of freedom of speech and following suggestions made by some civil society groups, the government has designated a space as the free speech corner at Hong Lim Park. The Park is a space dripping with historical, political 'significance', it being the space in which many fiery speeches were made in the days of anti-colonialism. The irony that this designation was itself an admission that there was and is no right to free speech in Singapore appeared to be lost on all who promoted such a scheme. In any case, one month after its celebrated opening, the space is now as free as it is empty.

As for the PELU, the cultural sphere most affected by its power is the performing arts. However, with the establishment of a National Arts Council, it has largely deferred to the Council the responsibility of screening artistic performances and now acts on the Council's advice regarding censorship or banning of a proposed performance. After the banning of a controversial play – a monologue of domestic violence in Indian Muslim families narrated by one of its victims – in 2000, which ended with the president of the theatre company being detained by police after a brief confrontation on the night in which the play was to be previewed before license was to be issued, the Ministry of Home Affairs has announced that the role of PELU *vis-à-vis* performing arts will be reviewed in the near future.

4 The most anti-democratic of all legislation is clearly the Internal Security Act (ISA). This Act empowers the Minister of Home Affairs to detain anyone for a period of up to two years, without the need for a public trial, so long as the Minister is subjectively satisfied that the one detained has acted against the national interest and is a threat to national security. In a country where the slogan for national defense is 'total defense', covering social, cultural, psychological, economic and military, 'national security' is a concept that casts a wide net. Accordingly, the Act casts a wide repressive shadow, even ordinary Singaporeans who are not in the slightest way critical of the government are well aware of its presence. It is thus the most commonly used index of how unfree is politics in Singapore. That the Act is invoked sparsely – only twice in fifteen years, between 1987 when a group of young Catholics were detained for an alleged 'Marxist' conspiracy till 2001, when it was used to detain thirteen alleged Muslim 'extremists' with links to Al-Queda organization, which was responsible for the bombing of the World Trade Center in New York on 11 September 2001 – is cold comfort to a population that is increasingly better educated and diversified in their opinions and sentiments. Finally, so long as the ISA remains as a piece of the legal arsenal for repression, it will always mark the absence of democracy in Singapore.

The combined effects of the legislations render the political sphere undemocratic. For example, freedom of expression is multiply constrained, in spite of the insistence by the government that Singaporeans can speak freely publicly. First, anyone wanting to make public speeches requires a license from PELU. Second, dissemination of critical statements through the media is constrained by media owners and editors who, guided by financial interest and the Newspaper and Printing Act, choose to interpret the 'national interest' narrowly, in accordance with that restrictively defined role. Third, and of greater consequence, is the fact that critical comments can be and have been reinterpreted, retrospectively and recontextualized within existing repressive laws to legally accuse particular speakers of intentions to disrupt social peace. For example, in the defamation case against the now fugitive politician Teng Liang Hong, the latter's statements made in several different contexts were reinterpreted as expressions and evidence of his Chinese chauvinism, which in Singapore is a code for someone trading close to political detention. The repressive shadow of existing legislation is always already present before an individual speaks, rendering the public sphere un-free.

Changes to the electoral and parliamentary systems combined with the anti-democratic legal constraints on basic freedoms of association and expression, effectively reduce the ability of non-PAP political parties to contest general elections on an uneven playing field. Furthermore, sustained national economic growth since 1960, which enables the government to subsidize many of the daily necessities of everyday life such as housing, basic medical care and mass education, translates into very tangible improvements in the material life of all Singaporeans, albeit unevenly. This achievement has paid high political dividends to the PAP, in terms of continuing and sustained popular support at the ballot boxes during general elections. The popular support and political dominance have been so immovable that, in desperation, all the other political parties have, since 1987, forged a united front during each general election to avoid three-corner contests. The coalition has also decided to contest in less than 50 percent of the electoral constituencies available at each general election. It is convinced that the electorate wants the PAP to continue in government. Thus, it reasoned that if on nomination day the PAP is already returned to power to form the government because it would have won more than half the seats available by default for absence of contest, then, the electorate might be more willing to vote for non-PAP party candidates to meet the electorate's other desire to have opposition voices in parliament. The success of this coalition strategy was short-lived: in the 1987 general election, the number of opposition MPs elected increased to four from one but by the next election it had dropped by two and at two it now stays, after the recent election in December 2001.

The less than democratic and illiberal character of the PAP government is nothing new to those familiar with Singapore's domestic politics. For outside observers, explanation for the lack of movement towards greater democratization tends to stop at attributing the regime's authoritarianism as the primary cause (Tremewan 1994; Tamney 1996). In contrast, I want to suggest that, beyond the obvious repressive legal and political structures, part of the underlying logic and thus explanation of the political practices of the PAP is its definition of the basic political unit to be governed. This basic unit is not individual citizens as conventionally assumed in a democracy but rather socially identifiable bounded groups, which can be loosely called 'communities'. This emphasis on conventionally recognized 'natural' bounded groups, such as family and 'race', underpins the PAP government's social policies, giving the policies a recognizably 'communitarian' orientation in their logic and effects. The effects manifest themselves, negatively, through the costs that are imposed on individuals who defy simple and simplifying bureaucratic assignation of themselves into socially 'bounded' groups.

My argument will thus contest the PAP government's self-claim that its 'communitarian' orientation is conceptually distilled from the major Asian civilizations of the Malay, Indian and Chinese populations, which it collectively called 'Asian Values' (Chua 1995); a claim that has drawn criticisms from journalists to political theorists like Habermas (2001). I will argue that the PAP's operating logic of administration by 'socially bounded groups' begins with the management of race relations within the city-state and its communitarianism is a generalization and reconceptualization of the totality of its administrative practices that issue from its race policies.

Management of race: the emphasis of boundedness

At the time of political independence in 1965, the demographic composition and the geopolitical conditions required the new nation to begin life as a constitutional multiracial nation. Demographically, there were three visible, component races – Chinese, Malay, Indians – with the rest nominally relegated to the residual category of Others (CMIO), among whom were local Eurasians and British left over from the colonial days.[5] Geopolitically, archipelagic Southeast Asia might be designated as the 'Malay' world, where Malays constitute the regional demographic majority. This necessitated that Singapore recognize its Malay population as the 'indigenous' population of the nation, although strictly speaking the number of Malays resident on Singapore was miniscule in 1819, when Raffles established the trading post for the Anglo East India Company that laid the foundation for the future city and nation.

The translation of the regional geopolitics into a domestic political necessity to preserve the Malay group boundary has been fundamental to the unfolding logic of the PAP domestic politics and social policies. If the racial boundary of Malays was symbolically 'necessitated' by regional geopolitical demand, the preservation of the Chinese group boundary was required by domestic conditions of the nascent Singapore nation: the Chinese were demographically dominant, constituting about seventy-five percent of the total population; as the dominant economic players in the trading economy at the time they had economic power; finally, politically, the mass support base of the left factions in the PAP was constituted by politically mobilized Chinese union members, Chinese educated youth and generally, the Chinese working masses. This was therefore a 'community' that a newly elected government, uncertain of its future, could only ignore at its own peril. Having established the respective boundary of the Malays and the Chinese, the logic of racial community could then be applied to the Indian population as well. As the smallest racial group, the functional importance of Indian community was to reinforce the very logic of 'racial' groups. That these 'racial' groups were in a conventional sense 'natural', hid the fact that the ideological 'significance' inscribed on the differences among the groups were intentionally constructed; 'nature' serving as alibi for ideology (Barthes 1993).

This ideological signification can be readily exposed. From a comparative perspective, one needs simply point to the fact that many countries with multiracial demographic compositions do not declare themselves constitutionally 'multiracial' societies; one of the most obvious and powerful examples is the USA. The ideological effect is however far more significant at the local level. It was and is obvious to everyone in Singapore that the 'Chinese' category was constructed out of suppression of language differences among the ethnic Chinese population. A multiple dialects society of Hokkiens, Cantonese, Hakkas, Teochews, to name just the major ones, had been reduced to a single, homogenizing category; as for the Indian category, the same flattening of linguistic differences was even more drastic, including, again, to name but the major ones, Bengali, Tamil, Malayalee and Punjabi. If the Chinese had at least a common written script that might serve to 'unify' them, most of the Indian languages were mutually incomprehensible to each other. The same applied to the Malay group which included Boyanese, Javanese, Achenese, Menangkabau, again with significant linguistic differences. In addition, there were also significant religious differences among each of the three racial groups. The regrouping and discursive homogenization of each of these groups is therefore an enforced erasure of differences, so as to facilitate the ease of government and administration, as we shall see in the next section (Purushotam 1997).

Foremost among the political entailments of constitutional multiracialism is the principle of 'racial equality' which must be, and be seen to be maintained and practiced in the management of race by the government. The government thus sets itself above the races, without siding with the demographic majority Chinese and without prejudice towards the demographically smaller communities of Malays and Indians. The constitutional demand to maintain racial equality enables the government to deflect rather than to succumb to the pressures from the overwhelming Chinese majority. It creates both the discursive and practical space for the government to delineate and define national interests as different and separate from the interests of the Chinese majority. The national interests would have to cover the three races equally, rather than being identical to the majority Chinese. This enables the government to place itself as structurally above the racial communities from which it defines its relative autonomy over the racially constituted 'society' as a whole (Chua 1998).

At the regional level, being an overwhelmingly Chinese predominant city-state enveloped in a region in which Malays constitute the overall majority, the displacement of the Chinese majority interests from the national interests reduced, if not erased completely, the opportunities for the Malay population to make racial discrimination a political issue and a potential source of conflict, at home and regionally; it reduces potential regional animosity.[6]

The logic of racial equality has, since the beginning of political independence, formed the basis of much of the politics of social redistributions in Singapore. In each of the social policies documented below, which together cover all the major aspects of daily life in Singapore, equality of races and the desired overall effect of its practice, namely to achieve 'racial harmony' as an abstract, generalized social good, mitigate against claims of individuals as citizens. Indeed, the idea of the individual cannot be categorically accommodated in all these public policies. It is this tension between abstract 'collective' good and the costs it extracts from or imposes on the individual that is central to the communitarian ideology in Singapore. Let us begin with the concerns with mass education, an area of sustained human capital investment, in a city-state where trained human resource is its only competitive edge in global economy.

Education

The education system was a site of serious contestations in the early years of 'self-government', when responsibility for domestic affairs on the island was transferred from the British colonial office into the hands of a fully elected assembly. The British colonial administration had provided very limited opportunity for English education and Malay vernacular education, leaving each of the Chinese and Tamil communities to finance the education of their respective children. Chinese schools were the most prominent. Their students the most politically radical during a period of political mobilization for decolonialization and independence, partly because of the rise of the People's Republic of China, their nominal 'homeland' and partly because of resentment against negligence and discrimination in the hands of the colonial regime. A multi-language stream education system was adopted after much negotiation during the self-government period. Education remained a contested terrain during time leading up to the formation of Malaysia. As a member of Malaysia (1963–1965), Singapore retained autonomy in education matters rather than adopted the 'Malay' language of national schools of Malaysia. After separation from Malaysia, a national education system with English as the primary language of instruction was adopted. To be consistent with multiracialism, racial equality is 'maintained' within an English-medium education system by the insistence that each primary and secondary school-going child compulsorily learn his/her racial language as a second language in school (Wong and Gwee 1972; Gopinathan 1974).

The issue of 'which' is the racial language of a racially mixed marriage is, of course, immediately a problem. Ambiguity is unintelligible in an administrative system that governs by the logic of groups. Rather than allowing a mix-marriage household to choose for itself, the 'race' of a child is settled by paternity: a child is officially automatically assigned the father's race. The system thus admits of no 'hybrids', without any irony of the nation's claim to be 'multiracial' and 'multicultural'; 'multi' simply means 'many' and not 'mixed'. This enforcement of a formal state-determined racial marker can potentially impose a high cost on individuals who are forced into the official categories. For example, a child of a Chinese father and Indian mother who is forced to learn Mandarin as his/her 'race' language may suffer poor performance in Mandarin because the parents, including of course the father, in such mixed marriages tend to be English-educated. That is, the family is an English-speaking one regardless of the fact the father is ethnically Chinese, thus without the presumed facility of any 'race' languages. The child may as a consequence be deprived of tertiary education as entry to local university is contingent upon his/her achieving a minimum standard in the second language. A further consequence is that the same child would face very limited employment opportunities as an adult. On the other hand, a child of Indian father and Chinese mother who is forced to take an Indian language as the second language may be deprived of the opportunity to study Mandarin, the language of the majority of educated Chinese and as a result suffer financially in the future, even socially,[7] in spite of the fact that the second language is called the 'mother tongue' of the child; again, the irony seems to escape the education authority. Fortunately, flexibility into the system has been introduced in recent years. Not only are children of mixed marriages given the right to choose a second language, more South Asian languages have been admitted as acceptable second languages. Obviously, the logical thing to do would be to let every student, regardless of race, choose freely from a slate of second languages, which would include languages that are not tied to the three races. Such freedom would minimize the hardship imposed on individual students who have difficulties learning the languages of their respective, presumed identifiable 'natural', racial communities. However, the point of the exercise is not just the learning of a second language but of a second language that is supposed to be the vehicle for transmitting culture and values of its race. It is a learning that is dictated by the logic of official multiracialism.

Housing

The national public housing program of the PAP government is the one of the most successful in the world. Eighty-five percent of the population lives in public housing, of which more than 80 percent own a 99 year lease on their flats; home ownership is almost universal and is the declared aim of the government. This is made possible by compulsory acquisition of private land holdings at very much below market prices, in the name of national interest, among which is the development of public housing estates. As a result, the government holds 90 percent of the land of the city-state and the public housing authority, the Housing and Development Board, emerges as the monopoly provider of housing to all but the top 10 percent of the highest income earners. The draconian compulsory acquisition of private properties obviously violates the common law understanding of rights of property. On the other hand, it could be argued that this displacement of private property rights to make available land for all public purposes is emblematic of the generalized communitarian claims of the PAP government.

As the government is the monopoly provider of housing for the overwhelming portion of the population, it is to be expected that housing is an area where the government will extract more than financial returns from its heavy investment. Indeed, many social policies ride on the back of housing provision; for example, in the interest of promoting family as a basic institution of society, severe restrictions are imposed the availability of public housing for single individuals (Chua 1997 2000). One should, therefore, also see the group logic of multiracialism playing itself out in housing policies.

Apparently, in the interest of the abstract collective good 'racial harmony', the government has enforced physical integration of the races within the housing estates. In pre-independence days, the three racial communities, particularly Malays and Chinese, lived quite separately in their own districts, with only a sprinkling of the families from the other races. Through the national public housing program, the government had broken up these racial districts through squatter clearance and re-housing the residents into high-rise, high-density public housing estates. The different races have been redistributed by quota into each housing estate and into each block of public housing. As its stands, each block of public housing will reflect approximately the proportion of the racial composition of the total Singaporean population; approximately 75 percent Chinese, 17 percent Malays and 8 percent Indians. This enforced physical integration of the different racial groups as immediate neighbors are rationalized, negatively in terms of preventing racial conflicts and in more positive terms as encouraging racial integration.[8]

Such policy of enforced physical integration unavoidably imposes hardships on individuals and households. Financially, it affects the ability of households to get the best price for selling their flats. For example, a Chinese household who wants to sell its flat to a prospective buyer who is Malay may be prevented from doing so if the quota of Malays in the block is filled. The household may then be forced to take a lower price by selling it to either a Chinese or an Indian household who remains eligible by quota. Meanwhile, the prospective Malay family may be forced to buy a house in a less than preferred housing estate or a particular housing block. This is especially ironic since part of the housing policy is to encourage married children to live in close proximity to their parents, in order to maintain mutual aid.

The policy also affects the social and cultural lives of the residents, particularly the two smaller racial groups of Malays and Indians. Take the Malays for example. As Muslims, aspects of daily life, including dietary items, are grouped into *halal* and *haram* (simplistically, permissible and not permissible by the religion). In the event of emergency, it would be more difficult for a Malay family to find a fellow Malay household to assume the care of the children, as the immediate neighbors would likely be Chinese, who do not observe similar injunctions. The same does not apply to the Chinese, who with the overwhelming majority of the population, cannot help but have fellow Chinese as immediate neighbors. It should be apparent that the costs imposed on different racial groups by enforced physical integration are unevenly distributed (Lai 1995). This may explain why Malays have been less likely to participate in state-initiated 'community' activities, such as becoming involved in resident committees, than in activities which are organized by the mosques in the housing estates; indeed, the mosque with control over its own spaces have become the center of Muslim activities in each public housing new town.[9]

The government's overriding interest, even anxiety, in 'achieving' racial harmony at the collective level, leaves the individual households without any legal recourse, as the relationship between public housing residents and the public housing authority are treated as private transactions between renters/purchasers and landlord/vendor. The housing authority is free to impose rules, including quotas and the residents are free to look somewhere else for housing. However, the 'freedom' of residents is merely a 'formal' right because, with the public housing authority as the monopoly provider, there is no alternative housing for all Singaporeans but the highest 10 percent income earners.

Ethnic self-help groups

The PAP government insists that it is ideologically against social welfarism for two primary reasons among others. First, it believes welfarism saps the work ethic. Second, it believes that it is undesirable for the state to substitute itself for the family in providing social and financial support as this would weaken the family and thus, weaken a fundamental bond in society. Yet, when one examines the government's social policies in education, health, housing and other infrastructure provisions, government subsidies are heavy and obvious. Indeed, its legitimacy and longevity in parliament are partly dependent on such public provisions, although they are discursively portrayed as 'human capital' investments rather than conventional welfarism. It did resist direct hand-out of cash to the needy, which was the sole basis for its claim to be anti-welfarist. However, in 2003, faced with sustained structural employment, a very generous package of up to 100,000 Singapore dollars of assistance, to be used for purchase of public housing, education for children and occupational training for the mother, has been offered to every small family who might conceivably be stuck permanently in poverty (*Straits Times*, 21 August 2003).

Prior to the recent initiative in welfare provision, in the early 1980s, the PAP Malay Members of Parliament were alarmed by the disadvantaged social, economic and educational position of their racial constituency, relative to the Chinese and Indians. With governmental financial support and the collaboration of other Malay-Muslim community organizations, they established Mendaki (*Majlis Pendidikan Anak-Anak Islam*, Council on Education for Muslim Children), an organization dedicated to helping Malay children from lower income families who are falling behind in their education. Once this was established, by the logic of equality of racial groups, the Chinese population set up its own organization, the Chinese Development Assistance Council, with initiatives taken by leaders in the Chinese community. This was followed by the Singapore Indian Development Agency (SINDA).

All the organizations are funded by their respective ethnic communities: the government undertakes the administrative work of deducting a very small sum of money, between one to two dollars, from the monthly social security savings, the Central Provident Fund (CPF), of each working Singaporean, as contributions to their respective racial community organization. Willingness to contribute to the collective funds is presumed unless one explicitly writes to the CPF board to opt-out. Among the small number who did, it is more a protest against the presumed volunteerism rather than against the idea of collectivization of welfare. Again, individuals are marked by official racial categories and not permitted to contribute across racial boundaries. Those who fall between the cracks of simplistic race markers are assigned one of the categories. In this instance, the case of South Asian Muslims stand out, as (s)he can be categorized either by religion and contribute to Mendaki or as 'Indian' and make contributions to SINDA.

Beyond the issue of how individuals may be differently assigned racial categories, a more serious problem concerns collective welfare of the nation. By sheer numbers, the Chinese community would collect more funds than the Malays and Indians. To this, one must add the relative economic strength of the Chinese community in a nation where a very significant portion of the domestic economy and wealth are in the hands of the Chinese business community; for example, the founding families of the largest private banks and other significant companies continue to control these enterprises which are now publicly listed. The smallness of the Malay and Indian communities coupled with their relatively weak economic positions, particularly the Malay community, compares unfavorably with the Chinese when it comes to generating public contributions and charities. The result, unavoidably, is that the Malay and Indian communities will net much less 'collectivized' funds than the Chinese and are, therefore, less able to provide the range of necessary services needed to upgrade the economic conditions of their respective communities. The possible long-term consequence that the 'racial self-groups' will intensify, or at least perpetuate economic divisions along racial lines cannot be denied in this arrangement (Lily Zubaidah Rahim Ishak 1994).

Yet, the government has persistently refused to be persuaded by the argument that in the interest of equality for all citizens, a national administrative unit, such as a ministry of the poor, should be established to administer educational 'upgrading' programs for all regardless of race. It argues that on such a 'sensitive' issue of persuading different racial groups to contribute and participate in upgrading themselves, government bureaucracies lack the 'personal' touch which only members of the same racial groups can provide for each other. Nevertheless, it has been pragmatic enough to recognize the inequalities of delivery capacities of the three racial organizations and has encouraged them to share their resources; now children of different races access educational help at centers closest to their homes, regardless of which organization runs the place.

Scaling group markers

This practice of marking and assigning every individual to a 'naturally' given socially bounded racial group and its attendant logic of governance can be transferred to other identifiable social units. Smaller than the racial group is the 'family', which can be ideologically attributed and invested with even greater 'naturalness'. Larger than the racial group is the 'nation', which is ideologically more imaginary and thus more difficult to constitute in substance; recognizing this difficulty, the Prime Minster had declared, almost forty years after self-government and political independence, Singapore to be a state without a nation.[10] This sequence of levels, from family to racial group to nation, is inscribed and enshrined in the national ideology, the White Paper on Shared Values.[11] This document embodies the PAP government's conception of communitarianism; a conception which is both derived from and translated into the Party's political and administrative practices of governing through socially bounded groups. The Shared Values statement specifies: 'nation before community and society above self' and 'the family as the basic building block of society', among other 'values'. The government's suggestion that the Values are a distillation of the values of the three Asian civilizations – Sino, Indic and Islamic – is but a retrospective ideological rationalization of its unvarying mode and logic of government of groups instead of individual citizens.

Significantly, the family and the national levels are often ideologically intertwined and discursively slide over each other as in 'family is like the nation' or 'nation is like a family'. Such ideological interpenetration of family and nation are commonly found, of which Confucianism may be a classical Chinese mode, while Swedish 'social democracy' (Kemeny 1992: 132) is an example in the West. Given this conceptual entanglement, 'communitarianism' cannot escape the fate of being often a form of 'patriachialism' (Woodiwiss 1998 and in this volume). This sliding between the two poles is nicely captured in the political philosopher, David Miller's characterization of PAP government as an extreme form of 'right communitarianism' that should, perhaps more accurately, be called 'authoritarianism' (2000); authority not only of the 'collective' over individuals but also of 'father/government' over children/governed. Miller's comment refers to the political reality that the PAP government, among other Asian countries, has been known to use the idea of the 'collective' well-being to suppress dissenting voices.[12]

In the case of the PAP, a further linkage between family and nation is one mediated by the Party's self-understanding as a social democratic organization. This ideological link is spelt out by PAP cabinet minister, George Yeo, the ideologue of the third generation party leaders. In defense of the political and economic systems, Yeo reminded party members of the Party's social democratic roots, which explains the government's 'collectivist' or 'socialist' ideological position. Then, in an attempt to link this social democratic claim to the idea of Singapore as an 'Asian' society, he concluded that socialism is a 'natural' tendency of humans, as the family will always be 'social' and 'communitarian' (*Straits Times*, 17 June 1994). Here, we find the ideological merging of the major ideological concepts of the PAP government: multiracialism, Confucian familialism and social democracy. One will certainly find many contradictions if one were to work out the logic at the meeting points of these 'master' concepts. However, in political practice, demand for conceptual systematicity is generally eschewed and contextual rationality in which anyone of these concepts holds sway will suffice.

In their everyday practices, Singaporeans have also grown adapt at shifting from race to family to nation. Focus on family is relatively unproblematic. The shift between race and nation can be seen in the way

Singaporeans deal with the highly visible presence of foreign labor, particularly South Asian and PRC workers. In principle, most Indian-Singaporeans and Chinese-Singaporeans can extend and establish race-based affinities with their counterparts in the foreign labor population. This is not happening. Instead Singaporean nationality is invoked to set Singaporeans apart from their foreign labor counterparts, privileging nationality over race. This is all the more ironic since all Singaporeans still claim to be of migrant stock. Furthermore, it is argued that this migrant past accounts for the hardworking and thrifty character of the present population that underpins the nation's economic success; in short, the migrant past underpins the presence of Asian Values. One should, therefore, logically expect Singaporeans to have sympathy for the newly arrived migrants who are hewed from the same 'homelands'. Alas, these arrivals are seen as individuals from underdeveloped countries, with all its supposed cultural 'backwardness', in contrast to the present day Singaporeans. This common attitude is reinforced by legislations that make it difficult for Singaporean citizens, particularly those with lower incomes, to marry low-end laboring new immigrants.

The emphasis on family, racial groups and nation as different manifestations of the idea of community has obliged the state to deliver some impressive provision of collective goods, including housing, education, health care and infrastructure, which contribute to the popular political support and the longevity of the PAP in power. There are however also costs to be paid by the citizenry, particularly in the political sphere.

Consequences

1 The emphasis on community, from family to race to nation, has led to the development of a political language that severely delimits political discussion. A very elaborate set of concepts of responsibilities to social units has been developed over time at the cost of language of rights. It should be obvious that 'responsibility' is heavily inscribed and embedded in the national ideology, the Shared Values. 'Responsibility' is pervasively embedded in government policies: very restrictive public housing access for singles because easy access will 'undermine' the family institution; every child must be responsible in learning his or her 'mother tongue' adequately so as to preserve tradition; in politics, voting is compulsory and in economics, the most conventional Singapore refrain, 'no one owe us (you) a living'. It is commonly asserted by both the political leaders and other moral gate-keepers that there is no right without responsibility. Furthermore, rights are not 'naturally' given as in liberalism but must be earned through responsible social behavior. The idea of human rights as natural rights

is unintelligible within Singaporean political vocabulary (Bell 2000: 173–276).

2 At an abstract level, it can be argued that, since the 'collective' is but the 'aggregate of individuals', the 'well-being of the collective' is only meaningful if it translates into well-being of individuals in general. In public discourse, therefore, an individual's interests are assumed to be taken care of by the achievement of collective interests. In practice, this 'truism' appears very persuasive at the societal level: for a duration of forty years, there has been an absence of racial violence, no child has been deprived of education by the system, every family is relatively adequately housed, there has been full employment and generally, rising standards of living.

Issues regarding individuals as individuals only arise when a specific individual with particularistic character or need is brought into focus. As illustrated by the above-discussed instances, such an individual is administratively unmanageable to the system of governance by group and is, therefore, coercively assigned an official category, often to the individual's detriment, as in the example of a child of Indian father and Chinese mother, being forced to take Tamil as second language or a Malay family being forced to live further away from its kin because of the racial quota system. As the boundaries of each officially designated bounded racial group is rigidly defined, admitting no boundary confusion or boundary crossing, the personal costs paid by individuals in any 'hybrid' situations is indubitable, although the costs vary according to issues at hand.

Conversely, an individual who, for whatever reasons, disavows the social group in which one is officially inscribed is placed in a marginal existence. Here, the logic of governance by group is often taken up by the racial groups themselves as instruments of community self-government. An illustration of the anguish of marginalization is that experienced by a Malay-Muslim who converts to another religion. Such individuals are often subjected to serious psychological pressures by others in the Malay community. This is a situation in which the logic of governing by racial groups reinforces the Islamic religious injunction against apostasy. It is these instances where disavowal of collectivity is made difficult that liberals, including those sympathetic to the values of community, would want group membership to be voluntary rather than officially ascribed. Furthermore, that membership should be open and subject to individual critical reflection and exit made possible (Kymlicka 1995).

'Exit' is something that the existing logic of the PAP mode of governance does not permit, which is apparent in its policies on citizenship. In Singapore, a citizen by birth can stand to lose the citizenship if he/she were out of the country for a period of ten years or more, on the presumption that one has no longer any stake in the survival of the nation. Dual citizenship is something not contemplated because, in the words of the Immigration and Registration department, 'We have not reached the state of nationhood where a Singaporean with a second citizenship would retain his identity and loyalty to Singapore'.[13]

3 Finally, to the issue of the 'nature' of politics in Singapore. It is, of course, the PAP government's conviction that the current practices in the social redistribution of collective goods, which contribute much to the improved material well-being of all Singaporeans, are only possible with its mode of government. In the desire to maintain 'social harmony', an abstract socially desirable good, the government has chosen to engage in 'preemptory' action as a mode of government, a strategy that is implicit in all the above-discussed anti-democratic legislations.

This mode of preemptory policing is closed in its reasoning and self-fulfilling in its consequences: in order to have social harmony, preemptory proscription against potential social disruption is necessary, however, whether the presumed potential social disruption will in fact materialize is never verified, because it has been prematurely removed. Take a concrete example, PAP government's management of dissent: freedom of speech may give rise to confusion among the populace, resulting in absence of social cohesion, therefore dissent must be suppressed, and unity of social purpose maintained. Whether dissent will have the anticipated result of chaos was never tested but repression continues. It is this logical consequence of repression that makes politics under the PAP irksome, to put it mildly.

Conclusion

What then should the politics of Singapore be? The hope of liberals that economic development and rise of the middle class will be the harbinger of democratization is, by now, obviously misplaced in the case of Singapore. Instead, the very impressive social policies of the PAP, which while allowing income inequalities to rise also ensures improvements at the lower-income levels, have indeed contributed greatly to its mass political support. For the overwhelming majority of the population, there are good reasons to be governed by the logic of groups: The housing policy has produced arguably the best housed citizens in the world, if there were some inconveniences to some families; the insistence of mother-tongue learning has satisfied most Singaporeans' minimalist demand for continuation of racial identity and culture, minimalist because there is a general fear of over-zealous identification with race; the pro-family social policies have kept the traditional emphasis on family life relatively healthy, if it also disadvantages singles in some areas of public policy and general social stigmatization; there is industrial peace and full employment, if it meant limits being placed on labor rights. Above all, all these social policies, in aggregate, have delivered a 'Developed World' standard of living in a country that could have been stuck in Developing World squalor. The overwhelming majority of citizens are relatively satisfied and support the system with good reasons.

An absolutist power, a healthy capitalist economy with a fully employed – although this is beginning to fray after the 1997 Asian financial crisis and subsequent sustained global downturn – well-housed, well-educated population enjoying the best of consumer capitalism has to offer! Indeed, it is this success of the PAP government that makes it something to be emulated by other absolutist governments, such as the PRC under the late Deng Xiaoping and other 'market socialist' nations. It is this very same success that makes the PAP government something to be 'fearful' of to the liberal minded.

One can readily understand the anguish of a segment, by no means the whole of the tertiary educated, upper-middle-class income individuals, who crave for liberal freedoms. For the rest of the population – only 25 percent of income earners in Singapore made enough money to pay income tax – the apparent benefits of emphasizing 'collective' well-being provide a sense of security, in spite of some lack of freedoms. The worst nightmare of a liberal in Singapore is to discover just how pro-family, pro-racial, pro-religious identification and nationalistic are the overwhelming number of Singaporeans. They may be quite happy with corporatism and willing to pay the price of membership or belonging in all three levels of collectives. And why should they not? The material benefits outweigh abstract principles, particularly when it is rather easy to show that the principles do not exactly work out as promised elsewhere anyway.

On the question of what kind of politics should there be in Singapore, liberal Singaporeans should nevertheless lament that there is no incentive for the PAP government to initiate political structural changes. There is no serious pressure from the ground for this. Recent expansion of civil society can be readily granted, even encouraged, with government grants; theatre performances that often provide critical social and political commentaries being a prime example. There can be liberalization of the social and cultural sphere without democratizing the political sphere. External pressure for greater democratization has very limited effect because the PAP government has been rather well behaved in the eyes of those governments that can exert serious pressure on Singapore. There are plenty of badly behaving states that demand more attention and action against them will win the critical governments more electoral support at home and in international relations. There in lies the anguish of liberal democrats in Singapore but sadly, perhaps, nobody else's.

References

Barthes, Roland (1993) *Mythologies*. New York: Vintage.

Bell, Daniel A. (2000) *East Meets West: Human rights and democracy in East Asia*. Princeton: Princeton University Press.

Bell, Daniel A., David Brown, Kaniska Jaayasuriya and David Martin Jones (1995) *Towards Illiberal Democracy in Pacific Asia*. London: Macmillan.

Chen kuan-Hsing (ed.) *Trajectories: Inter-Asia cultural studies*. London: Routledge, pp. 186–205.

Chua Beng Huat (1995) *Communitarian Ideology and Democracy in Singapore*. London: Routledge.

Chua Beng Huat (1997) *Political Legitimacy and Housing: Stakeholding in Singapore*. London: Routledge.

Chua Beng Huat (1998) 'Culture, multiracialism and national identity in Singapore' in Chua Beng Hsing (ed.) *Trajectories: Inter-Asia cultural studies*. London: Routledge, pp. 186–205.

Chua Beng Huat (1999) '"Asian Values" discourse and the resurrection of the social', *Positions: East Asia cultures critique* 7(2): 573–592.

Chua Beng Huat 2000) 'Public housing residents as clients of the state', *Housing Studies* 15(1): 45–60.

Clammer, John (1983) 'Deconstructing values: the establishment of a national ideology and its implications for Singapore's political future' in Garry Rodan (ed.) *Singapore Changes Guard*. New York: St. Martin's Press.

Gopinathan, S. (1974) *Towards a National System of Education in Singapore 1945–1973*. Singapore: Oxford University Press.

Habermas, Jürgen (2001), 'Remarks on legitimation through human rights' in Habermas (ed.) *The Postnational Constellation: Political essays*. Cambridge, Mass.: MIT Press, pp. 113–129.

Kemeny, Jim (1992) *Housing and Social Theory*. London: Routledge.

Kymlicka, Will (1995) *Multicultural Citizenship*. Oxford: Clarendon Press.

Lai Ah Eng (1995) *Meanings of Multiethnicity: A case study of ethnicity and ethnic relations in Singapore*. Singapore: Oxford University Press.

Lily Zubaidah Rahim Ishak (1994) 'The paradox of ethnic-based self-help groups' in Derek Da Cunha (ed.) *Debating Singapore*. Singapore: Institute of Southeast Asian Studies, pp. 46–50.

Miller, David (2000) 'Communitarianism: left, right and center' in *Citizenship and National Identity*. Malden, Mass.: Polity Press, pp. 62–80.

Open Singapore Society Report (2000) *Elections in Singapore: Are they free and fair?*

Purushotam, Nirmala S. (1997) *Negotiating Language, Constructing Race: Disciplining difference in Singapore*. New York: Mouton de Gruyter.

Rodan, Garry (1989) *The Political Economy of Industrialization of Singapore*. London: Macmillan.

Rodan, Garry (1996) 'State–society relations and political opposition in Singapore', in Rodan (ed.) *Political Oppositions in Industrializing Asia*. London: Routledge, pp. 95–127.

Seow, Francis T. (1998) *The Media Enthralled: Singapore revisited*. Boulder, Colo.: Lynne Rienner.

Tamney, Joseph (1996) *Struggle over Singapore's Soul: Western modernization and Asian culture*. New York: Walter de Gryuter.

Tan, Kevin and Cherian George (2001) 'Civil Society and the Societies Act', *Straits Times* 27 March.

Tan Teng Lang (1990) *The Singapore Press: Freedom, responsibility and credibility.* Singapore: Institute of Policy Studies Occasional Papers No. 3.

Tremewan, Christopher (1994) *The Political Economy of Social Control in Singapore*. New York: St. Martin's Press.

Woodiwiss, Anthony (1998) *Globalization, Human Rights and Labor Law in Pacific Asia*. Cambridge: Cambridge University Press.

Wong, Francis Hoy Kee and Gwee Yee Hean (1972) *Perspectives: The development of education in Malaysia and Singapore*. Singapore: Heinemann Education Books (Asia).

Notes

1 For critical assessment of the Shared Values, see Clammer (1993); for critical commentary on the idea of communitarianism in Singapore, see Chua (1995: 184–213).

2 The most cogent argument for independent commission is provided by the Roundtable, a civil society group on political issues. Its position is published in the *Straits Times* (10 November 2001), penned by Lam Peng Er, Harish Pillay, Chandra Mohan and K. Nair.

3 During the 2001 general election, the cash deposit was raised to $13,000 per candidate; a GRC team of six candidates would thus require $78,000, a sum which one of the most serious opposition parties, the Worker's Party, found it hard to raise. For a critical view of the electoral system and process from the other political parties, see Open Singapore Society Report (2000).

4 For a free-ranging critical discussion of the press in Singapore, see Seow (1988).

5 The term 'race' instead of the more 'neutral' term ethnicity, will be used throughout this chapter because race and racial are the terms used by the Singapore government, perhaps, to emphasize the difference so that public policy can be more readily rationalized in terms of 'difference'.

6 Regional sensitivities are very concrete and real. For example, at the height of the 1997 Asian regional financial crisis and the subsequent political disruptions in Indonesia, President Habibie, who succeeded Soeharto, pointed out to the Singaporean Minister of Defense, who was in Indonesia to present some food aid to the Indonesian people, that Singapore is but a 'little red dot' in the sea of green of Indonesia. Green is of course symbolically the color of Islam.

7 For ethnographic evidence of such dilemma in Chinese-Indian families see Purushotam (1998).

8 The last serious racial violence took place in 1964. However, the fear of racial violence has been ideologically invested with mythic proportion and inscribed on the social and political body so as to rationalize and facilitate the imposition of social regulations, policing and discipline.

9 Arguably, one preferential treatment of the Malay community as the indigenous population is the allocation of a very prominent site in each new town for the construction of a mosque, which government agencies help to design and administer the collection of monthly contributions of the faithful through

deductions from the latter's compulsory monthly social security savings that are deducted from income.

10 This statement was made during the year 2000, annual National Rally Speech, a state-of-nation report.

11 This White Paper on Shared Values was tabled in parliament in the January 2000 sitting of the government.

12 The most common criticism from the 'West' regarding Asian leaders claim that 'Asian Values' underpinned the rapid capitalist economic development in Asia, was to point to slippage of the Asian governments political use of the idea of 'collective' good as a means of suppression of difference and dissent; for detail discussion on this point and references to material on Asian Values see Chua (1999).

13 *Today*, 21 January 2002.

6

THE ETHICS OF CARE AND POLITICAL PRACTICES IN HONG KONG[1]

Ho Mun Chan

Introduction

This chapter examines the governing strategies and social policies adopted by administrations in Hong Kong during the colonial and post-colonial eras to maintain their political legitimacy. It argues that during both eras, government policy has largely been shaped by the doctrine of benevolent government and the idea of *minben* (people-as-basis) in the Confucian tradition. Based on textual analysis, the paper further argues that the philosophical foundation of the doctrine of benevolent government and the idea of *minben* can be traced to the Confucian ethic of care. At the end of the paper, empirical findings which show that people uphold the Confucian values that underpin social policy in Hong Kong are presented. Finally, the paper concludes that because it is deeply rooted in a Confucian tradition widely supported by the public, social policy in Hong Kong is an essential means for the government to secure its political legitimacy.

Legitimacy problem during the post-colonial era

Political stability and legitimacy[2] are not easily maintained under an authoritarian regime. This is particularly the case in Hong Kong because of the tension between two rival factors. While the political system is far from being democratic by Western standards, opposition forces are none the less present both inside and outside the system and there is a tradition of respecting civil and political liberties, such as the freedom of the press. Before the change in sovereignty, because of doubt that Beijing would honour the promise of 'one country, two systems', there was public support for a quicker pace of democratization; this was regarded as a way of building a shield to protect Hong Kong from interference by the central government in Beijing after the handover. Yet society was divided over how radical and how quick the pace should be. The Chinese government, on the other hand, was skeptical about the intentions behind the political reforms launched by the colonial regime. As a result, democratic reforms and human rights legislation introduced during the last years of the colonial era led to serious Sino-British strife and internal divisions.

Since the handover, Beijing has to a great extent, though not entirely, kept its promise to not interfere in the internal affairs of the Hong Kong Special Administrative Region (SAR). The need to build a democratic shield has therefore been less pressing. Furthermore, during his first term of office, Tung Chee-hwa, the Chief Executive of the SAR government, adopted a strategy of depoliticalization; deliberately drawing people's attention away from highly politicized issues, such as democratization, and towards social, economic and livelihood issues (Lau 2002: 8). For decades, the colonial government had employed the same strategy to secure its legitimacy and to maintain the political stability of the colony. Tung's style of governance is therefore a continuation of a political tradition rooted in Chinese culture.

Unexpectedly, the origin of the first real crisis the new SAR administration had to face was economic. Hong Kong has been unable to recover from the economic recession triggered by the Asian financial crisis, which has greatly handicapped the administration's ability to maintain broad economic opportunities and security for all. Given the external origin of the recession, it is unlikely that the SAR government could have coped with the problem alone. This is not to deny that there were some fundamental flaws in Tung's governing strategy. During his first term of office, Tung was unable to build a broad-based political coalition (Lau 2002). This failure almost paralyzed the SAR government and made it incapable of alleviating the pain caused by the economic crisis. Eventually many people placed all the blame on Tung, which led to an outburst of political conflict, as he was about to finish his first term of office.

Although Tung was able to secure a second term of office in 2002, it was obvious that he needed to modify his governing strategy. Yet there was no widespread support for the idea that democratic reforms were necessary to solve the problem of governance, and support for a quicker pace of democratization seemed no stronger than during the last years of the colonial era. Though democracy has it own intrinsic values,[3] many people in Hong Kong only treasure it instrumentally if they treasure it at all; they do not believe that there is a strong link between democratic reform and economic growth and so democracy has not been widely regarded by the public as a key solution. Many believe that the heart of the matter is whether the government could adopt the right strategy to recover economic prosperity and deal effectively with livelihood issues. However, the continuing economic recession has made it increasingly difficult for the SAR government to deliver the goods, especially for the grassroots and vulnerable in society. The repeated failure to recover the economy has resulted in erosion of legitimacy of the SAR government, which has led, by mid 2003, to a rising public demand for a quicker pace of democratization and more radical political changes.

A caring society

Social policy in Hong Kong has consistently been guided by the values of care and compassion. Both the British colonial and SAR administrations have made the obligation to provide care for the needy a central element in social policy development. This has been repeatedly asserted since it was outlined in the first 'White Paper' on social welfare in 1965 (Hong Kong Government 1965). In the 1991 consultation paper on the development of government welfare policy, it was stated: 'social welfare should not be regarded as some form of charity, confined to the socially and financially disadvantaged. The services are and should be made available to all who need them' (Hong Kong Government 1991). Chris Patten, the last governor of the colony, reaffirmed the ethos of care in society in his address to the Legislative Council in 1995: 'One of the most insistent messages which this Council and the community send to the Government is that it expects us to accept a duty to care for the vulnerable' (Hong Kong Government 1995a). There is evidence that social development during the colonial era was shaped by the political culture of Hong Kong people. It was, therefore, not coincidental that the values that underpinned the social policy of the colonial government were in agreement with the values upheld by the public.

The 1967 riots triggered by the Cultural Revolution in China created a legitimacy crisis for the colonial government. Nevertheless, for largely political reasons there was no strong demand for democratization, let alone radical political reform. Firstly, democratization would have jeopardized Sino-British relations because China would have seen it as a step towards independence. It would not then have tolerated the continual presence of the British Administration in a territory that it regarded as an inseparable part of China, until agreement about the future of Hong Kong had been reached. The British Government also regarded it as a political reality that independence was impossible, and was thus very cautious in launching any political reforms in Hong Kong. Secondly, democratization would have politicized society and would then have provided room for conflicts between the Chinese Communist Party and the Chinese Nationalist Party to be drawn into Hong Kong politics. These conflicts had been a major source of political instability before; both the colonial government and the general public would have wanted to contain these conflicts.

While there was no demand for democratization, there were, nevertheless, conscious efforts to promote political consolidation and active consensus building from the top of the government down to the bottom (Jones 1990: 67–68) by aligning policy orientation closer to the political culture and values of Hong Kong society. The most significant reorientation in rebuilding the legitimacy of the colonial government in post-1967 Hong Kong was the commitment to the ideal of a caring society. In his speech to the Legislative Council, Sir (latterly Lord) Murray MacLehose, the governor of Hong Kong from 1971 to 1982, nicely epitomized this new policy orientation: 'People will not care for a society which does not care for them' (Hong Kong Government 1976). Many policy initiatives were introduced in the 1970s to strengthen care for the poor and vulnerable, and housing, healthcare, education and social welfare were regarded by the government, as the 'four pillars' for building a better society (Jones 1990: 210, Leung 1996: 126). It was clear that in the post-1967 era the colonial government was trying to strengthen its political legitimacy by correcting its past mistake of just encouraging people to take care of themselves. Since the new political orientation of the colonial government was reactive rather than proactive, the commitment to a caring society was merely a response to the expectations and demands of the general public, the values and political culture of the community.

Since the change in sovereignty, the SAR government has been quite explicit in asserting that its policies are rooted in the traditional values and culture of Hong Kong people. There has been a deliberate and proactive attempt to adopt traditional Chinese values as guiding principles for policy development. Even while Tung Chee-hwa was still a candidate for the first Chief Executive of the SAR government, he indicated clearly respect for Chinese values and culture (Lau 2002: 3–7). Hence, it was no surprise that after the handover on 1 July 1997, Tung Chee-hwa adopted the concept of 'A Compassionate and Caring Society' as the overarching theme of his first Policy address: 'As we work hard together to build our future, caring for those in need, supporting the elderly and helping the disadvantaged are fundamental to the quality of our society' (Hong Kong SAR Government 1997). The same stance was reiterated in his second Policy Address under the theme of 'Taking Care of People in Need'.[4] Finally, in spite of the economic downturn, Tung reconfirmed the commitment to a caring society in his 2001 Policy Address, under the theme of 'Helping and Caring for One Another': 'Current economic restructuring will result in some profound adjustments in our society. Inevitably, this will bring about various social problems and exacerbate some existing problems. More than ever, we need a caring society with a spirit of participation and dedication' (Hong Kong SAR Government 2001).

The ethos of care has not been regarded only as a social ideal or asserted merely in broad terms either by the colonial or the SAR government. The development of all major social policy areas in Hong Kong has been shaped by this ethos for decades. In housing, the government had already asserted by the early seventies that public responsibility was necessary because 'the inadequacy and insecurity of housing' and the harsh situations that result from it, 'offends alike our humanity, our civic pride and our political good sense' (Hong Kong Government 1972); after years of development, more than 50 percent of the population now live in public housing estates. Also, since 1974, it has been the government's policy that no one should be denied adequate health care services due to lack of means (Hong Kong Government 1974). Though Hong Kong has a dual public and private health care system, more than 93 percent of the hospitalization service is provided by the public sector and is highly subsidized by the government. The current daily rate for hospital services is HK$68 (approximately US$8.5), which only amounts to 2–3 percent of the average daily cost of providing the service. In education, the government accepts 'a special responsibility to ensure that no one is deprived of a place in the education system because of a lack of means' (Hong Kong Government 1994). Although only a very small number of primary and secondary schools are directly operated by the government, the majority of which are aided schools run by religious bodies, voluntary agencies, welfare organizations and trade associations, are funded and fully supported by the government; only very few schools are privately funded. In social security, the government's policy undertakes the responsibility to help 'the disadvantaged members to attain an acceptable standard of living' (Hong Kong Government 1995b). However, despite a strong commitment to the provision of care, it is not the policy of the government to make Hong Kong a welfare state. This view was reasserted in Tung's Policy Address of 2001: 'Our aim is to help our people to enhance their ability to help themselves and to boost their will-power to do so. Under this social contract, the Government is firmly committed to providing a reliable safety net as a basic guarantee for our citizens' (Hong Kong Government 2001. See also Hong Kong Government 1996, 1997; Social Welfare Department 1999).

In other words, unlike the situation in a welfare state, the provision of care is maintained at a level that will not lead to erosion of the values of meritocracy, work ethic, self-reliance and individual responsibility, which is consistently with the belief of many Hong Kong people. Consequently, the government has consistently maintained the level of public expenditure at around 20 percent of Gross Domestic Product (GDP) by placing all major policy areas under tight budgetary control. For example, total health care expenditure has been capped at consuming around 12 percent of total public expenditure and 2 to 2.5 percent of GDP. This control of public expenditure has enabled the government to keep taxation low; less than 40 percent of the working population are required to pay tax and only 0.3 percent need to pay the standard rate of 15 percent, but their contribution amounts to 19.5 percent of the total salary tax collected.

In Hong Kong, it is generally believed that economic growth can be best achieved by the free market system, and that the widespread economic prosperity created will enable most people to flourish without relying upon the government. Many people look to the free market rather than to the government for fulfillment of their hopes, but the government is firmly expected to undertake the obligation of taking care of the needy so that they can eventually help themselves. Of course, because of the economic downturn, it has become harder for the government to maintain the widespread prosperity that members of Hong Kong society have been enjoying over the past two decades or so. The burden of taking care of the needy has become also heavier. However, the general public still expects that the first priority of the government be to strengthen the economy of Hong Kong rather than to make drastic changes in its social policy to provide more direct support for the needy; many perceive the current problem in Hong Kong therefore as economic rather than one which requires a quick fix resulting from changes in social policy. There has so far been no strong drive for the government to extend the coverage and loosen the means testing for its social security programs, though there is resistance to tightening the purse strings.

If budgetary situation continued to worsen, however, some downward adjustment will still have to be made. After the realty market collapsed, the government has weakened its commitment to the provision of public housing to avoid competing with the private housing sector, hoping that this sector can reposition itself and recover at a quicker pace in the absence of competition. In healthcare policy, the economic recession has indirectly pushed the government towards moving more quickly with its reform of healthcare financing. In mid 2002, the Hospital Authority launched a trial in some public hospitals where patients are no longer supplied with non-essential drugs free of charge. A nominal charge for the accident and emergency service was introduced at the end of this year. Several surveys in Hong Kong had shown that the public generally supported the introduction of this new charge, new measures. This support seemed to stem from people's commitment to the value of individual responsibility. In 2003, further measures to revamp the fees structure of the public healthcare system have been introduced with no strong objection from the general public.

In sum, examination of social policy in Hong Kong shows that there is a strong vision of care and compassion in the community and that the government has a strong commitment to a caring society. Yet society also adheres firmly to the values of work ethic, self-reliance and individual responsibility as in generally, people look to the free market to secure their well-being. After the Asian Financial Crisis, this moral ethos has manifested itself again in many people's expectation that, despite their economic hardships, the first priority of the government should be to adopt appropriate measures to strengthen the economy rather than to loosen its purse strings. Of course, under the strong vision of care, this does not mean that the government should weaken its commitment to provide direct assistance to the vulnerable; the wider general public also expects the government to exercise its care and concern by creating a healthy economic environment so that they are able to flourish as a result of their own efforts. I will argue in this chapter that the social policy of enabling people to help themselves by guaranteeing a reliable safety net for all is grounded in the Confucian tradition.

The doctrine of benevolent government[5]

It can be argued that the public expectation of the role of the government in Hong Kong has largely been shaped by the doctrine of benevolent (*ren*) government in the Confucian tradition. Though Mencius is a well-known proponent of this doctrine (Hsu 1975; Li 1999), Confucius had already stated the idea in the *Analects* (1999: 12.7): 'Zigong asked about government. The Master said, "Sufficient food, sufficient weapons, and the confidence of the common people".'

To practice the governance of benevolence (*ren*) is to look after the well-being of the common people. If a ruler can take good care of the people, they will trust him and he can then maintain his political legitimacy; so being caring is the way of becoming a wise ruler. This idea was further developed by Mencius (1999):

> a wise ruler will decide on such a plan for the people's means of support as to make sure that they can support their parents as well as their wives and children, and that they have enough food in good years, and are saved from starvation in bad.
>
> If your Majesty wants to run a benevolent government, why not turn to what is of fundamental importance? Let mulberry trees be planted about each homestead to five *mu* of land, and those who are fifty will have floss silk garments to wear. Let fowls, pigs and dogs be raised without neglecting their breeding seasons, and those who are seventy will have meat to eat. Let farm work be done without interference in a hundred *mu* of land, and a family of eight mouths will not go hungry. Let careful attention be paid to education in local schools, where the significance of filial and fraternal duties is stressed repeatedly, and grey haired people will not be carrying loads on the roads. In a state where old people are clothed in floss silk garments and have meat to eat, and the masses do not suffer from hunger and cold, what prince can fail to unify the whole world? (*Mencius* 1.7).

Mencius had seen people being taken away by the ruler during farming seasons, making them unable to support their families. He believed that taking good care of the common people was essential to good governance and political legitimacy; a ruler who cares about his people can gain legitimacy by popular support if he can ensure that people do not miss their farming seasons, have good harvests in good years and are prepared for bad years. In contrast, a despotic ruler who does not care about the well-being of his people loses legitimacy and Mencius believed that 'there is duty not just to oppose but also to *depose*, any unjust ruler' (Hall and Ames 1999: 171).

Although the idea of a democratic form of government cannot be found in Confucianism, it nevertheless has some quasi-formulation, elements or seeds of democracy in the doctrine of *minben* (people-as-basis). In the *Book of Documents*, it is written: 'The masses ought to be cherished, not oppressed, for it is only the masses who are the root of the state, and where this root is firm, the state will be stable' (Legge 1960, Vol. 3: 158). In *Mencius* (14.14), we read, 'Of the first importance are the people, next come the good of land and grains, and of the least importance is the ruler. Therefore whoever enjoys the trust of the people will be emperor'. So in the Confucian tradition, cherishing the common people and allowing them to flourish is of utmost importance in good governance. However, the idea of *minben* (people-as-basis) cannot be simply equated with that of a full-fledged democracy. According to Ambrose Y.C. King: '*[Minben]* contains the essence, perhaps, of what Lincoln meant by "of the people" and "for the people", but it does not extend to "by the people"' (1997: 172).

Based on the earlier review of how the colonial and post-colonial administrations in Hong Kong have tried to maintain their political legitimacy, we can see that the governing strategy in Hong Kong has largely been shaped or is at least in agreement with the doctrine of benevolent government and the idea of *minben*. Maintaining widespread economic prosperity and security, and taking care of the well-being of the vulnerable have been key to governments building up their popular support and securing their political legitimacy. The absence of a fully-fledged democracy had not been a major concern to the general public during the colonial era because the administration had shown a strong commitment to the ethos of care and was able to keep the economy growing at a rapid rate, though there was greater support for more radical political reform during the transitional period. The same governing strategy has been adopted by the SAR government since the handover, and the legitimacy problem encountered seems to be mainly concerned with the government's inability to recover the economy after the Asian financial crisis; people in general do not believe that there is a direct link between the legitimacy problem and the absence of a fully-fledged representative government.

The Confucian ethic of care

The philosophical foundation of the doctrine of benevolent government and the idea of *minben* can be traced to the care ethic in Confucianism.

Such an ethic can be derived from the notion of benevolence (*ren*). According to Chan (1993), the concept of *ren* has two senses. As a particular virtue, it refers to the virtue of benevolence and altruistic concern for others. As a general virtue, *ren* stands for perfect virtue, goodness or moral perfection. *Ren* in the general sense provides the overarching, unifying ethical framework in Confucian ethics; it encompasses all the other particular virtues such as benevolence, propriety, courage, filial piety, loyalty, etc. and so is the virtue of virtues. Li (1999) makes a similar distinction: *ren* affection vs. *ren* of virtue. As an affection, *ren* 'stands for the tender aspect of human feelings and an altruistic concern for others' (p. 96). In the second sense, a person of *ren* is a morally perfect person and the virtue of *ren* can only be realized 'among other virtues' (p. 97).

The first sense of *ren* is captured in the notion of care found in the work of Confucius and Mencius: 'Fan Chi asked about the benelovent. The Master said, "He loves men."' (*Analects* 12.22); 'A benevolent man loves everybody' (*Mencius* 13.46). The same usage of the notion of *ren* can also be found in the writings of other ancient Chinese philosophers (Tao 1998). According to Mencius, the source of this first sense of *ren* can be traced to the natural heart that is sensitive to the sufferings of others. He wrote, 'The reason why I say all men have a sense of compassion is that, even today, if one chances to see a little child about to fall into a well, one will be shocked, and moved to compassion, neither because he wants to make friends with the child's parents, nor because he hates to hear the cry of the child The sense of compassion is the beginning of benevolence' (*Mencius* 3.6). Thus, the ethic of care and compassion occupies a cardinal place in the Confucian notion of *ren*. However, it is a mistake to interpret the philosophy of *ren* as a philosophy of universal love, in which one ought to care for everyone equally.

Both Confucius and Mencius advocate that the practice of *ren* should start within the family: 'Filial piety and brotherly respect are the root of benevolence' (*Analects* 1.2); 'It is benevolence to love one's parents' (*Mencius* 13.15). Family ethics are central to Confucianism and this makes some scholars such as Bertrand Russell uphold the mistaken view that filial piety is the weakest point of Confucian ethics because it prevents the growth of public spirit (Russell 1922). Confucianism in fact advocates that people should extend the practice of *ren* from within the family to other people. Mencius is well known for this principle of 'care by extension'. The following are his formulations of the principle: 'Do reverence to the elders in your own family and extend it to those in other families; showing loving care to the young in your own family and extend it to those in other families' (*Mencius* 1.7) and, 'A benevolent man extends his love from those dear to him to those he does not love' (*Mencius* 14.1). The extension of love to those who are not related to you does not mean that you should love your father and a stranger equally. That extended love should be guided by the principle of 'love with gradation': 'A benevolent man loves everybody, yet his relatives and the virtuous should be given first place in his heart' (*Mencius* 13.46). The principles of love with gradations and extension of care are therefore two sides of the same coin.

The usefulness of these two principles can be demonstrated. For example, it can provide a coherent framework for resolving a dilemma in the feminist debate about the role of care in public life (White 2000). Some feminists, such as Nel Noddings (1984), believe that the duty to care is limited and delimited by relation. Upholding this view leads one to go down the road of parochialism, which denies the existence of any caring relationship among distant people, non-related beings become moral strangers, the ethos of care is eroded and the public domain regulated by the minimalist ethic advocated by the libertarian. Other feminists, such as Susan Okin (1989), go to the other extreme and maintain that Rawls' egalitarian liberalism 'is a voice of responsibility, care, and concern for others.' Yet this sounds psychologically implausible because people in general can hardly have such strong motives to maximize the well-being of the worse off who are likely to be strangers to them. This is actually confirmed by the empirical findings discussed later in this paper.

In a culture dominated by Confucian tradition, the true picture is likely to fall between these two extremes. The principles of care by extension and love with gradations imply that the commitment to the care for distant others will fall somewhere between that of equalitarian liberalism and libertarianism. So people in Hong Kong support the government's strong commitment to a caring society but maintain that the commitment should not lead to a welfare state, a principle adopted by the government as a guiding principle for social policy development. The strong commitment to care has also allowed room for the Confucian values of meritocracy, work ethic, self-reliance and individual responsibility to flourish and unfold themselves in the free market. These are key values in the Confucian tradition and can be traced to the doctrine of equal moral worth. Mencius wrote: 'all men may become Yaos and Shuns' (*Mencius*, 12.2) and, in the *Analects*, Confucius remarked: 'By nature, men are alike; by practice, they become different' (*Analects* 17.2).[6]

In the Confucian tradition, everyone has equal potential and obligation to strive for good. Good can only be achieved through self-cultivation and self-realization and that is why Confucianism upholds the values of meritocracy, work ethic, self-reliance and individual responsibility. The unfortunate should be taken care of so as to enable them to have the opportunity to strive for perfection. Having been shaped by this cultural tradition, people in Hong Kong generally give much stronger support to the notion of equality of opportunity than to those of equality of conditions or outcome. The empirical findings discussed below will show that Hong

Kong people in general accept some sort of safety net principle as the principle of social justice.

A Chinese conception of social justice

So far the arguments developed in this chapter have been largely based upon documentary and textual analyses; one may ask whether there is evidence that people in Hong Kong uphold the Confucian ethic of care and believe that it should be the guiding principle of government policy in Hong Kong. A further question is whether such a value commitment is distinctively Chinese and not solely a Hong Kong phenomenon. In order to answer these questions, my colleagues and I have conducted in Hong Kong, Beijing and Taipei an experimental study on social justice, which was developed by Norman Frohlich and Joe A. Oppenheimer (1992) and which has been conducted in other locations/countries, including the US, Canada, Poland and Korea.

The basic design of the study is based upon Rawls's (1971) liberal theory of justice. His argues that people will manifest their sense of justice if they are kept behind a 'veil of ignorance' and have no special knowledge about themselves so that they cannot make choices to advance their self-interests.[7] He believes that people behind a veil of ignorance would perceive themselves being related to one another in the original position characterized by the assumption that everyone is free and equal, mutually disinterested and rational in the sense that everyone will maximize his/her self-interests. In other words, they would perceive themselves to be regulated by a liberal ethic. Based on this liberal assumption, Rawls believes that subjects would choose the 'Difference Principle' – where a distribution is just if it is to the greatest advantages to the worst off – as the guiding norm for the just distribution of wealth. The experiment conducted by Frohlich and Oppenheimer was designed to simulate Rawls's argument to see if his theory could stand empirical scrutiny.

Objectives of the experimental study

The objectives of the study were as follows:

(a) To identify the principle(s) of justice that Chinese subjects in Hong Kong, Beijing, and Taipei choose under experimental conditions which facilitate them engaging in a process of impartial reasoning as near as possible to the one characterized by Rawls' idea of a 'veil of ignorance', and to examine the underlying reasons for the choices made by the subjects under such conditions;

(b) To examine whether subjects perceive themselves to be related to one another in a way as if they are in the 'original position' stipulated by

Rawls and whether the 'difference principle' is chosen under the above experimental conditions;

(c) To compare the results of this project with the findings of similar studies in Poland, Canada, the United States (Frohlich and Oppenhiemer 1992), and South Korea (Bond and Park 1991).

Research design

Twenty experimental sessions were conducted in each of the three Chinese cities. Each session consisted of (1) a structured observation, (2) a focus group discussion, and (3) a questionnaire survey. The group size for each session was five, and a total of 300 subjects participated in the whole study.

In the first part of the experiment, i.e., structured observation, each subject was asked to make an individual choice between the following four principles:

> **Difference Principle:** The most just distribution of income is that which maximizes the floor (the lowest) income in the society.
>
> **Principle of Maximization:** The most just distribution of income is that which maximizes the average income in the society.
>
> **Floor Constraint Principle:** The most just distribution of income is that which maximizes the average income only after a certain specified minimum income is guaranteed to everyone.
>
> **Range Constraint Principle:** The most just distribution of income is that which maximizes the average income only after guaranteeing that the difference between incomes (i.e. the range of income) in society is not greater than a specified amount.

A scheme of income distribution that satisfied the principle chosen by the subject was then selected, and the subject was randomly assigned to a class in the scheme. The pay-off for the subject was tied to the income of the social class they were assigned to. The experimental design to a certain extent simulated the effect of the 'veil of ignorance' because the subjects did not know how they would fare before they made their choices, and had to suffer the consequences of their choices.

In the second part of the experiment, subjects were asked to participate in a focus group discussion leading to agreement on a preferred principle. This step was used to simulate Rawls's idea of a contractual agreement in the original position. Again subjects did not know how they would fare before they made their decision. The final part of the study consisted of a questionnaire survey of the subjects' backgrounds, and social and political attitudes.

Sampling method

The snowball sampling method was used to recruit subjects in all three Chinese cities. Subjects were selected according to five background criteria, including gender, age, education level, monthly income and occupation. Subjects were selected from three different age groups (age 18–30, age 31–55 and over 55 years old), three education levels (junior high school or below, senior high school, and tertiary or over), three income levels set according to the living standards of the three cities, and from five occupational groups (professionals and executive positions, supporting staff or non-technical workers, sales or service-oriented personnel, technical or skilled workers and non-productive individuals). Attempts were made to ensure that the backgrounds of the five subjects participating in each session were as diverse as possible. No more than three people from the same gender, age, education and income groups, and all five occupational groups were represented in each session.

Major findings of the study and their implications

In the questionnaire survey, subjects were asked to respond to 35 statements; the responses were used to measure their social and political values on a 5-point Likert scale, ranging from strongly disagree to strongly agree. Results of ANOVA (Analysis of Varience) indicate that there are significant differences in the responses to 20 statements among subjects from the three Chinese cities ($p < 0.01$) studied. However, the significant differences are non-substantial in the sense that they only represent differences in the degree of agreement, with the two exceptions shown in table 6.1. The overall response of subjects in Beijing suggests disagreement for these two statements, while the corresponding responses in Hong Kong and Taipei suggest agreement. Yet multiple regression analyses show that results for such value items do not predict the choice of principle of justice made, and that the values significantly predicting

Table 6.1

	Mean			
	Beijing	*Hong Kong*	*Taipei*	
Q28 I quite accept the Western style of living.	2.51	3.48	3.51	$F(2, 297) = 38.304$, $p < 0.01$
Q29 The less the government intervenes in the market the better.	2.74	3.39	3.29	$F(2, 297) = 11.904$, $p < 0.01$

subjects' choices were broadly similar across the three groups of subjects examined. Hence, the three groups of subjects were combined for further analysis.

Preference for floor constraint principle

The Floor Constraint Principle was the predominant choice of the subjects from the three Chinese cities. Subjects in 17 sessions (out of 20) in Hong Kong unanimously chose this principle, while the corresponding figures in Beijing and Taiwan are 16 and 12 respectively. This result is in agreement with findings of similar experiments conducted by Norman Frohlich and J.A. Oppenheimer (1991) in Poland, Canada and the US. The result, however, differed from that of a similar experiment carried out in South Korea, where the most popular choice was found to be the Range Constraint Principle (Bond and Park 1991). In all these experiments, statistical analysis of the data obtained from the questionnaire survey showed no evidence that the choices made by the subjects were related to their social and economic backgrounds. In other words, it could be concluded that the choices made were likely to be the result of the impartial reasoning of subjects.

Let us deal with Rawls's liberal theory of justice first. Rawls has argued that people under condition of 'veil of ignorance' would choose the Difference Principle that would maximize the income of the worse-off. It was found that the Difference Principle was the least popular choice among Chinese subjects in this study. Indeed, no experiment conducted elsewhere in the world has so far has affirmed Rawls's argument. In not choosing the Difference Principle, the Chinese subjects showed that they were not as averse to risk as Rawls has presupposed; they did not seek maximal protection against the risk of being worse-off. They also did not believe themselves to be in the original position regulated by a liberal ethic because they did not perceive their being related to one another as mutually disinterested beings and were concerned solely about their individual well-being. Contrary to Rawls's assumption, the Chinese are not by nature liberal. The results of the present study in the three Chinese cities contradict both of Rawls's argument and assumption.

Within the context of East Asia and this volume, the differences between findings of Korean and Chinese subjects warrant some interpretations. There are two possible reasons. First, Bond and Park had made modifications to the experimental design used in the Korean study; the structure of income distribution schemes to be selected by subjects was changed to zero sum in nature. Under the assumption of playing a zero sum game, the incentive to earn more would play a weaker role in subjects' deliberations about the moral choice between different principles of justice. They would be induced to be more egalitarian and consequently tend to opt for the Range Constraint Principle as their first choice. The Difference Principle is also a very egalitarian principle; the zero sum game assumption may also explain why this principle was rated a close second to the Range Constraint Principle in the Korean study, even though it was ranked very low in other studies.

Second, the findings of the Korean study may also manifest a conflict between values and preferences in Korean society. As Chang argues in his chapter in the present volume, Korean society still has a strong ethos of Confucian familism. Such an ethos, as I have argued earlier, would not lend ready support for an egalitarian approach. Bond and Park, in their study, did find that Korean subjects held fast to a hierarchical view of society, and so they argued that their choices reflected 'the hierarchically organized community's responsibility to its lowest members' (Bond and Park 1991). Confucianism does not contradict and actually supports the idea that there is an obligation to take care of the needy, but this does not mean that Confucianism endorses an egalitarian approach, on the contrary. Perhaps under the shadow of the democratisation of Korea and its heavy rhetoric in public discourse, people may have switched to choosing egalitarian options, but deep down they still hold fast to Confucian values.

We can further make sense of the choice of the Chinese subjects by examining qualitatively the rationales for the support of the Floor Constraint Principle cited by the subjects during the focus group discussion.[8] Many of the subjects admitted that the worse off might not be able to meet their basic needs in the free market and agreed that the government should ensure that poor people are able to afford a decent standard of living. This made the Principle of Maximization an unpopular choice among the Chinese subjects; however, they also upheld a strong work ethic and gave little support to promoting equality of outcome, which, they believed, would dampen people's motivation to work harder in order to earn more. They maintained that people with the ability to earn more should be allowed to do so; this led to the rejection of both the Difference Principle and the Range Constraint Principle. The notions of care, compassion, a friendly society, social harmony, social stability and so on were used in justifying subjects' acceptance of the Floor Constraint Principle. The focus group discussions in the three Chinese cities showed that the rationales behind subjects' acceptance of the Floor Constraint Principle had a distinctly cultural flavour. The rationales for the support of the Floor Constraint Principle seem to stem from the Confucian ethics shared by the subjects in the three Chinese cities for the following reasons. First, the notions of care and harmony are fundamental to Confucianism. Second, the rationales seem to embrace the values of meritocracy, work ethic, self-reliance and individual responsibility rooted in the Confucian doctrine of equal moral worth.

Although subjects in the experiments conducted by Frohlich and

Oppenheimer (1992) in Poland and North America also predominantly chose the Floor Constraint Principle as the most just, unfortunately no similar rationales were reported in their studies. They recognise that the choice of a just principle was related to subjects' social values in their experiments but provided no detailed explanation of this relationship. The fact that they used only college students as subjects, which may have made the samples too homogenous, may explain why they failed to generate results that are able to facilitate an understanding of the relationship between justice and culture. Their main concern appeared to be to establish the hypothesis that people universally accept the Floor Constraint Principle across different cultures under conditions of impartial reasoning. Notwithstanding the agreement of findings between the Chinese subjects with subjects of their experiments, the present study does not lend ready support to their hypothesis of universality of acceptance of the Floor Constraint Principle.

Setting aside earlier discussed counter-evidence obtained in the South Korean experiment, the experimental results for subjects from the three Chinese cities show that subjects' choices of a just principle were dependent upon their social values and political attitudes. This is consistent with the critique of Rawls's theory of justice by Sandel (1982): the choices made by subjects behind the 'veil of ignorance' hinge upon who the contractors are and how they perceive themselves to be tied morally to one another in a political community. If this is the case, then the similarity of results obtained from Chinese subjects and those in Poland and America may be based on very dissimilar reasons and dissimilar underlying conceptions for justice. Furthermore, it is obviously entirely possible that results different from those obtained in Poland, North America, and Hong Kong could be generated in other cultures. For example, there are studies which indicate that Swedish and Indian people take claims of need more seriously than people in other countries (Miller 1992). Performing the Rawlsian experiment with subjects from Sweden and India would therefore probably yield different results. In both instances of similarity and difference of possible findings, Frohlich and Oppenheimer's universality hypothesis is not sustainable.

Finally, in the studies conducted in Poland and North America, it was found that the specific minimum income set by the subjects when choosing the Floor Constraint Principle was substantially and significantly correlated with their attitude towards redistribution of wealth. Yet no such correlation was identified in the study of the three Chinese cities. Most of the time, groups who chose the Floor Constraint Principle easily reached a consensus in setting the size of the minimum income, and the difference between amounts set by different groups from the same city was found to be small. This finding is not difficult to explain, at least, in the case of Hong Kong.

Rawls rejected the Floor Constraint Principle mainly because he believed that it leaves the floor level incompletely defined. If this principle is to be adopted by contractors in the original position, negotiation is needed to fix the floor and there is no guarantee that they can reach a unanimous agreement; and even if agreement is reached, it may not be widely accepted by the public once the 'veil of ignorance' is lifted. Yet whether this is a problem in reality depends upon the political and cultural conditions of the community in question. The Rawlsian experiments conducted in various locations have shown that subjects do generally reach consensus when determining the proper level of the floor without much difficulty. The findings in Hong Kong show that individual disagreements regarding the floor level may be less of a problem for people in some cultures than for those in others. Of course we cannot rule out *a priori* that the problem raised by Rawls is a real issue for *some* political communities, but we cannot in the abstract say that the problem is a serious one for *every* political community either.

Conclusion

The guiding principle of the social policy in Hong Kong is to guarantee that everyone can maintain a minimum decent level of living but at the same time allow the free market to flourish without too much government intervention. This suggests that Hong Kong abide by the Floor Constraint Principle. The results of the experimental study reported in this chapter show that the rationales for choosing this principle manifest a distinctive conception of justice. Philosophically this conception can be derived from the doctrine of benevolent government, the idea of *minben*, the Confucian ethic of care, and the doctrine of equal moral worth, and among these four principles, the Confucian ethic of care is central and fundamental. The results show that the values underpinning the conception are widely held not just by Hong Kong people but also by people in different Chinese communities. Social policy in Hong Kong is therefore rooted in the Chinese tradition widely supported by the public and is a fundamental means by which the SAR government can maintain its political legitimacy and the political stability of the territory. However, the success of this strategy heavily relies upon the government's ability to maintain the economic prosperity of Hong Kong. The repeated failure to recover the economy after the Asian financial crisis has made it increasingly difficult for the SAR government to acquire its legitimacy by using this political strategy alone.

References

Beetham, D. (1991) *The Legitimation of Power.* Basingstoke: Macmillian.

Bond, D. and Park J. (1991) 'An Empirical Test of Rawls's Theory of Justice: A Second Approach, in Korea and the United States', *Simulation & Gaming*, 22(4): 443–462.

Chan, S. Y. (1993) An Ethic of Loving: Ethical Particularism and the Engaged Perspective in Confucian Role-Ethics. Unpublished dissertation. The University of Michigan.

Confucius (1999) *The Analects*. (Arthur Waley, trans.) Hunan: Hunan People's Publishing House.

Frohlich, N. and Oppenheimer, J. A. (1992) *Choosing Justice: An Experimental Approach to Ethical Theory*. Berkeley and Los Angeles, CA: University of California Press.

Hall, David L. and Roger Ames (1999) *The Democracy of the Dead: Dewey, Confucisus, and the Hope for Democracy in China*. Chicago and Lasalle, Ill.: Open Court.

Hong Kong Government (1965) *Aims and Policy for Social Welfare in Hong Kong*. Hong Kong: Government Printer.

Hong Kong Government (1972) Address by the Governor, Sir Murray MacLehose, at the opening of the 1972–1973 session of the Legislative Council, October, 1972. Hong Kong: Government Printer.

Hong Kong Government (1974) *White Paper on the Further Development of Medical and Health Services in Hong Kong*. Hong Kong: Government Printer.

Hong Kong Government (1976) Address by the Governor, Sir Murray MacLehose, at the opening of the 1976–1977 session of the Legislative Council, October, 1976. Hong Kong: Government Printer.

Hong Kong Government (1991) *Social Welfare into the 1990s and Beyond*. Hong Kong: Government Printer.

Hong Kong Government (1994) *Hong Kong 1994*. Hong Kong: Government Printer.

Hong Kong Government (1995a) *Hong Kong: Our Work Together*, Address by Governor Rt. Hon. Christopher Patten at the opening of the 1995–1996 session of the Legislative Council, 11 October. Hong Kong: Government Printer.

Hong Kong Government (1995b) *The Five Year Plan for Social Welfare Development in Hong Kong – Review 1995*. Hong Kong: Government Printer.

Hong Kong Government (1996) *Hong Kong 1996*. Hong Kong: Government Printer.

Hong Kong Government (1997) *Hong Kong 1997*. Hong Kong: Government Printer.

Hong Kong SAR Government (1997) *Chief Executive's Policy Address*. Hong Kong: Government Printer.

Hong Kong SAR Government (1998) *Chief Executive's Policy Address*. Hong Kong: Government Printer.

Hong Kong SAR Government (2001) *Chief Executive's Policy Address*. Hong Kong: Government Printer.

Hsu, L. (1975) *The Political Philosophy of Confucianism*. London: Curzon Press.

Jones, Catherine (1990) *Promoting Prosperity: The Hong Kong Way of Social Policy*. Hong Kong: The Chinese University Press.

King, Ambrose Y. C. (1997) Confucianism, Modernity, and Asian Democracy. In Ron Bontekoe and Marietta Stephaniats (eds), *Justice and Democracy: Cross Cultural Perspectives*. Honolulu, HI: University of Hawaii Press, pp. 163–179.

Lau, Siu-kai (ed.) (2002) *The First Tung Chee-hwa Administration*. Hong Kong: Chinese University Press.

Legge, James, trans. (1960 repr.) *The Chinese Classics*. 5 vols. Hong Kong: University of Hong Kong,

Leung, Benjamin K. P. (1996) *Perspectives on Hong Kong Society*. Hong Kong: Oxford University Press.

Li, Chengyang (1999) *The Tao Encounters the West*. Albany NY: State University of New York Press.

Mencius (1999) *Mencius*, (Zhentao Zhao *et al.*, trans.). Hunan: Hunan People's Publishing House.

Miller, D. (1992) 'Distributive Justice: What the People Think.' *Ethics* 102(3): 555–593.

Noddings, Nel (1984) *Caring: A Feminine Approach to Ethics and Moral Education*. Berkeley and Los Angeles: University of California Press.

Okin, Susan (1989) Reason and Feeling in Thinking about Justice. *Ethics* 99(2): 39–53.

Rawls, J. (1971) *A Theory of Justice*. Cambridge, MA: Harvard University Press.

Russell, Bertrand (1922) *The Problem of China*. London: Allen & Unwin.

Sandel, M. (1982) *Liberalism and the Limits of Justice*. Cambridge: Cambridge University Press.

Social Welfare Department (1999) *Departmental Report 1997/98*. Hong Kong: Government Printer.

Tao, Julia Po-Wah Lai (1998) Confucianism. In *Encyclopedia of Applied Ethics*, Volume 1. London: Routledge.

White, Julie Anne (2000) *Democracy, Justice, and the Welfare State: Reconstructing Public Care*. University Park, Penn.: The Pennsylvania University Press.

Notes

1 The work described in this chapter was fully supported by a SRG grant (Project No. 7000982) and an RCPM grant for the project 'An Investigation on the Conception of Social Justice in Taiwan – A Comparative Study' from City University of Hong Kong. Thanks are due to Andrew Brennan for his valuable comments, and needless to say any mistake made in this chapter is mine.

2 Political legitimacy is not a single and simple concept. A political regime can establish its legitimacy by satisfying a number of criteria (Beetham 1991). It can be legitimate to the extent that (1) it is acquired and exercised in accordance with the law; (2) its source of authority is widely accepted as rightful; (3) it serves the moral ends of government in accordance with the socially acceptable standard; (4) its authority is confirmed by express consent or affirmation of its subjects; (5) it is recognized by other legitimate authorities. This list of criteria is not exhaustive. The criteria are not exclusive either because all contribute to legitimacy to a certain extent. Political authorities across different cultures may have different emphasis on the importance of these criteria. This chapter argues that both the colonial and post-colonial governments in Hong Kong have relied heavily on criterion (3) to establish their legitimacy although this political strategy has become less effective because of the recent economic and political changes.

3 I myself believe that there is a strong moral justification for democracy and support a quicker pace of political reform. From an instrumental perspective, I also believe that there are positive links between democratic reforms and

economic growth in Hong Kong. However, these are not the issues that I want to address in this chapter. Rather one of the major questions that I want to ask is whether Hong Kong people in general see that there is a direct link between economic development, political legitimacy and democracy. This question is largely cultural and empirical and is different from the normative question of whether democracy is desirable for Hong Kong.

4 'No matter how successful we are in fulfilling our mission to meet the forces of change and turn them to our advantage, there will always be people who need the community's support and care. We must work to improve the living conditions of those in need. Our success in this area is a measure of the true quality of our society' (Hong Kong SAR Government, 1998).

5 An earlier version of the following two sections appears in Ho Mun Chan 'Justice is to be Financed Before It is Done: A Confucian Approach to Hong Kong Public Health Care Reform', R-Z Qiu (ed.) (2003). *Bioethics: Asian Perspectives*. Netherlands: Kluwer Academic Publishers (forthcoming).

6 This is my modified translation of the Chinese text.

7 Being kept behind this 'veil of ignorance' is only an ideal situation, and Rawls only tried to derive his theory by conducting a thorough experiment.

8 Further statistical analysis indeed shows that preference for the Floor Constraint Principle is positively related to how strongly subjects treasure the value of care as measured by the statements in the questionnaire, but the relationship between the choice of this principle and the commitment to individualistic values is found to be negative. For further details of the analysis, see Ho Mun Chan 'A Chinese Conception of Social Justice' (unpublished manuscript), and Anthony Fung and Ho Mun Chan 'Chineseness in Contemporary Chinese Societies: A Comparison of Cultural Values among Hong Kong, Beijing and Taiwan' (unpublished manuscript).

7

SHARIAH FORMALISM OR DEMOCRATIC COMMUNITARIANISM?

The Islamic resurgence and political theory

Robert W. Hefner

> All cultures have a certain degree of ambivalence that allows for contesting prevailing perceptions and seeking to replace them with new or formerly suppressed conceptions through an internal discourse within the terms of reference of the particular culture and in accordance with its own criteria of legitimacy.
>
> (An-Nai'im 1999: 159)

One of the least welcome features of recent debates on Asian values has been the revival of nineteenth-century stereotypes of 'Asia' and the 'West'. As in Prime Minister Mahathir's comments on the primacy of community and social harmony over individual rights in Asian culture, or Samuel Huntington's (1996: 207–237) remarks on the uniqueness of Western rationalism, the models of civilization invoked in these discussions tend to be ahistorical and bipolar. The ironies of the contrast are many. Until recently, for example, Asian leaders did not typically think of themselves as sharing unitary values (Pertierra 1999). Many ordinary Asians today still do not. More generally, as Inoue Tatsuo has observed, 'the concept of Asian values does not convey Asian voices in their fully complexity and diversity ... [but rather] depends on, or even abuses, the West-centric frameworks that it claims to overcome' (1999: 29). The same generalization applies in spades to conservative Islamist and Occidentalist characterizations of Islam. Although disagreeing in the substance of their characterizations, the two camps agree in posing a caricature of Islam in opposition to an equally stereotyped West.

Against the backdrop of these bipolarities, the debate between communitarians and liberals in Western political theory provides a welcome opportunity to remind participants on all sides of these debates that no civilization is a seamless whole, and all carry rival and alternative potentialities within their varied streams. Just as there is ideological diversity in Asia and the Muslim world, the debate between communitarians and liberals has shown that there are profound differences of value and practice in the West, even among people who regard themselves as unequivocal democrats. Unfortunately, however, so far there is little to indicate that this message of civilizational pluralism has been heard much beyond the hallowed halls of political and cultural theory. For specialists of Islam and Southeast Asia like myself, for example, it is striking that, while fiery blasts on the 'clash of civilizations' have heated the sermons of populist Muslim preachers in *kampung* across Malaysia and Indonesia, the cooling breeze of the liberal-communitarian dialogue has hardly been felt at all. In part this is the case, of course, because there is no constituency in these countries interested in reflecting on the liberal-communitarian exchange. By contrast, Mr Huntington's warnings about radical Islam have been seized on by anti-liberal Muslims around the world. To the consternation of democratic Muslims, the anti-liberals delight in citing Mr Huntington's hoary remarks as proof that the West does indeed see Muslims as the new global enemy.

Another reason the communitarian dialogue with liberalism has failed to attract the attention of political thinkers in Asia and the Muslim world, however, is the sheer complexity of the theoretical issues in question. It is hard enough to get a consensus on citizenship or the proper relationship of individual to community in Western democratic circles. When the discussion is moved into a cross-cultural setting, the resulting density of interpretations is so great as to make even a limited meeting of horizons difficult.

At the risk of only adding to the confusion, I want in this paper to relocate a few of the issues raised in the liberal-communitarian debate from their Western setting to a modern Muslim one. Using what is, loosely, a historical sociological framework, I want in particular to examine the world-wide Islamic resurgence, with an eye toward appreciating its similarities and differences with religion, democracy, and modernity in the West. Having presented a general model, I will then attempt to illustrate some of its contextual dynamics in the largest of the Muslim world's nations, Indonesia. Toward the end of this paper, finally, I will hazard a few comments on the possibility of democracy across cultures, and the relevance of the communitarian-liberal debate for exploring that question.

The greatest benefit of this comparison, I will suggest, is that it alerts us to the plurality and rivalry intrinsic to all civilizations. That diversity has become all the more apparent and important under the globalizing circumstances of our late modern age. In particular, just as the communitarian critique of (neo-) liberalism reminds us that democracy can be constructed in varied ways, so too ferment in the contemporary Muslim world reminds us that political Islam comes in a variety of forms. Recognizing the internal diversity of all civilizations allows us to escape from the dire dualities of the clash-of-civilizations thesis. It also provides us with a better point of entry to an examination of the conditions of the possibility (to use an old post-structuralist saw) of democracy, human rights, and tolerance across cultures. Many features of modern Muslim experience, for example, are more intelligible in light of the communitarian critique of liberalism than they are the rarefied heights of liberal philosophy alone. Conversely, and perhaps more surprisingly, some of Western communitarianism's cross-cultural limitations – especially as regards the modern challenge of pluralist diversity – become more apparent in light of Muslim modernity.

Tradition and reform

Any effort to compare Muslim historical experience with liberalism and communitarianism in the West immediately runs up against the general problem of how to characterize the great transformation that has swept the Muslim world since the late 1970s. Iran's Islamic revolution of 1979 stands as a landmark in this world-wide resurgence, but it is only a particularly dramatic example of a general increase in Islamic piety and activism since that decade. Prior to the 1970s, the dominant political discourse in the Muslim world was loosely nationalist and socialist, to varying degrees of secularity and populism. Today, while it has its supporters (and in a few nations, like Iran, it is actually experiencing a new lease on life), secular nationalism is being bitterly contested by Islamist discourses and organizations.

The question this poses for a comparative historical sociology, of course, is whether this religious effervescence is evidence of a movement toward a modernity similar to that seen in the West, East Asia, and other parts of the world, or whether it reflects a fundamentally different, and essentially undemocratic, evolution. Some analysts have argued that the Islamic resurgence is neither modern nor democratic, but merely the latest in a cycle of reform and purification that has punctuated the whole of Muslim history. In a similar vein, others have characterized the resurgence as a nativistic reaction against modernity and, in particular, against the Western institutions that dominate so much of our global economy and culture.

Each of these characterizations touches on real problems, but, in the end, neither does justice to the internal diversity of the Islamic resurgence. To begin with the first of these arguments, one can note that it is both historically true and sociologically significant that, unlike Western Christianity, movements of resurgence and purificatory reform have taken place over the course of Muslim history, in a way that highlights a basic civilizational difference between Western Christianity and Islam.

In an influential, if problematic, article published 20 years ago, the philosopher and social anthropologist, Ernest Gellner (1981), made just this point. He observed that there has been a cyclical 'flux and reflux' of religious reform throughout Muslim history. The flux is marked by the oscillation between, on one hand, periods of relative laxity or (from the perspective of normative Islam) moral decadence, and, on the other, epochs characterized by great upsurges of religious purification and reform.

Gellner drew on the work of the great fourteenth-century Arab historiographer, Ibn Khaldun (1967), to argue that what underlay this cycle of religiosity in Islamic history was a sociology profoundly different from that of Church and state in the premodern West. The cycle was anchored, Gellner argued, on the dual ecology of nomadic pastoralism and town-dwelling sedentarism so widespread in the classical Middle East. As Ibn Khaldun had earlier observed, town dwellers tend over time to lower their moral guard and sink into social laxity, as the pleasures of urban life lure them away from strict religious observance. Immunized from this decadence by the demands of desert living, the nomadic population can better resist the moral temptations of urban life.

To these familiar Khaldunian themes, Gellner offers the additional observation that, because of the austerity of their social circumstances, the Muslim world's nomads provided a ready sociological reserve for the religious reformers who periodically arise, decrying urban decadence and calling for a return to the pristine ways of scripture. Alarmed by what they regard as believers' deviation from the Word, reformers channel the nomads' antipathy for cosmopolitan ease into a general crusade for religious and societal reform. Where the reform movement succeeds, it manages for a generation or two to press the urban population back toward scriptural ways. Eventually, however, the temptations of town life drag the urban population back down into a corrupted version of the faith. But the fall is not for forever. It is only a matter of time before the flux begins anew, as Muslim society generates another purifier of the faith and cycle of reform.

Gellner's adaptation of the Khaldunian model has the benefit of reminding sociologists of religion that models of reformation based on Christianity in the early modern West, with its pattern of momentous historical rupture, should not be taken as the prototype for all traditions. The history of religious reform in the Muslim world looks more like a periodically punctuated equilibrium, rather than a singular great transformation. The Gellner-Khaldun model is also useful because it draws our attention to, but never fully explains, a pattern of religious authority and organization quite different from that recognized in sociologies of religion based on Christian prototypes. It is clear that the Muslim example has most of the ingredients of a Christian sociology, including scripture, scholars, and state authorities. But all of them are embedded in an institutional framework with a dynamic quite different from that of classical Christianity.

What is the nature of this dynamic? A few variants of Shi'ism Islam excepted, in the Muslim case there is no central ecclesiastical authority or 'Church' as such; nor are there bishops or even priests. In place of a centralized Church, the religious infrastructure is networked and pluricentric, organized as it is around a loose association of scholars and jurists, known as *ulama* (lit., 'those who know'). The *ulama* are dispersed across a variety of loosely coordinated institutions, including religious schools, pilgrimage centers, mystical clubs, and other religious associations. From a religious perspective, the function of the *ulama* is to lead public worship, preserve and transmit knowledge derived from the Qur'an and Sunna (canonically recognized actions and sayings from the life of the Prophet), study the great religious commentaries, interpret holy law (*shariah*), and otherwise manage the many-stranded culture of textuality and devotion at the heart of Muslim tradition.

Because some *ulama* may be recruited to state administration, it is difficult or impossible to speak of a clear separation of religion and state in most of the premodern Muslim world. However, contrary to the claims of some Western historians as well as conservative Islamists, there is no single institutional formula for how the two are to be conjoined either. The canonical commentaries say simply that a good Muslim ruler is one who upholds Allah's laws in his land; however, exactly how the ruler is to do so is, institutionally speaking, left vague. As Abdullahi A. An-Nai'im observes:

> Traditional Islamic notions of the rule of law through the supremacy of *Shariah* over political expediency require effective enforcement mechanisms, which have always been weak in *Shariah* as a regime designed for small traditional communities radically different from the impersonal urban centers of present Islamic societies.
>
> (1999: 158)

In classical times, Muslim rulers might appoint *muftis* or chief jurists to serve as liaisons between the state and the community of religious scholars. Rulers might also engage scholars to serve in Islamic courts, help in collecting religious alms (*zakat*), or assist in other activities designed to demonstrate the ruler's piety, as well as keep the energies of the faithful in line.[1] Although these institutional ties might give state officials significant leverage over the scholarly community, some, indeed, most in the religious community managed to escape state controls. In part this reflected the fact that the recruitment and training of 'those who know' was never a state monopoly. The process of *ulama* education was carried out in numerous centers – in local society and in far-away lands where pilgrims studied with renowned scholars. The existence of multiple centers of education and worship created the potential for rival religious authorities in the Muslim community. This pluricentrism also meant that ideological unanimity was rare. Indeed, it was common for 'center–periphery' tensions to develop among scholars, most frequently between those in the service of state authority and those at the subaltern margins.

The relationship among central and peripheral scholars was, and is still today, also affected by scholars' ties to the community of believers. All pious Muslims are supposed to orient their profession of the faith by recognizing the authority of a particular scholar, to whom they look for counsel on religious matters, including the law. But the constraint works the other way as well. That is, lacking a Church authority and dependent as they are on the social estimation and economic support of believers, *ulama* tend to be responsive, not merely to the abstract concerns of the holy Qur'an, but to their community of fellow-believers. This dependency increases the likelihood that some *ulama*, particularly those remote from centers of power, may at times come to conclusions at odds with established views.

Inevitably, of course, the counter-hegemonic potential of the *ulama* network varied over time. In periods of peace and stability the Muslim community might recognize a more-or-less regularized hierarchy of religious scholars. *Ulama* at the periphery might differ little in their opinions from those at the center; even where they did, they might receive a very limited public hearing. The legal pronouncements (*fatwa*) of respected scholars, conversely, could command respect among a broad community of believers. During periods of social discord, however, the balance of power among religious scholars could shift away from centrally-located scholars to heretofore peripheral ones. During these unsettled times, the pluricentric potential of the scholarly community could be vividly realized, generating new leaders and a counter-hegemonic message of religious renewal. Marginal scholars could be catapulted to the center, carrying a reformed understanding of Allah's commands and mobilizing followers behind a campaign to demand social and religious reform.

One should not overstate the critical potential of the scholarly community. As Henry Munson has noted (1993: 82), Gellner exaggerated the frequency of religious reform *cum* political rebellion in Middle Eastern history. In addition, rulers' awareness of the subaltern potential of peripheral scholars often led them to impose strict limits on the scholars' public activities, including (as in some contemporary nations in the Middle East) limiting the topics that may be discussed during Friday mosque sermons.

But let me return for a moment to the Gellner-Khaldun model of reform, with its dual ecology of town dwellers and nomads. My comments on the subaltern potential of *ulama* networks are intended, among other things, to free Gellner's basic insight on the punctuated equilibria of Muslim civilization from its original Middle Eastern ecology. The latter is really too limited to apply to most areas of the Muslim civilization or to Muslims in modern times. Gellner's model really applies to only a few portions of the premodern Middle East, where urbanites lived in a sea of incompletely pacified nomads. The great (and, relatively speaking, nomad-poor) agrarian kingdoms of Mesopotamia, Turkey, and Islamic Spain – not to mention the Islamic kingdoms in South and Southeast Asia – fit poorly if at all in this account. The model is even less relevant for understanding the modern Muslim world, most of which is, so to speak, nomad free. I leave it to the judgment of readers as to whether Osama bin Laden should not be considered a modern-day heir to the status of reformer-among-the-nomads.

Viewed from the perspective of the sociology of religious authority I've outlined here, one can see that Gellner's model conflates what is primary and secondary in the flux and reflux of Islamic reform. The critical influence on this religious dynamic is not the social ecology of town and desert, but the networked nature of religious authority, center–periphery tensions in the *ulama* network, and the dialogical relationship of scholars with the surrounding society. Reform comes not through founding a new church or seizing the reins of an existing one, but through the entrepreneurial efforts of scholars' carrying a message of renewal to a community of believers. In appealing to nomads or today's urban poor, Muslim reformers respond to social imbalances and injustice by interpreting the divisions as proof of believers' deviation from Allah's commands. If his message is to move society, however, the reformer must press forward on two fronts. He must consolidate his position in the network of religious scholars, and simultaneously win the backing of masses and at least some patrons.

Rather than nomad ecology, it is this uniquely Muslim sociology of religious reform that has underlain the flux and reflux of Muslim religious life over the course of the ages. Rather than the Khaldunian dichotomy of urbanite and nomad, the real fount of Islamic reform is this three-sided dynamic among networked scholars, powerful elites, and the community of believers.

An important point follows from this model. Conservative Islamists today point to the historical pattern of cooperation between religious scholars and state officials as proof that there can be no separation of religion from state like that thought characteristic of Church and state in Christianity. But Islam's civilizational history shows us that the collaborations effected in most Muslim societies were invariably limited, and at times the relationship between ruler and scholars became openly antagonistic. Viewed from the perspective of actual historical practice rather than canonical memory, after the death of the Prophet there was always a significant separation of religious from state authority. The centrality of divine law to the religious tradition and center–periphery dynamics in the *ulama* network made it inevitable that some scholars would recognize that rulers' actions respond to interests more varied than the law alone.[2]

Herein lay one of the great paradoxes of Muslim civilization. Although the Prophet Muhammad provided a model for the union of religion and state, the very hallowedness of Allah's laws, and the fickleness of humans, guarantee that any absolute union after the age of the Prophet is impossible. The secessionist battles that marked the caliphate after the Prophet's death showed this quite clearly. There was no prophet after Muhammad, and never again would it be possible for the law to be implemented in a consensually absolutist manner. Again and again, the transcendent truth of the Law compels some *ulama* to dissent from their comrades, and to insist that they and the Law must never become mere appendages of state power. Even if many scholars did not and do not understand this paradox as such, the urgency of the Law and the center–periphery dynamics of *ulama* authority mean that there is always a practical separation of religious and political authority. Getting believers to recognize *in principle* that this is the case, and that such a separation is good for politics and for religion, has proved to be one of the central obstacles to the reform of Muslim politics in the modern era.

A different modernity

In modern times the reformist dynamic described above has been given a new and distinctive twist. As both Ernest Gellner and Benedict Anderson have argued, the rise of ethno-nationalisms in the nineteenth century West took place against a backdrop of the declining influence of the Church in public life. Critics have rightly faulted both authors for exaggerating the secularity of modern Western nationalism (van der Veer 1994). After all, Irish, English, Polish, and Spanish nationalism, among others, have regularly drawn on religious symbolism to strengthen their appeal. Since the end of World War II at the very least, and by comparison with the contemporary Muslim world, however, nationalist idioms in the late modern West have relied less on religion and, by contrast, more on secular social markers like language, culture, and ethnicity.

In the Muslim world in the mid-twentieth century, it seemed at first as if secular nationalism were also destined to consign religious authority and discourse to the margins of history. With the notable exception of Saudi Arabia, the dominant political discourse in the Muslim world during the middle decades of the twentieth century was a notably secularized nationalism. This nationalism's social imagery was only lightly inflected, at best, by references to the past glories of Islam. However, the religious resurgence of the late twentieth century changed all this, as Islamist movements rose to challenge and, in a few places, even displace nationalist regimes. In some countries, the Islamist advance was helped along by a pervasive delegitimation of corrupt nationalist regimes. However, there were more positive influences on the resurgence as well, the most notable of which illustrate basic differences between Muslim and Western modernities.

During the first years of the twentieth century, most Muslims still lived in agrarian societies, some of which were under Western colonial rule. In the aftermath of World War II and national independence, Muslim societies underwent unprecedented social change.[3] Developmentalist regimes introduced new roads, markets, and mass media, along with more intrusive state administrations. Most countries also experienced a great and sudden explosion of urban population. The large and impersonal landscapes of towns and cities created a social world in which the traditional ties of kinship and locality proved less able than before to provide an effective compass for social life.[4] Drawn to the message of a new generation of Muslim preachers, some among the populace turned to Islam for the answer to how to live in a brave new world.

There was an important infrastructural dimension to the Islamic resurgence. The developmentalist states launched ambitious programs of school-building and mass-education. Between 1950 and 1979, the population in most Muslim countries went from being massively illiterate to being predominantly literate (Eickelman 1992). Enrollments in high school and universities also soared. With this basic change in literacy, there soon developed a popular Islamic version of the 'print capitalism' Benedict Anderson (1991: 37–46) has argued was so important to the development of nationalism in the West. A mass market in inexpensive Islamic books and magazines emerged. These products offered commentaries on everything from how to pray or cleanse oneself after sexual relations to the need for an Islamic state. Although the nationalist elite had expected otherwise, mass education and modern communications were being put to uses anything but secular.

There was another important dimension to this revolution in knowledge and authority. The classically educated scholars (*ulama*) who, as I have suggested, long lay at the heart of the Islamic tradition came to find themselves challenged by a new and less centrally located class of 'people who know'. These new Muslim leaders, a sort of subaltern *ulama*, were diverse in background and ideology. They emerged from the ranks of religious activists, secularly educated Muslim intellectuals, independent preachers, and others of unconventional educational background. Traditionally trained and establishment-recognized *ulama* now found that they were not the only ones laying claim to the mantle of Islam. Everywhere, it seemed, there was heightened 'competition and contest over both the interpretation of [religious] symbols and control of the institutions, formal and informal, that produce and sustain them' (Eickelman and Piscatori 1996: 5).

The question these developments raise is whether the pluralization of religious authority is likely to be a force for repressive regimentation or civic freedom and democratic participation. On this point, scholars disagree. Some analysts, for example, have emphasized that the overall effect of mass education and religion's pluralization will be unambiguously democratic. Distinguished observers of Muslim politics, the anthropologist, Dale F. Eickelman, and the political scientist, James Piscatori, assert that:

> mass education opens the way to "democratized" access to sacred texts and overcomes restrictions as to who is "authorized" to interpret them. As a consequence, the monopolistic control by elites ... is countered by the greater number of would-be interpreters from diverse backgrounds yet commonly possessing modern-style education.
> (1996: 111)

Over the long run, Eickelman and Piscatori insist, the break down of religious monopolies and the rise of new *ulama* will create 'multiple centers of power and contenders for authority' in the Muslim community, greatly increasing the prospects for a broader democratization of society and culture (1996: 132).

Other observers of Muslim society, however, are not so sanguine. The French sociologist, Olivier Roy (1994), has developed a model of Muslim politics and social movements that agrees with Eickelman and Piscatori in emphasizing the pluralization of knowledge and authority taking place across the Muslim world. Rather than viewing this change as a harbinger of democratic things to come, however, Roy views the resurgence more ominously. He points out that many of what I am calling the 'new *ulama*' come from the ranks of secularly-educated students of science and engineering. Unfamiliar with the rich diversity of Islamic civilization, and biased by a peculiarly positivistic understanding of the exact sciences, these Islamists view religious law as a set of lifeless formulas to be mechanically imposed on the world. The irony here, Roy observes, is that, although this 'militant rationalism' pretends to be anti-Western, its formalism represents a latent internalization of the worst features of Western scientism.[5]

To make matters worse, Roy argues, the new Islamists link this positivistic understanding of religious law to a state-centered and corporatist model of political power. As with the Leninist left, the new Islamists aim for nothing less than the conquest of state. From there, they intend to use its leviathan powers to subject society to a new and totalizing plan. However much the new Islamist movements emerge from civil society, then, Roy believes their ultimate impact is deeply antithetical to civility and democracy.

Shariah formalism or civic pluralism

Most observers of the resurgence agree that, in certain respects, Islamic modernity does indeed diverge from that of the West and East Asia. The networked and pluricentric organization of religious authority has shown a remarkable ability to adapt to modern opportunities and challenges. Rather than being pushed to the margins or reduced to a system of purely personal ethnics, Islam has catapulted itself back into the public sphere. However, just what it is to do now that it is there remains an issue on which the Muslim community remains deeply divided.

Before speculating on the future of intra-Muslim rivalries, it might be useful to provide a few preliminary observations on the resurgence from the perspective of Western communitarianism and liberalism. One intriguing cultural effect of the resurgence is that in modern Muslim societies few ordinary people subscribe to the mythology, so widespread in Western societies, that the 'real' institutions of public life are markets and the state, while all else is a matter of private interests or superstructural amusements. Spurred by the modern fragmentation of markets, lifestyles, and communities, popular ethics in the late modern West have tended, not merely toward individualism, but toward what William James (1941) once called a 'medical materialism'. Medical materialism acknowledges the reality of individual and physical needs, but has greater difficulty recognizing social collectivities and shared sensibilities.

Popular culture in majority-Muslim societies, by contrast, tends to have an entirely different blind spot. Most Muslims readily accept the proposition that ethics and morality must be matters of public and political concern. Although its philosophical idioms might be unfamiliar, the communitarian argument that individuals are 'encumbered' with social identities and that politics must concern itself with public ethics does not have to swim against the Muslim current. However, although Muslims might agree that politics must involve more than a 'procedural republicanism',[6] they have greater difficulty agreeing on just what ethical values should be promoted, and how.

In light of the centrality of the *ulama* network to Muslim tradition and shariah law to *ulama* concerns, the crux of the debate for pious Muslims often comes back to the question of the precise intent of Allah's commands. Some scholars will insist that social justice and popular welfare can only be advanced through the strict and literal application of divine laws, the details of which are fixed for all time. Moreover, inasmuch as Allah, not the people, is the ultimate sovereign, divine commandments can never be made matters of democratic negotiation or legislation.[7]

Other Muslims will insist, however, that this shariah formalism confuses the letter of the law with the deeper divine intent. After all, the Muslim democrat argues, Allah's commands were meant to bring blessing to all of humankind through the realization of universal ideals of justice, equity, and morality. These ends can only be served if believers are responsive to the realities of their age. To apply the law justly, then, one must look beyond the literal text to the context of its enactment. In the modern world, the realities commentators must consider include the creative instability of scientific investigation, the movement of women into public life, human rights, constitutional law, and the growing pluralism of modern societies.[8]

For students of political theory, the rivalry between these two Muslim ethics reminds us that, rather than a starkly individualized liberalism facing off against a socially responsive communitarianism, the central ideological struggle of the Muslim world can be more aptly described as a rivalry between two opposed visions of Islamic communitarianism. Both are 'communitarian' in that they acknowledge the embeddedness of individuals in moral communities larger than the individual. Both are communitarian in that they aim to establish ethico-political structures responsive to the needs of individuals and communities. The two visions differ profoundly, however, in their ethical ambitions and the practices they recommend for their realization.

Which vision will likely prevail? To answer this question, it is necessary to take a brief detour into the sociology of democratic transitions. The Islamic resurgence has been marked by the heightened participation of masses of once-marginal people in the determinant events of Muslim society. However, as we all know, mass participation need not be democratic in its organization or outcomes. Where the participation involves the mobilization of large numbers of people, even majorities, with the aim of denying equal citizen rights to ethnic, religious, or ideological minorities, we cannot speak of democratization but something more appropriately called 'massification'.

It was in part as a result of their recognition that popular participation is not sufficient to guarantee democratization that political theorists, such as Putnam (1993) in the 1990s moved beyond the analysis of formal elections and constitutions to the study of the informal social and cultural conditions in society that 'make democracy work'. Recognizing that, even in the West, formal constitutional prescriptions have not prevented majorities from depriving minorities of their rights, neo-Tocquevillians like Robert Putnam began to speak of the importance of citizen associations and 'civil society' for socializing the habits of the heart required for democratic citizenship. From a different philosophical tradition but with a similar analytic concern, Jürgen Habermas spoke of the importance of developing a 'public sphere' of dialogue and exchange to nurture democratic values and provide opportunities for citizen input above and beyond the horizons of formal politics. Similarly, the political sociologist Peter Evans (1996) spoke of democracy's dependence on a 'social capital' of communication and coordination across the state–society divide.

However much they might disagree on other aspects of communitarian discourse, these analytic approaches agreed with one of its central premises, namely that democracy depends on, not just markets or formally democratic institutions, but cultural resources distributed across the whole of society. The sociologist Peter Evans adds an additional and, I believe, especially important element to this argument. He observes that, left to themselves, democratic cultures and organizations are still insufficient to guarantee democratic outcomes. For these resources to contribute to an effective democratic outcome, they have to be 'scaled up' into larger and more encompassing structures within and between state and society.

As I have suggested elsewhere (Hefner 2001: 1–58), Evans' generalization takes on even greater analytic importance when we take it a bit further than he does, and explore its implications for societies marked by deep divisions of ethnicity, religion, or ideology. Contrary to the utopian idealizations of some theorists, many associations in civil society have decidedly narrow horizons. Left to themselves, most do little more than what their founders intended them to do: not instill a democratic spirit, but provide entertainment, facilitate business deals, satisfy a hobby or sporting appetite, or serve any number of other close-at-hand interests. Along the way, the bowling association, the business club, or the bird-watchers league might socialize attitudes compatible with a democratic spirit. However at other times the activity may have exactly the opposite effect. After all, many ethnoreligious sodalities arise, not to deepen their members' commitment to tolerance and equality, but to compete with or even exclude those who lie on the other side of an ethnic, racial, or religious divide. To state the matter more theoretically, many associations that might be regarded as 'civic' according to their location in society are not civic in their impact on politics and public culture. Like white supremacist clans in the US, or Unionist marching clubs in Northern Ireland, some associations may diminish rather than expand their members' democratic commitments. History reminds us all too often that many 'civic' associations can become founts for hateful sectarianism.

If civil society groupings are to foster democratization, then, they must not only meet certain structural or locational criteria (i.e., existing outside of the state), but must contribute to the 'scaling up' of a public culture that promotes equal citizen rights for all regardless of their race, ethnicity, gender, or religion. Moreover, the scaling remains incomplete and vulnerable if it does not also reach into and reinforce a similar disposition in the state. Societies change, and even the most democratic society is at some point subject to anti-democratic challenges. The US's treatment of Japanese Americans during World War II offers a painful case in point. To diminish the chances that uncivil trends in society might lead to a democratic collapse, then, the scaling up of civility and participation in society must at some point be accompanied by a parallel consolidation of democratic powers in the state and judiciary. Against the romanticism of the civil society discourse of the 1990s, this example reminds us that, when it comes to 'making democracy work', there can be no opposition between state and society. If democracy is to endure, there must be a 'civilizing' synergy across the state–society divide.

Here, then, are a few standards to assess the implications of the Islamic resurgence for democratization in majority-Muslim societies. Not surprisingly, when we turn from general analysis to particular cases, it becomes apparent that, on matters of public participation and democratic ethics, the Islamic resurgence is itself torn by an internal 'clash of civilizations' fiercer than anything taking place between the West and Islam.

For some shariah conservatives, the resurgence's pluralization of religious authority is but a prelude to a full-scale assault on the state. Once captured, the state is to be used to create a new religious monopoly, designed to reverse the tide of modern differentiation and cultural pluralization. Whether with the Taliban in Afghanistan or some of the *jihad* fighters in eastern Indonesia (from 1999–2002), the terms for participation offered in this political system differ profoundly from those of democratic citizenship. The most basic difference is that, in the eyes of conservative Islamists, religious law requires a strict differentiation of men from women and believers from unbelievers (*kafir*). In these conservatives' eyes, equal rights are contrary to religious law. Rather than every adult enjoying an equivalent package of citizen rights, then, the social contract on which shariah politics (under this conservative interpretation) depends involves segregating people according to gender and religion.

Sensitive to the criticism that such a differentiation might be inegalitarian, shariah formalists respond that, on the contrary, all religious communities enjoy equal rights under the terms of this Islamist social contract. People are only equal, however, in the sense that each believer is required to affiliate with one religious community and submit totally to its authority. Once Muslim believers are distinguished from *kafir* in this way, the shariah formalist introduces the additional restriction that non-believers must not exercise authority over Muslims. Some conservatives will insist this restriction applies only to non-Muslims who wish to serve in the highest ranks of government. But others will proclaim that the restriction applies to all positions of authority in state and society, including those outside formal politics. A similar escalating logic of exclusion and inequality is applied to women.

All this is to say, then, that, for the shariah formalist, the 'Western' concept of equal citizenship must give way to the classical Islamic category of 'protected minorities' or *dhimmi*.[9] *Dhimmi* are nominally free and equal in the sense that they regulate their own religious affairs, as long as their religious law does not contradict Islam. Again, however, their equality is based on a prior segregation by religion. Because they are not allowed to exercise authority over Muslims, *dhimmi* cannot serve in the armed forces. As non-Muslims, they are also spared the obligation to pay the religious alms (*zakat*). In turn, however, they must pay a tax that recognizes their status as protected minorities. The tax is designed to demonstrate that the *dhimmi* accept the authority of the Islamic state. The law further stipulates that, should the *dhimmi* take actions against the state, they will have acted as enemies of Islam, with all that implies in terms of capital punishment.

However much shariah formalists may insist otherwise, however, while the word of Allah is divine and inalterable, its interpretations are varied. Democratic Muslims will insist that, rather than beginning with the distinction between Muslims and non-Muslims (or men and women), the Qur'an begins with 'a recognition of the rights of human beings simply as human beings' (Othman 1997). Islam, the Muslim democrat will say, is designed to bring blessing to all humankind, not just to those who self-identify as Muslims. It does so by struggling to realize, not a new and more totalizing truth regime, but the substantive principles of justice, equality, and peace. For the message of Islam to be realized, then, it is not the letter of the law that must be respected, but the spirit. To abide by the latter, the law must always be interpreted in light of the history and social context of its original enunciation and contemporary realization. For the modern age, this means that the conditions for civility and participation are such that government must not segregate by confession or gender. On the contrary, the Islamic commitment to justice and equality can only be realized through the institutions of modern democracy, undifferentiated citizenship, and universal human rights.

From civil society to democratic coalitions

Stated in so dry a manner, this contrast between civic pluralist Muslims, who see their faith as consistent with modern democracy, and shariah formalists, who argue otherwise, makes clear that the Islamic resurgence is not in the least unitary. Again, however, can we make any determination as to what the outcome of the rivalry among its assorted varieties will be? To answer this question, let me take my remarks on the 'scaling up' of democratic capital a bit further, especially as regards the role of civil-society groupings during political transitions.

During transitions of this sort, I would argue, the more decisive influence on political outcomes is not the condition of 'horizontal' groupings in civil society alone, but the jockeying for power among rival coalitions that link 'vertical' elites to society-based horizontal associations. For the sake of discussion, let me refer to these vertical alliances as 'transformative coalitions'. There is a bittersweet irony to much political theory in our age. It is that those of us who care deeply about democratic ideals often find it difficult to admit that 'good' political ends are sometimes served in ways more complex than our democratic instincts might wish, including the reliance on powers and solidarities other than those of a majoritarian, egalitarian, or horizontal sort. To state the point more bluntly, we allow our normative preferences to cloud our empirical sociological vision.

However decent its moral bias, this sociological blind spot, I believe, helps to explain much of the recent fascination with, and sociological poverty of, the concept of civil society. In particular, it explains the tendency for so many scholars to visualize political processes in civil society as fundamentally egalitarian, undifferentiated, and horizontal, while overlooking the frequency with which civil societies are cross-cut by powerful vertical allegiances, segmentary coalitions, and linkages of elites and masses. The transformative coalitions that have supported many of the most decisive political contests of our age succeeded only because they were able to mobilize vertical as well as horizontal coalitions. As with the civil rights movement in the United States during the 1960s, some of the most effective alliances link well-situated elites in the state and other elite institutions with horizontal groupings in society. Precisely because the vertical elites in these coalitions command great political resources, they are able to influence political events to a degree much greater than their proportionate representation in society.

The point here, then, is that we have to move beyond the well-meaning but sociologically naive musings of civil society theory, and recognize that civil societies tend to be highly differentiated and vertically segmented – not just homogeneous or peaceably horizontal, as received models so often imply. Like society as a whole, real-and-existing civil societies show the imprint of divisions based on ethnicity, race, religion, gender, and ideology. Equally important, laterally organized groupings in society may often be drawn up into segmentary mobilizations that pit rival vertical coalitions against each other. Each of the segmentary coalitions competing in such contests will be intent on scaling up *its* interests and values into a hegemonic position in state and public culture.

Just as civil society and 'social capital' can be put to civil or uncivil ends, then, these segmentary coalitions can be, and typically are, dedicated to opposed political outcomes. For democratic theorists, the key question is not whether such vertical alliances influence political transitions – it is obvious that, whether our democratic instincts approve or not, they do – but whether they can be channeled in such a way as to have a democracy-enhancing effect.

Indonesian transformations

To illustrate this point about the centrality of transformative coalitions in the scaling up of values and organizations in state and society, let me turn for a moment to the society in which I have done most of my empirical work over the past 25 years, the majority-Muslim country of Indonesia. Over the course of its modern history, politics in this society has undergone a series of decisive transitions, each characterized by bitter struggles between rival transformative coalitions. In fact, contestation between rival vertical alliances has been so pervasive in Indonesian history it has earned a term all its own: *politik aliran*, or the politics of (vertical) 'streams' (Geertz 1965).[10]

On occasion, some of the coalitions involved in Indonesia's political transitions have been expansively pluralist and democratic in orientation; others, however, have been anything but democratic. During the country's war of independence (1945–1949), Indonesia developed what was perhaps the most brightly inclusive of republican ideologies in the Southeast Asian region. As independence-leaders rallied the population to the anti-colonial fight, they appealed across ethnic and religious divides to all segments of society. The leadership even reached out to Chinese Indonesians – a population that, up to this time, they had viewed with some misgivings – with promises of full and equal citizen rights for all who supported the republican cause (Suryadinata 1992).

In this initial phase, then, the Indonesian experience differed profoundly from that of Malays and Chinese in nearby Malaysia. In 1946, the Malay elite succeeded in rallying the Malay community against British proposals to extend equal citizen rights to Chinese and Indians, in addition to Malays. The result was that, when Malaysia finally achieved independence in 1957, the terms of citizenship were differentiated along ethnic and religious lines. In particular, Muslim Malays were promised numerous political privileges that Chinese and Indians were not (Milne and Mauzy 1999). By contrast, Indonesia's national ideals during the first years of the republic were officially free of ethnic and religious differentiations – with the notable exception that the constitution stipulated the president must be 'indigenous'.

Unfortunately, however, the unsettled state of Indonesian politics insured that the country has been regularly thrown into deep political crises. During these times high democratic ideals are sacrificed for low tactical advantages. During the 1950s, the national leadership was divided into three major power blocs: the armed forces, Muslim parties, and secular nationalist parties (of which the Nationalist and Communist Parties, themselves rivals, were the primary constituents). As competition among these groups intensified in the early 1950s, government officials reneged on their promises of equal rights for Sino-Indonesians, implementing openly discriminatory programs against the Chinese. This discrimination was taken to new heights during the New Order government of President Suharto (1966–1998). During this period, public celebrations of Chinese holidays were banned; newspapers, books, and public signs printed in Chinese characters were forbidden; and the government pursued a heavy-handed if inconsistent policy of ethnic assimilation.

In these and other cases, the fatal vulnerability of Indonesian politics has been the inability of the political elite to agree on and implement the terms of public policy or, more seriously, the constitutional bases of the nation. Nationalists and the military pressed for various forms of multi-ethnic citizenship, most of which were based in some sense on the 'five principles' or Pancasila, a nationalist philosophy formulated by President Sukarno and other nationalist leaders in 1945. Islamists insisted that, as a majority-Muslim society, Indonesia must be governed according to some form of shariah constitutionalism. It was not the severity of this ideological divide alone, however, that condemned Indonesia to periodic outbreaks of fierce political violence. Far more damaging was the tendency of some in the political elite to respond to standoffs in the capital by opting out of the democratic game and deliberately exacerbating tensions in society, a pattern I have described as sectarian trawling. In the late 1950s and early 1960s, in particular, some members of the elite sought to press their advantage by exploiting regional and religious tensions. Having amplified these sentiments, the elites then attempted to tap them for the purpose of building transformative coalitions able to strike at rivals and change the balance of power at the center.

The most extreme example of this anti-civil politics occurred in late 1965 and early 1966, with a series of events that brought down the left-leaning government of President Sukarno and ushered in General Suharto and the military-dominated New Order regime (1966–1998). In the aftermath of a failed left-wing officers' coup (which may have enjoyed the tacit support of some in the Communist Party leadership), conservative factions in the armed forces accused the Communist Party of having masterminded the coup. They also alleged that the communists had planned to carry out mass killings of their opponents if the coup had succeeded, with most of their intended victims coming from the Muslim community. In the weeks following the failed coup, mysterious documents outlining just such a plan were 'discovered' in villages across Indonesia. Regime officials made much of the alleged plot, and used the resulting public outrage to mobilize religious organizations (especially but not exclusively Muslims) into a campaign of mass killing. Upwards of a half million people were killed in the subsequent violence; most of them simple peasants who had the misfortune of having joined organizations affiliated with the Communist Party (Cribb 1990). Here, then, was a 'scaling up' of religious sensibilities and organizations that was anything but democratic in its ambitions. The effects of the violence are felt still today.

In the aftermath of the campaign, the military-dominated elite surprised its allies by imposing new restrictions on Muslim political organizations. Worse yet, as was so vividly illustrated in its policies against Chinese language and culture, the regime ratcheted up its policy of playing ethnic and religious groups against one another. It used tensions among ethnoreligious groupings to keep opponents off balance, undermining the prospects for a broad-based opposition coalition. This divide-

and-rule tactic was a hallmark of regime policy during the entire the New Order.

Although the tactics deployed by the regime remained generally the same, the social constituency given momentary advantage changed over time. In the early years of the New Order, for example, secular nationalists, nominal Muslims, military conservatives, and Christians were given the lion's share of regime favors on matters related to religious policy, to the disappointment of Muslim party leaders. In the last ten years of Suharto's New Order, by contrast, the regime reversed tack, and cultivated support among conservative Muslims – while systematically harassing secular nationalists and democratic Muslims. In the last six months of the Suharto regime, as the nation reeled from the effects of the Asian financial crisis, government ideologues made open appeals to anti-Christian and anti-Chinese sentiment. More quietly but equally alarmingly, they provided funding and tactical support to ultraconservative Islamists who railed against the democracy movement as secularist, Christian-dominated, and anti-Islam (Hefner 2000).

Even after Suharto's fall, a few hardliners in the government and military continued to exploit ethnoreligious tensions. As is well known, for example, in 1999 regime hardliners implemented their policies in East Timor by arming local paramilitaries against pro-independence Timorese. Less well known but even more revealing, regime hardliners also attempted to rally conservative Muslim sentiment to the Timor cause by portraying Western concern for the troubled island as part of an international Jewish and Christian conspiracy to weaken Muslim Indonesia. When violence broke out in September 1999 after East Timorese voted in favor of independence, hardliners attempted to portray the violence as the result of Western interference and 'horizontal' tensions between local groupings. However, it was all too clear that the bulk of the violence was not the result of horizontal antagonomisms but vertical meddling. It was carried out by paramilitaries armed, organized, and funded by elements in the Indonesian armed forces. In a similar manner, there is evidence to suggest that some (but only some) of the ethno-religious violence that afflicted Indonesia in the first three years following Suharto's overthrow was stoked by *ancien régime* elites striking bargains with ascendant (and 'aliranized') regional bosses. The backers of this alliance scaled up ethno-religious tensions in an effort to scuttle the multi-ethnic and multi-religious coalition pressing for democratic reform (Tomagola 2000: 21–32).

In short, the New Order regime made regular use of vertical organizations and transformative coalitions. Most of the alliances it chose to support, however, were of an anti-democratic and anti-pluralist sort. In its final years, the regime's primary political allies were Islamic ultra-conservatives hostile to Christians, Chinese, and moderate Muslims. The regime provided these hardliners with a political influence greater than their actual numbers in society. Regime initiatives also forced much of the real politics of state underground and out of public scrutiny. Not surprisingly too, after Suharto fell and the center's grip on the provinces weakened, regional bosses seized on these same methods of divide and rule and made them their own.

Indonesia provides a vivid illustration, then, of the centrality of vertically organized coalitions in political transitions. In the case of Indonesia's New Order government, the Suharto regime scaled up support for Muslim hardliners, while marginalizing Muslim groupings committed to pluralism and democracy. The regime's promotion of ultraconservative Islam was not sufficient to allow the conservatives to seize power. It was enough, however, to handicap moderate Muslim efforts to forge a broad-based democratic coalition. Moreover, as the central government's hold on the provinces has weakened, it has also opened the regions to a maelstrom of ethno-religious violence. Although the situation is not yet clear, Indonesia today (2003–2004) appears to be emerging from the worst of this conflict, in part because a new military-backed elite has asserted itself.

Conclusion: democracy across cultures

In the West, communitarianism is but the latest in a series of social and intellectual movements that have sought to challenge the 'growing power of atomist modes of thought', and the political policies they inform (Taylor 1989). We know, of course, that political cultures are the product of complex and multi-sided interactions. To cite, and disagree with, the old Althusserian saw, there is no 'determinant in the last instance' when it comes to the determinants of political and economic cultures. It would be a serious oversimplification to conclude, then, that the atomistic proclivities of some Western ideologies are merely a superstructural by-product of, say, modern capitalism. The influences on public culture and politics in the West have been many, and the balance of values they strike will continue to be many, not one.

Inasmuch as this is the case, we should not be surprised to see that, as Asia and the Muslim world become more involved in global capitalism and communications, their religious and ethical systems need not go down the exact same cultural path as the West. There will certainly be some cultural convergences, particularly where a business, media, or political structure diffuses across national borders and brings with it specific (and effective) modules for organization and culture. Modern societies are not seamlessly integrated wholes, however, and modern hegemonies are often not as powerful as they first appear. No sooner may a business or media culture implant itself in a new national home than local communities and organizations premised on a different ethico-cultural regime may challenge its operations. As the Islamic resurgence illustrates so well, globalization need not imply cultural homogenization. On the contrary, globalizing processes are just as likely to intensify myriad cultural contestations.[11]

Public ethics and politics in the West, too, have long given evidence of counter-currents to the putative atomism of neoliberal models. As Benedict Anderson, Ernest Gellner, and Charles Taylor have all emphasized, for example, the age of capital was also the age of nationalism. And nationalism has always assumed varied ideological incarnations, not just one. Some nationalist discourses have offered strong cultural counterpoints to the atomism of economistic policies. Still today, in fact, some vaguely communitarian thinkers, like Charles Taylor, argue that a revised version of democratic or liberal nationalism (which Taylor refers to as 'republican patriotism') might yet offer a better balance between liberalism's individual freedoms and communitarianism's 'common identification with a historical community founded on certain values' (Taylor 1989: 178).

I confess that I find aspects of Taylor's civic republicanism compelling. I also believe that modern Western history has shown a good deal more anti-atomist ferment than some critics of Western neoliberalism acknowledge. Indeed, consistent with this last point, Taylor and Bernard Yack have both observed that communitarians have sometimes conflated ontological questions concerning how human identity is constituted (communitarians arguing that all human subjectivities are socially constituted and thus 'encumbered') with normative arguments as to *which* type of encumberedness or responsiveness is best for the individual and society (Sandel 1982).[12] The former view, concerning the socially inflected nature of human subjectivity, is one with which most in the human sciences would probably agree. As we all know, however, the latter, normative question generates no corresponding agreement.

This last point, I believe, takes us to the crux of the matter concerning the cross-cultural limitations of Western communitarianism. As I have tried to illustrate by way of the Islamic resurgence, the central ideological question in most non-Western societies is, not how to restore a sense of communitarian responsiveness in an atomized social landscape, but which among several 'communitarian' options is best, and how to build the transformative coalition to implement its aims. As is also the case in East and Southeast Asia, the Muslim world has no dearth of sociologically encumbered designs for living. The real ideological divide in these countries centers, not on the question of atomization vs. communitarianism, but on *which* socially responsive plan to pursue.

At least in the romantically undifferentiated form popularized by activists in the 1990s, the concept of civil society was initially designed to provide one answer to this question, but I have suggest here that it lacks the precision to do so convincingly. The concept of civil society suffers from many of the same conceptual limitations as the idea of 'community' in communitarian thought. Left to themselves, communities are not necessarily pluralism-tolerant or democracy-friendly. Civil societies, too, are ethnically, religiously, and ideologically differentiated. While they may help to embed politics and 'encumber' social actors, civil societies do not inevitably strengthen democratic attitudes or institutions. The critical issue, again, is whether communities and civil organizations can work with pivotal people in state and society to create coalitions that scale up the civic cultures and practices found in certain segments of society into citizenship institutions available to all.

In the Western democratic tradition, communitarian thought has served as an important reminder that democracy and political civility are vitally dependent on resources in society, rather than on the formal structures of government or market alone. In an age of economic globalization, it is important that locally based resources of this sort be protected from policies and powers that, while professing their support for freedom and equality, effectively corrode the community resources required for the realization of democratic ideals. Equally important from a cross-cultural perspective, communitarian criticisms of neoliberalism have provided support for the arguments of non-Western actors that there is not one, but numerous roads to modernity and democracy. The road may allow balances of public and private, individuality and social responsibility, different from those prevalent in the late-modern West. In this sense, however self-interested the promoters of Asian or Islamic values might be, their initial premise, concerning the right of different societies to make markets and polities responsive to their own needs, is certainly correct.

All this is to say that communitarianism offers vital lessons for global debates on the politics of late modernity. At the same time, however, communitarian proposals suffer from the same sociological vagueness that has afflicted discussions of civil society. Theorists from both schools are right to emphasize that democratic societies cannot take for granted public commitments to dignity, freedom, and tolerance. When it comes to specifying the structures or organizations that can best scale up these cultures, however, the communitarian, like the civil theorist, often falls back on vague generalities. In the Muslim world, as in east Southeast Asia, there are any number of home-grown communitarianisms. But many of them, perhaps even the majority, are neither pluralistic nor democratic.

My conclusion, then, is that what Western communitarianism has to offer non-Western theorists is more a general spirit of democratic pluralism rather than specific policies or programs. If pressed a bit further, however, this general lesson can lead to a useful insight. It is that high democratic ideals always depend for their realization on local cultures and coalitions. The transition to democracy is impossible without transformative alliances that emerge, not from abstractions like 'civil society' or the 'people', but from specific coalitions and communities. To say that these coalitions must scale up existing social resources and meanings into more encompassing state-societal forms is to say that, however high their ideals, they always depend on the local and provisional.

Inasmuch as this is the case, those of us who hail from the West should welcome the claims of those in Asia and the Muslim world who insist that the balance of values in their democracies can differ from that in the West. In reality, as the struggle for civil rights in the United States illustrated, there has been no static balance to the cultures or practices of democracy in the West either. Democracy is a form of governance that lays claim to universality. The richest and most unusual aspect of its universality, however, is that it always and everywhere depends on local meanings, solidarities, and communities. This simple insight is consistent, I believe, with the spirit if not the letter of the communitarian critique of neoliberalism. The point is that, not only are individuals culturally 'encumbered', democracies are as well.

The diffusion of democratic governance to non-Western societies, then, will not lead to the extinction of cultural difference, but facilitate its new and more vivid expression. We are still in an early phase of this great historical transformation, but this much already seems clear. Inasmuch as this is the case, it is time that we – especially 'we' in the West – get used to the idea that, even as democracy brings a few procedural commonalities, it will facilitate greater cultural differentiation in other spheres. All this reminds us that we have arrived, not at the end of history, but at another of its breathtakingly complex beginnings.

References

An-Na'im, Abdullahi A. (1990) *Toward an Islamic Reformation: Civil Liberties, Human Rights, and International Law.* Syracuse: Syracuse University Press.

An-Nai'im, Abdullahi A. (1999) 'The Cultural Mediation of Human Rights: The Al-Arqam Case in Malaysia', in Joanne R. Bauer and Daniel A. Bell, eds, *The East Asian Challenge for Human Rights.* Cambridge: Cambridge University Press, pp. 159.

Anderson, Benedict (1991) *Imagined Communities: Reflections on the Origins and Spread of Nationalism*, 2nd edn. London: Verso.

Antoun, Richard T. (1989) *Muslim Preacher in the Modern World: A Jordanian Case Study in Comparative Perspective.* Princeton: Princeton University Press.

Awang, Abdul Rahman (1994) *The Status of the Dhimmi in Islamic Law.* Kuala Lumpur: International Law Book Services.

Bowen, John R. (1993) *Muslims Through Discourse: Religion and Ritual in Gayo Society.* Princeton: Princeton University Press.

Cribb, Robert (1990) *The Indonesia Killings, 1965–1966: Studies from Java and Bali.* Clayton, Australia: Monash Papers on Southeast Asia, No. 21, Centre of Southeast Asian Studies, Monash University.

Eickelman, Dale F. (1985) *Knowledge and Power in Morocco: The Education of a Twentieth Century Notable.* Princeton: Princeton University Press.

Eickelman, Dale F. (1992) 'Mass Higher Education and the Religious Imagination in Contemporary Arab Societies', *American Ethnologist* 19(4): 643–655.

Eickelman, Dale F. and James Piscatori (1996) *Muslim Politics*. Princeton: Princeton University Press.

Engineer, Asghar Ali (1994) *The Islamic State*, 2nd edn. New Delhi: Vikas.

Evans, Peter (1996) 'Government Action, Social Capital and Development: Reviewing the Evidence on Synergy', *World Development* 24(6): 1119–1132.

Geertz, Clifford (1965) *The Social History of an Indonesian Town*. Cambridge, Mass.: MIT Press.

Gellner, Ernest (1981) 'Flux and reflux in the faith of men', in Ernest Gellner *Muslim Society*. Cambridge: Cambridge Studies in Social Anthropology No. 32, Cambridge University Press, pp. 1–85.

Hannerz, Ulf (1992) *Cultural Complexity: Studies in the Social Organization of Meaning*. New York: Columbia University Press.

Hefner, Robert W. (ed.) (1998) *Market Cultures: Society and Morality in the New Asian Capitalisms*. Boulder: Westview.

Hefner, Robert W. (2000) *Civil Islam: Muslims and Democratization in Indonesia*. Princeton: Princeton University Press.

Hefner, Robert W. (2001) 'Multiculturalism and Citizenship in Malaysia, Singapore, and Indonesia' in Robert W. Hefner (ed.) *The Politics of Multiculturalism: Pluralism and Citizenship in Malaysia, Singapore, and Indonesia*. Honolulu: University of Hawaii Press, pp. 1–58.

Huntington, Samuel P. (1996) *The Clash of Civilizations and the Remaking of World Order*. New York: Simon & Schuster.

Hussain, S. Showkat (1997) *Minorities, Islam, and the Nation State*. Kuala Lumpur: Islamic Book Trust.

Inoue, Tatsuo (1999) 'Liberal Democracy and Asian Orientalism' in Joanne R. Bauer and Daniel A. Bell, eds, *The East Asian Challenge for Human Rights*. Cambridge: Cambridge University Press, pp. 27–59.

James, William (1941) *Varieties of Religious Experience*. London: Longman, Green.

Khaldun, Ibn (1967) *The Muqaddimah: An Introduction to History*, Trans. by Franz Rosenthal, Edited by N.J. Dawood. Princeton: Bollingen Series, Princeton University Press.

Kurzman, Charles (ed.) (1998) *Liberal Islam: A Sourcebook*. New York: Oxford University Press.

Kymlicka, Will (1995) *Multicultural Citizenship: A Liberal Theory of Minority Rights*. Oxford: Clarendon Press.

Lapidus, Ira M. (1975) 'The Separation of State and Religion in the Development of Early Islamic Society' *International Journal of Middle East Studies* 6(4) (October): 363–385.

Milne, R.S. and Diane K. Mauzy (1999) *Malaysian Politics under Mahathir*. London: Routledge.

Milner, A.C. (1983) 'Islam and the Muslim State' in M.B. Hooker (ed.) *Islam in South-East Asia*. Leiden: E.J. Brill, pp. 23–49.

Moussalii, Ahmad S. (1992) *Radical Islamic Fundamentalism: The Ideological and Political Discourse of Sayyid Qutb*. Beiruit: American University of Beiruit.

Munson, Henry Jr (1993) *Religion and Power in Morocco*. New Haven: Yale University Press.

Othman, Norani (1997) 'Shari'a and the Citizenship Rights of Women in a Modern Nation-State: Grounding Human Rights Arguments in Non-Western Cultural Terms'. Bangi, Malaysia: IKMAS Working Papers, No. 10, Universiti Kebangsaan Malaysia.

Pertierra, Raul (1999) 'Introduction: Asian Values' *Sojourn* 14(2) (October): 275–294.

Putnam, Robert D. (1993) *Making Democracy Work: Civic Traditions in Modern Italy.* Princeton: Princeton University Press.

Rahnema, Ali (ed.) (1994) *Pioneers of Islamic Revival.* London: Zed Books.

Roy, Olivier (1994) *The Failure of Political Islam.* Cambridge, Mass.: Harvard University Press.

Sandel, Michael J. (1982) *Liberalism and the Limits of* Justice. Cambridge: Cambridge University Press.

Sandel, Michael J. (1996) *Democracy's Discontent: America in Search of a Public Philosophy.* Cambridge: Harvard University Press.

Schrauwers, Albert (1999) *Colonial 'Reformation' in the Highlands of Central Sulawesi, Indonesia, 1892–1995.* Toronto: University of Toronto Press.

Shamsul, A. B. (1997) 'Identity Construction, National Formation, and Islamic Revivalism in Malaysia' in Robert W. Hefner and Patricia Horvatich (eds) *Islam in an Era of Nation-States: Politics and Religious Renewal in Muslim Southeast Asia.* Honolulu: University of Hawaii Press, pp. 207–227.

Singerman, Diane (1995) *Avenues of Participation: Family, Politics, and Networks in Urban Quarters of Cairo.* Princeton: Studies in Muslim Politics, Princeton University Press.

Soroush, Abdolkarim (2000) *Reason, Freedom, and Democracy in Islam.* Oxford: Oxford University Press.

Suryadinata, Leo (1992) *Pribumi Indonesians, The Chinese Minority, and China.* 3rd edn. Singapore: Heinemann Asia.

Taylor, Charles (1989) 'Cross-Purposes: The Liberal-Communitarian Debate' in Nancy L. Rosenblum, (ed.) *Liberalism and the Moral Life.* Cambridge, Mass.: Harvard University Press, pp. 159–182.

Tomagola, Tamrin (2000) 'The Bleeding Halmahera of North Moluccas' in Olle Tornquist, ed., *Political Violence: Indonesia and India in Comparative Perspective.* Oslo: SUM Report No. 9, Centre for Development and the Environment, University of Oslo, pp. 21–32.

van der Veer, Peter (1994) *Religious Nationalism: Hindus and Muslims in India.* Berkeley: University of California Press.

Yack, Bernard (1988) 'Liberalism and its Communitarian Critics: Does Liberal Practice "Live Down" to Liberal Theory?' in Charles H. Reynolds and Ralph V. Norman (eds) *Community in America: The Challenge of Habits of the Heart.* Berkeley: University of California Press, pp. 147–169.

Notes

1 Not all Muslim rulers even bothered to appoint *qadi*. Some Muslim states in premodern Southeast Asia dispensed with the institution entirely, see A.C. Milner (1983).

2 On the separation of state and religion in Islamic history, see Ira M. Lapidus

(1975). Henry Munson Jr's (1993) provides a vivid illustration of a similar tension between *ulama* and rulers in Moroccan history.

3 For anthropological studies of this transition, see Antoun (1989), and Eickelman (1985). For an Indonesian counterpart, see John R. Bowen (1993).

4 One should not exaggerate the decline. Many ethnographic studies have demonstrated the resilience of kinship networks and family politics in urban Muslim societies; see, for example, Diane Singerman (1995).

5 In his study of young *dakwah* militants in Malaysia, Shamsul A.B (1997) noted a similar tendency toward positivistic readings of Islam.

6 A communitarian theme developed most extensively in Michael J. Sandel (1996).

7 For a discussion of these themes in relation to specific Islamist thinkers, see Ahmad S. Moussalii (1992) and Ali Rahnema (1994).

8 For a representative sampling of English-language commentaries from the liberalizing side of this debate, see, Abdolkarim Soroush (2000); Abdullahi Ahmed An-Na'im, (1990); Engineer (1994) and Charles Kurzman, (1998).

9 For two recent defenses of the institution of *dhimmi*, see Abdul Rahman Awang (1994), and S. Showkat Hussain (1997). For a philosophical analysis of *dhimmi* as a non-liberal form of tolerance, see Will Kymlicka, (1995: 155–158).

10 The Indonesian concept is, of course, directly related to the familiar concept of 'pillarization' applied to vertically organized religious groupings in Dutch politics and society. For a recent comparison of the usage in Netherlands and Indonesian sociology, see Albert Schrauwers (1999).

11 On the contestive interaction of the local and the global, see Ulf Hannerz, (1992) and Robert W. Hefner (1998).

12 Coming from the liberal rather than Sandel's (1982) communitarian side of the debate, Bernard Yack (1988) has made the same point Taylor does concerning this confusion of (social) ontology and normative advocacy in communitarian arguments. More generally, and quite elegantly, he argues that the actual *practice* of liberalism has been far more responsive to social and community concerns than some liberal *theory* would imply. However, Yack neglects to add that atomized social theories can and do lead to practices that strip mine the public cultural resources on which democratic life depends.

8

THE FAILURE OF STATE IDEOLOGY IN INDONESIA

The rise and demise of *Pancasila*

Vedi R. Hadiz

Introduction

For over half a century '*Pancasila*', or the Five Principles,[1] remained a contested concept in Indonesia, in spite of its closest association with the statist and developmentalist ideas that underpinned the stifling and oppressive long rule of Soeharto's New Order. It is argued here that the contest primarily had to do with competing interests that variously claimed to be heirs of the legacy of Indonesia's nationalist revolution. Thus, the ascendance, and near-hegemony, of conservative and reactionary interpretations of *Pancasila* was linked to the victory in the mid-1960s of a coalition of interests led by the army over the potentially fundamental challenge posed by the presence of the Indonesian Communist Party (PKI) and other radical populist forces. Apart from the army, this coalition embraced a variety of urban and rural petty bourgeois interests threatened by the agitation of the communists, and which ultimately consented to the rule of an authoritarian state and its corps of officials. In the absence of a viable national bourgeoisie and the small size of the urban middle class, this allowed the New Order to deploy the notion that the state should intervene in the market in the national interest. Furthermore, it was frequently able to represent politically connected private interests as identical to the national interest principally defined in terms of the safeguarding of order and stability – in turn, viewed as essential to successful material development.

Nevertheless, it is also suggested here that a wide range of critics of the New Order almost never ceased to attempt to re-appropriate *Pancasila* from the state. Instilling it primarily with social justice concerns, they used the official language of *Pancasila* to advance a critique of a capitalist project presided over by interests taking an increasingly oligarchic character – fusing politico, bureaucratic and corporate elements – that had instrumentally captured the institutions of state power.[2] As late as the mid-1990s, for example, labour leader Muchtar Pakpahan was to claim that his trade union activities – then effectively outlawed – were inspired by a vision of '*Pancasila* Socialism' (as quoted in Hadiz 1997: 149). Generally, however, critics were to focus attention especially on the disjuncture between the reality of predatory capitalism and the social justice and egalitarian ideals of the national revolution.

These critics emanated from a broad range of groups and represented interests newly formed by the very process of capitalist industrialisation successfully ushered in by the New Order. They included a variety of middle-class-based NGOs and student movements, as well as political and human rights groups, and labour-based organisations. This demonstrates that the *Pancasila*, rather than mere state ideology, was also deeply ingrained in the collective memory as an integral part of Indonesia's National Revolution – the struggle to create a just society. However, there were also liberal reformist opponents of the New Order's organic-statist use of *Pancasila* who advocated an agenda of economic liberalism based on free markets. These were notably less equipped to develop a critique couched in the language of *Pancasila*, largely because of the difficulty in presenting individualist, market-oriented world-views in the terms of a largely communitarian ethos born of a nationalist and anti-imperialist struggle. Nevertheless, issues such as democratisation and human rights were often advanced in public debates by liberal intellectuals and by NGO activists, criticising the official proscribing of these on the basis of a claimed incongruity with national cultural values.

Political history

Until recently, *Pancasila* – Indonesia's Five Principles – has been remarkably resilient. 'Formulated' by Soekarno in 1945 to represent the 'authentic' expression of Indonesian culture, it was enshrined as 'sole ideology' (*azas tunggal*) by Soeharto 40 years later. In between, Indonesia went through an armed national revolutionary struggle, major constitutional changes, the rise and fall of parliamentary democracy and of 'Guided Democracy', the violent eradication of communism, as well as the ascendance of a capitalist project presided over by a highly centralised authoritarian and corporatist state. In 1998, *Pancasila* lost the privileged status especially bestowed during the long Soeharto era, as new freedoms followed the unravelling of the New Order's institutions of social and political control. Still enshrined as state ideology, it has now lost much of its lustre as new political parties and organisations are no longer obliged to profess strict ideological adherence.

But *Pancasila*'s legacy cannot yet be fully erased: though discredited as the major component of the New Order's ideological armoury of repression, it arguably still speaks to the hearts and minds of several generations of Indonesians who were brought up constantly being reminded of the egalitarian and social justice aims of the Indonesian Revolution and Nation. For whole generations, *Pancasila* was not only state ideology, but also the shorthand for these ideals. The anti-Soeharto student demonstrators of 1998, for example, were no doubt the recipients of a life-long formal education on the virtues of such ideals and their demands for 'total reform', as noted below, were partly an expression of disappointment that Indonesia's elites were not upholding them. Significantly, that many student activists regarded themselves as part of a 'moral' rather than 'political' movement (Aspinall 1999: 222–223) can be partly explained by the lingering influence of the notion of selfless youthful heroism – perpetuated in the New Order's own recounting of recent Indonesian history.[3]

Furthermore, especially during the nation's infancy *Pancasila* arguably helped to cement Indonesia's fragile early nationalism. It was specifically a pragmatic compromise between disparate and potentially antagonistic social forces – most notably secular nationalism and organised political Islam. Indeed, Soekarno re-invoked the 1945 Constitution – which the New Order of Soeharto later proclaimed to be organically inseparable from the *Pancasila* – in 1959, to brush aside debates about the basis of the Indonesian state. These debates had been dragging on for several years in the Constituent Assembly, the body then charged with drawing up a new constitution (Nasution 1992).

However, this act arguably paved the way for the long process of centralising state power that would be taken to much greater lengths by Soeharto. What Soekarno did was to effectively prop up his own authority by imposing curbs on political parties, refashioning parliament to reflect representation by interest groups, and centralising more power on the state bureaucracy and Presidency. In many ways, therefore, Soekarno's Guided Democracy, in which *Pancasila* already occupied a special place, opened the door for Soeharto's New Order, which then introduced such concepts as *Pancasila* Democracy and *Pancasila* Industrial Relations.

Under the New Order, the codification of *Pancasila* – through drab and mind-numbing indoctrination courses that countless cohorts of students, civil servants, and ordinary citizens had to suffer – was most closely identified with conservative, reactionary social and political projects. In many ways the *Pancasila* advanced by the New Order's ideologues – including the cunning and ruthless General Ali Moertopo during its earlier days – was an organicist one which seemed more akin to the reaction of European fascisms and increasingly distant from the more egalitarian and revolutionary appeal of Indonesia's nationalist, anti-colonial struggle.

This *Pancasila* essentially emphasised the benign role of an omnipresent state, acting as father figure to societal groups, for the purpose of maintaining national unity and social integration. But the manifestation of such a concern was invariably severe restrictions on civil and political rights. Though *Pancasila* indoctrination courses would regularly conjure up the heroic deeds of bamboo-wielding nationalist youths against colonial oppression, the new emphasis was on its function in relation to stability, development and unity. Born of a period of turbulent revolutionary struggle, *Pancasila* came to be ironically drained of its revolutionary resonance.

Though not inevitable, this was not entirely surprising either. Reeve (1985) has suggested that the root of ideas which seek to express purportedly authentic Indonesian values of harmony, cooperation, and the family, and which eschew conflict, can be found in indigenous Javanese social and political thinking. Thus, the ideas of Ki Hadjar Dewantara, the educationist, for example, are rooted in the traditional philosophy of the Javanese conservative aristocracy. It was such 'traditional' notions that the New Order particularly referred to in its *Pancasila* courses. David Bourchier (1996), on the other hand, has traced organicist thinking in Indonesia – which found full expression in the codification of *Pancasila* by the New Order – to early twentieth and late nineteenth century European legal thinking, which in some of its offshoots, was instrumental to the rise of fascism. These were transported to Indonesia via Dutch legal thinking, and much later, through Catholic intellectuals surrounding General Moertopo, who feared both the mass movements of communism and of organised Islam. He notes, for example, that New Order thinking on labour and class struggles closely resemble the organicist and anti-class struggle stance taken by the Catholic Church in Rome in the time of Mussolini (Bourchier 1996: 205–206).

But we are less concerned here about whether such figures as the prominent Indonesian legal and constitutional scholar and aristocrat, Raden Soepomo, were primarily Javanists or the intellectual cousins of European fascists. It is sufficient to note that organicist thinking seemed to be attractive to a wide range of modernising aristocratic or traditional elites, especially in historical contexts characterised by the absence of challenges from a viable liberal bourgeoisie or a coherently organised working class. This recalls Jayasuriya's (1998) observations about the diverse expressions in recent world history of 'reactionary modernisation', an alternative vision of modernity to the liberal or social democratic varieties.

Rather than seeking to trace its genealogy, we take an approach that emphasises the use and abuse of *Pancasila* to support often contradictory political projects underpinned by a range of entrenched interests. As mentioned earlier, given *Pancasila*'s position at the birth of the Indonesian nation, the sometimes-antagonistic heirs to Indonesia's revolution – with the notable exception of significant sections of organised Islam – have laid claim on its legacy.

Pancasila and economic power

According to the often-cited article 33 of the 1945 Constitution, all vital sectors of the economy ought to be run by the state in the name of the collective interest. Moreover, it is said that the economy should be run according to 'family principles'. Thus, some Indonesian thinkers and statesmen, like former Vice President Mohammad Hatta, were adamant that the cooperative should be the defining feature of the Indonesian economy, as opposed to the capitalist enterprise (Reeve 1985: 36–41). They also tended to romanticise the idyllic life of the traditional village based on mutual cooperation. Hatta was a great supporter of article 33 and its communitarian vision of the organisation of the economy. But he was not alone. Indeed, his erstwhile ally and eventual nemesis, Soekarno, was also keen on the idea of *gotong royong*, or mutual help, as an essential characteristic of Indonesian culture.

These ideas, of course, were prominent because they emerged in the context of nationalist struggle that was in many ways simultaneously anti-capitalist. For the Indonesian nationalists of the first half of the twentieth century, capitalism was tantamount to colonialism and imperialism, and therefore professing adherence to it was no less than heresy. No Indonesian leader, until more recently, could get away with calling himself a supporter of the idea of capitalist free markets, so deeply ingrained was the aversion to materialistic pursuit of self interest left behind by the nationalist struggle. Indeed anti-capitalist sentiment was common across the political spectrum and was in no way the sole domain of the communists – nor of radical nationalists like Soekarno. Early Muslim political leaders and intellectuals were to decry the injustices inherent in 'sinful capitalism' (McVey 1965: 104) which was seen as being contradictory to the community-oriented ideals of Islam.

Also virtually across the political spectrum, it was the state that was expected to curb the ravages of unbridled capitalism and to deliver on the social justice promises of the national revolution. The problem, however, was the hijacking of such nationalist-statism by the state's corps of officials led by Soeharto, and the eventual ascendance of a capitalist class whose fortunes ultimately depended on a fusion of its interests with that of a predatory as well as authoritarian state. Ironically, state power, which was supposed to be the great bastion against the ravages of an un-Indonesian 'free fight' style of capitalism, was itself to be the incubator and protector of a most savage and rapacious form of capitalism.

There were dilemmas involved, however, as capitalist development proceeded and produced much starker social and economic disparities and introduced new forms of social marginalisation and dislocation. Soeharto himself was to reiterate many times over that the Indonesian nation, and his government, was against free fight liberalism because it went against the essential character of the Indonesian people and to the ideals of *Pancasila* and the 1945 Constitution. However, the claim that his government was the protector of the common interest was increasingly difficult to maintain at least since the mid-1980s, and thus Soeharto often had to go to great lengths to emphasise his aversion to the pursuit of private interest over the collective good. Both economic liberalisation during that decade – spurred by the fall in oil revenue that had been such a crucial source of the state's capacity to act as the main engine of development in the 1970s – and the rise of giant conglomerates had threatened to compromise this claim. The dilemma was especially acute given that Soeharto's own children had become major economic players by this time and had clearly benefited from the state's interventions into the market.

Moreover, it was also becoming evident that they were appropriating the process of economic deregulation that was being pushed in the post-oil boom period and which was heavily supported by the World Bank and by Western investors and creditors. Though the state was supposed to retreat from the economy, what transpired was often the blurring of the spheres of public and private economic interests as state-owned monopolies merely gave way to private, politically connected ones. Moreover, the economic deregulation process was highly selective and did not touch upon sectors – e.g. automotives and forestry – within which rent-seeking predatory interests remained ascendant. Even the opening up of the banking sector merely allowed for the establishment of countless new banks – typically owned by politically connected business groups – that merely served as a new avenue to self-finance illicit corporate expansion and projects of dubious economic merit (see Rosser 2002, especially pp. 51–83).

Aware of this dilemma, In 1989 Soeharto went as far as to order the Indonesian Association of Economists (ISEI) to deliver a theoretical blueprint that demonstrated how the operations of markets in Indonesia suited egalitarian *Pancasila* ideals. The economists had to engage in a great deal of intellectual acrobatics to do so (ISEI 1990). Perhaps more tellingly, Soeharto also summoned the owners of Indonesia's largest conglomerates to his private ranch in 1990. In a nationally televised address, he lectured them on the virtues of egalitarianism and requested that they transfer 25 per cent of their assets to cooperatives. This, not surprisingly, came to nothing. The act was clearly meant to be a more symbolic than substantive attempt at addressing grievances regarding social and economic inequities.

It was significant, though, that those summoned were Chinese-Indonesian owners of business conglomerates. Soeharto was obviously playing the race card – reinforcing popularly held notions about the rapacity of big Chinese business interests. This was done clearly to underline to these tycoons that it was state power that protected them (rather than to seriously force them to relinquish assets), and also to demonstrate to the predominantly *pribumi* television audience that he was the protector of their collective interest. In reality groups of *pribumi* business groups – the Bakries, Kodel, along with the business empires of the Soeharto children themselves – had also grown prosperous on the basis of state nurturance and protection.

But it was probably hoped that popular sentiment against particularly Chinese conglomerates would be useful in shielding the Soeharto family against public criticism. Bambang Trihatmodjo, one of Soeharto's sons, and head of his own determinedly expansive Bimantara business empire, disingenuously suggested at one point that the privatisation of state companies should be undertaken to benefit *pribumi*-owned businesses. This was supposedly in order to reduce the gap in the economic wealth of *pribumi* and Chinese Indonesian (*Media Indonesia*, 24 May 1991). By making this suggestion, he was claiming a place as a representative of some imaginary collective *pribumi* interest, though the extent to which this was successful was extremely doubtful given the levels of public resentment of the ill-gotten wealth of the Soehartos so evident by the end of the New Order.

It is significant that Soeharto's attempts to reassert his egalitarian credentials took place in the context of a growing public debate about 'economic democracy' as a feature of an economy based on *Pancasila*. Populist critics of the New Order, including student movements and NGOs had long been drawing attention to the growing disjuncture between the New Order's claims of furthering the collective interest and the undisguised growth of politically connected business conglomerates. One student activist, for example, was to suggest that the 'family principle' prescribed by article 33 of the 1945 Constitution has been distorted to mean rule by certain families only who have benefited the most out of development, while the mass of the Indonesian people suffered (Supriyanto 1989, 1997).

Significantly, such a sentiment was echoed nearly a decade later when student activists after the fall of Soeharto called for a transitional government that, among other things, would correct the 'distorted' implementation of *Pancasila* and the 1945 Constitution under the New Order. These students demanded a government that would apply these in a 'pure' and 'consistent' way (Forum Kota 1998). Ironically, this is precisely what Soeharto claimed to be doing when he took power – criticising his predecessor, Soekarno, for allowing the distortion of *Pancasila* and the 1945 Constitution by giving ample political space for the un-*Pancasila* communists.

Moreover, respected academics like Mubyarto (1979) and Arief Budiman (1982) had earlier been debating the substance of an economic system based on *Pancasila*. To Mubyarto, this meant an emphasis on the role of cooperatives and grassroots-oriented development schemes, while to Budiman, such a system was only possible within a wider socialist context. He claimed that the capitalist path pursued by the New Order was essentially inimical to an egalitarian *Pancasila* economic system.

But there was also a decidedly more liberal critique of New Order economic policy, which had to dispense with much of the egalitarian imagery invoked by *Pancasila*. Sjahrir (1990), the liberal economist, quite boldly proclaimed that the legacy of Indonesia's revolutionary 'founding fathers' was a hindrance to more vigorous economic development. He argued that it merely provided the ideological legitimacy for the pursuit of inefficient state economic policies, fostered abuse of power, and stifled the development of a competitive private sector. Though the views of intellectuals like Sjahrir were highly prominent due to their regular expression in the print-media, in reality they lacked a coherent social base. And though in line with the general outlook of such international development organisations like the World Bank – which were gaining in influence due to Indonesia's greater reliance on international assistance since the fall of oil export revenues – the bulk of Indonesia's bourgeoisie and middle class were essentially quite comfortable with the stability accorded by the New Order's authoritarian rule until the onset of the Asian economic crisis in 1997.

Pancasila and the organisation of society and politics

The early years of the New Order saw the process of furthering centralisation of powers in the hands of the state and its corps of officials. By 1973 a new state corporatist structure had taken shape, the hallmarks of which included a three-party system dominated by the state (and army-created) electoral vehicle, Golkar, corporatist-forms of societal 'representation' (Moertopo 1975), and so-called floating mass politics.

Under this system, heavily controlled parliamentary elections were always handily won by Golkar, to be followed by the unanimous re-election of Soeharto to the Presidency in a meeting of the People's Consultative Assembly (MPR). The two other political parties, the 'Islamic' United Development Party (PPP) and the 'nationalist' Indonesian Democratic Party (PDI) were mere ornaments: their ineffectiveness was already guaranteed by the fact that they housed, respectively, mutually antagonistic streams of political Islam, and a hotchpotch of formerly nationalist, socialist, Protestant and Catholic political vehicles with very little in common. Also under this system, mass membership of political parties was discouraged by a rule that they would not have branches at the local level (which favoured Golkar, given its identification with the state bureaucratic apparatus). The Indonesian people were designated a 'floating mass' to be disassociated from politics for the good of the development effort. Meanwhile corporatist organisations of societal representation, e.g. for workers, peasants, youths, were established under the auspices of the state to deter independent organising within civil society.

The essential logic of this system based on the political demobilisation of the great mass of the Indonesian people was that of an integralistic unity between ruler and ruled, government and people, state and society. It frowned upon political opposition, labour strikes, and freedom of expression and association as inimical to traditional Indonesian values based on cooperation and harmony. Such Indonesian values, were typically defined – negatively – as being in contradiction to both Western individualistic liberalism and to communist or socialist notions of class conflict and struggle. These were the values of a uniquely Indonesian *Pancasila* Democracy based on consensus.

Interestingly, school text books, by this time, had both demonised the Indonesian Communist Party as well as the period of liberal parliamentary democracy which lasted from 1950 till Soekarno established Guided Democracy. The communists were portrayed as national traitors and atheistic – therefore un-*Pancasila* – while political parties in general were said to cause national disunity and fragmentation of society according to particularistic interests. (Notably, the disdain toward political parties echoed that of Soekarno's, who at one point in the 1950s, called for them to be 'buried'). It was then left to a strong benign state to rise above these and uphold the interests of the nation as a whole. Significantly, at the same time, they continued to idealize the deeds of long gone nationalist heroes that had helped forge Indonesian nationhood.

In the mid-1980s these early tendencies were brought to their logical conclusion by legislation that enshrined *Pancasila* as *azas tunggal*, and which forced all political and societal groups to espouse their allegiance to it. Significantly, Soeharto saw this as his greatest personal triumph (Soeharto 1989: 382–383), an act that would allow Indonesia to abandon political ideology and to move ahead with national development. Indeed, the existing system of political and societal representation was also codified at the same time in related legislation, thereby outlawing the formation of new political parties, labour unions, or other kinds of societal organisation. This was the ultimate representation of the aim of systematically disorganising civil society in the name of the national interest.

Pancasila and opposition

Political opposition was never entirely absent in New Order Indonesia, however incoherently organised it mostly was. Student protests would break out from time to time, most prominently in 1974 and 1978, while he 1980s saw peasant protests (e.g. in Kedungombo and Cimacan, both in Java) over the transformation of land use for the building of dams, real estate or industrial development projects, or for new golf courses for the rich. In the 1990s, labour strikes also took off at unprecedented levels in the New Order, and a host of alternative labour organising vehicles emerged to challenge the state corporatist system of labour representation (Hadiz 1997; Kammen 1997). This growing industrial unrest contrasted starkly with the notion of state-capital-labour harmony under *Pancasila* Industrial Relations. Equally significantly, student movements, though severely crippled after 1978, would have a more than minor part to play in some of the instances of peasant and labour unrest. Moreover, new forms of social marginalisation and dislocation, environmental degradation, along with cases of human rights abuses provided an endless set of issues for Indonesia's NGO movement to develop, largely in a relationship of unease with the government.

But there were also critics from within the regime: a group called the Petition of 50, mostly composed of former top generals, bureaucrats and political figures charged Soeharto with abusing *Pancasila* and the Constitution in the early 1980s (Bourchier 1987). Also, the Forum Democracy emerged in the 1990s, which called for broad political reforms and for democratisation. This grouping was led by former MPR member and future President Abdurrahman Wahid – and mostly comprised of liberal intellectuals and activists, some of whom had been early supporters of the New Order.

The existence of such groups, many of which were engaged in open conflict with state policy over a broad range of issues, and some of which questioned the fundamental structure of economic and political power, clearly did not fit with the organicist notion of unity between all groups in society presided over by a benevolent, omnipotent state. Their very existence essentially questioned the very tenets of *Pancasila* Democracy, supposedly rooted in the cultural inclination towards harmony and consensus. Thus, it was not uncommon for state planners to explain away the existence of opposition voices by stating that they were either the expression of an alien, and illegal, remnant of communism, or of the interests of foreign countries or organisations.

The greatest potential threat to the New Order, however, was probably organised political Islam, which unlike communism or liberalism, was difficult to dismiss as an expression of a foreign influence detrimental to the national interest. The solution was to portray the challenge of some organized Islamic groups as a threat to national unity, given Indonesia's religious diversity.

It was no coincidence that organized Islam was regarded as a foe. As mentioned earlier, the New Order clinically pursued a policy of politically demobilizing civil society groups. With the eradication of the communists, political Islam was the only remaining social force with a strong grassroots basis in society. Although Islamic associations and political parties were a major part of the coalition that brought the New Order to power, there had already been serious dissatisfaction by the early 1970s about New Order officials' supposed lack of attention to arresting the decline of Muslim trading groups and their preference for alliances with Chinese Indonesian and multinational business interests. This disgruntlement was expressed typically as a kind of petty bourgeois populism against big business and criticism that the state did not do enough to raise the economic status of the *pribumi* (e.g. Bratanata 1981).

Head-on clashes were sometimes to occur between the state and representatives of political Islam. The most famous of these was probably the case of the Tanjung Priok riots in 1984 which saw security forces in the northern port area of Jakarta open fire on a group of demonstrators – led by one Amir Bikie, a disillusioned early supporter of the New Order. Many of these demonstrators, the exact number of which remains unknown, met their deaths, including Bikie himself.

Importantly, organized Muslim groups were among the most vocal opponents of the enshrinement of *Pancasila* as *azas tunggal*. Groups like the Association of Islamic Students resented that Islam had to take second place to a mere secular creed (HMI 1983; Prawiranegara 1983). Some also pointed out during heated debates on the issue that Muslims had already made a major concession in 1945 and were now being forced to give more way. They referred to the defunct so-called 'Jakarta Charter' version of the Pancasila, supported by major Muslim groups during the nationalist struggle, which had required that Muslims observe Islamic law.[4]

In spite of the debates, mainstream Islamic organisations eventually relented and formally accepted the *Pancasila* as *azas tunggal*. More significantly, however, much of the opposition from political Islam to the New Order was eventually defused with the establishment of ICMI (The Indonesian Association of Muslim Intellectuals) in 1990, under the sponsorship of Soeharto. This vehicle essentially provided an avenue to bureaucratic power for members of the new Muslim middle class produced by the modernisation process, and thus the organisation came to be filled with not only bureaucrats, but also formerly critical and vocal Muslim political activists (see Hefner 2000 for an account).

Pancasila after the new order

Pancasila is still enshrined as state ideology. But an MPR decree of November 1998 stipulated that organisations were free to adhere to other ideologies as long as they did not contradict *Pancasila*. The qualifier must be seen primarily as a continuing safeguard against the possible rise of a communist party. Indeed, efforts by then-President Abdurrahman Wahid in 2000 to introduce the idea of revoking the ban on Marxism/Leninism imposed by the New Order, were met by stiff resistance among the political elite (*Kompas*, 24 May 2000). This is not surprising: the political genealogies of key post-Soeharto political actors are embedded in the organisations and institutions that played a part in the alliance that eliminated the communist 'threat'. In this regard, with some possible exceptions within President Megawati Soekarnoputri's Indonesian Democratic Party for Struggle (PDIP), which houses, among other groups, the remnants of the old pro-Soekarno Indonesian Nationalist Party, they almost uniformly have a stake in maintaining the original *raison d'être* of the New Order: the eradication of communism.

Nevertheless, the downgrading of the status of *Pancasila* was a dramatic development, the broader context of which was the overall incapacity of Soeharto's successors to maintain the New Order's intricate system of repressive controls without him. With Soeharto gone, the system had essentially become unviable. Thus, Soeharto's immediate successors in the government of President Habibie realized that they could not survive except by opening up the political process and reinventing themselves in new alliances and vehicles – in other words, by democratizing (Hadiz 2000).

Nevertheless, *Pancasila* will not yet go away completely. It remains a useful part of the ideological armoury of powerful groups. The immediate practical value to them is that it is a potentially handy tool to legitimise the kind of statism that allows for the exercise of power by predatory groups in control of the institutions and resources of the state. The secular nationalist PDIP, for example, states that the 'Pancasila is ... truly the most suitable national ideology', and that past wrongs emanated from its 'corrupt implementation' during the 32 year rule of the New Order (PDIP 1999: 10).

A major source of challenge to *Pancasila* emanates from some sections of political Islam, particularly those that harbor the aim of establishing a state based on Islam and whose economic agenda is a kind of statism that would allow for the pursuit of a Malaysian-style NEP. But the support base of such groups arguably remains relatively small given Indonesia's great diversity, including within the adherents of Islam itself. A more fundamental challenge will probably emanate from economic neo-liberalism and the pressures of globalisation, imposing the harsh discipline of the market that predatory interests will no doubt continue to resist whenever convenient, even as they embrace the economic opportunities that may arise. The tension between statism, in its Islamic populist or secular-nationalist variants, and economic neo-liberalism will run especially high in the years to come, especially as Indonesia continues to crawl its way out of economic crisis. The implication is that future governments will continue to be pressured to abandon the commitment to a vision of an egalitarian Indonesia, which has remained attractive through the vicissitudes of the past half-century, even as it has been badly abused. But the unambiguous victory of a neo-liberal economic agenda, largely imposed by such organisaations like the World Bank and the IMF, is not at all inevitable (Robison and Hadiz 2004). At the same time, Indonesia's now open political system provides a wider avenue through which liberal agendas of rule of law and rights could be advanced, although this opportunity cannot be fully exploited in the continuing absence of a well-organized, coherent, and truly liberal party. Interestingly, however, a reassertion of the social justice tendencies within *Pancasila* would most likely result only from the revitalisation of an essentially long-gone political actor – the radical Left. This is hardly immediately likely in spite of the strenuous efforts of some small student and labour-based groups to reclaim this vanquished tradition.

References

Aspinall, Edward (1999) 'The Indonesian Student Uprising of 1998', in Arief Budiman, Barbara Hatley and Damien Kingsbury (eds), *Reformasi: Crisis and Change in Indonesia*, Clayton, Monash Asia Institute, Monash University.

Bourchier, David (1987) 'The Petition of Fifty', *Inside Indonesia*, No. 10, April: 7–10.

Bourchier, David (1996) 'Lineages of Organicist Political Thought in Indonesia', unpublished Ph.D. thesis, Melbourne, Department of Politics, Monash University.

Bratanata, Slamet (1981) 'Kebijaksanaan Baju Politik', *Prisma*, 10(4): 56–59.

Budiman, Arief (1982) 'Sistem Perekonomian Pancasila, Kapitalisme dan Sosialisme', *Prisma*, January: 14–25.

Forum Kota (1998) Pernyataan Sikap Komunitas Mahasiswa se-Jabotabek, 28 May.

Hadiz, Vedi R. (1997) *Workers and the State in New Order Indonesia*, London, Routledge.

Hadiz, Vedi R. (2000), 'Retrieving the Past for the Future? Indonesia and the New Order Legacy', *Southeast Asian Journal of Social Science*, 28(2): 10–33.

Hefner, Robert (2000) *Civil Islam: Muslims and Democratisation in Indonesia*, Princeton, Princeton University Press, 2000.

HMI (Himpunan Mahasiswa Islam) (1983) *Pandangan Kritis terhadap RUU Keormasan*, Jakarta, HMI.

ISEI (Ikatan Sarjana Ekonomi Indonesia) (1990) *Penjabaran Demokrasi Ekonomi*, Jakarta, ISEI.

Jayasuriya, Kanishka (1998) '"Asian Values"' As Reactionary Modernization', *Contemporary Politics*, 4(1): 77–91.

Kammen, Douglas (1997) 'A Time to Strike: Industrial Strikes and Changing Class Relations in New Order Indonesia', unpublished Ph.D. thesis, Cornell University.

Kompas, 24 May 2000.

McVey (1965) *The Rise of Indonesian Communism*, Ithaca, NY: Cornell University Press.

Media Indonesia, 24 May 1991.

Moertopo, Ali (1975) *Buruh dan Tani dalam Pembangunan*, Jakarta, Center of Strategic and International Studies.

Mubyarto (1979) 'Koperasi dan Ekonomi Pancasila', *Kompas*, 3 May.

Nasution, Adnan Buyung (1992) *The Aspiration for Constitutional Government in Indonesia: A Socio-legal Study of the Indonesian Konstituante 1956–1959*, Jakarta, Pustaka Sinar Harapan.

PDIP (Partai Demokrasi Indonesian Perjuangan) (1999) *PDI Perjuangan Menjawab*, Jakarta, PDIP.

Prawiranegara, Sjafruddin (1983) open letter to President Soeharto, 7 July.

Reeve, David (1985) *Golkar of Indonesia: An Alternative to the Party System*, Singapore, Oxford University Press.

Robison, Richard and Vedi R. Hadiz (2004) *Reorganising Power in Indonesia: The Politics of Oligarchy in an Age of Markets*, London, RoutledgeCurzon.

Rosser, Andrew (2002) *The Politics of Economic Liberalisation in Indonesia: State, Market and Power*, Richmond, Curzon.

Sjahrir (1990) 'The Indonesian Deregulation Process: Problems, Constraints and Prospects', in John W. Langford and K. Lorne Brownsey (eds), *Economic Policy Making in the Asia Pacific Region*, Nova Scotia, Institute for Research and Public Policy.

Soeharto (1989), *Pikiran, Ucapan, dan Tindakan Saya*, Jakarta, PT Citra Lamtoro Agung Persada.

Supriyanto, Enin (1997) 'Growth Oriented Development Strategies and Authoritarianism', in Ian Chalmers and Vedi R. Hadiz (eds), *The Politics of Economic Development in Indonesia: Contending Perspectives*, London, Routledge.

Notes

1 The Five Principles are Belief in One God, Humanity, Indonesian Unity, Consultative Democracy, and Social Justice.

2 This is a major theme addressed in Robison and Hadiz (2004).

3 This recounting portrays youths as having played key roles in 1) the Youth Oath of 1928, during which representatives of various regions pledged loyalty to the idea of an Indonesian nation; 2) The 1945–1949 armed struggle for independence; 3) the ascension of the New Order in 1966.

4 I am grateful to Priyambudi Sulistiyanto for reminding me of this aspect of the debate in the 1980s.

9

'COMMUNITY IN THE EAST'

Towards a new human rights paradigm

Anthony Woodiwiss

The discourse of 'Asian Values' has most often been seen as a threat to that of human rights, by proponents as well as opponents. I do not agree with this perception. On the contrary, it seems to me that, when understood and responded to not politically but social scientifically and with an eye for unintended consequences, the appearance of 'Asian Values' has provided a very necessary challenge to a version of human rights discourse that, had it become hegemonic, would have represented a very considerable threat to the possibility of a truly cosmopolitan world order; that is, a world order within which values in addition to those associated with individualism and liberalism, namely various kinds of communitarianism, could continue to command respect and provide guides for both individual and social development.[1]

The more specific benefits that follow from the 'Asian Challenge for Human Rights' (Bauer and Bell 1999) are several. In this paper, however, I will only spell out one of these which is that it foregrounds the presently pressing question of the relative status of, and the relationship between, civil and political rights, on the one hand, and social, economic and cultural rights, on the other. As very quickly becomes clear in any encounter with the human rights literature or indeed its politics, this is a very fraught and contextually sensitive area which divides North from South as well as East from West. Moreover, it is also one whose most problematic aspects, principally that related to the supposed non-justiciability (legal enforceability) of economic and social as opposed to civil and political rights have yet to be resolved. In my view, this failure is largely a consequence of too many of the participants in the debate allowing themselves to be drawn into taking sides in an overly abstract debate about whether rights are universal or culturally relative – contributions to which unintentionally but all too often give credence to the pernicious doctrine of the 'clash of civilisations' (Huntington 1997) – rather than simply accepting the differences involved and seeking practical means of articulating them with one another within a concretely cosmopolitan framework (for some exceptions, see An-Na'im 1990, 1992; Wilson 1996).

Globalization, imperialism and the threat to human rights

Globally these are interesting, dangerous and therefore challenging times. This is not simply because there is a very obvious lack of clarity as to what exactly globalization might mean for the world, but also because this lack of clarity appears to be unacceptable to more and more political actors. More particularly but to simplify, an interesting and long-running debate about whether globalization refers to a gradual process of multilaterally governed global integration or a new kind of empire has suddenly become rather threatening because, in the run-up to the attack on Iraq and since, the political associations of the two theories have been reversed. Thus an anti-globalization movement that was formerly guided by the imperialism thesis has become a staunch defender of multilateral global governance, while some pro-globalization states, notably the US and Britain, appear to have given up their erstwhile multilateralism and acknowledged the necessity of imperialism. What makes these shifts a source of danger is, first, that a thesis – globalization = imperialism – that was formerly deployed for critical and defensive purposes has been transformed into a rationale for affirmative and offensive actions; second, the thesis now has great military power behind it; and, third, the thesis remains, in my view, a mistaken one. The net result of the change in the political associations of the imperialism thesis is therefore much more likely to be endless war than a rapidly achieved hegemonic tranquillity since, notwithstanding the availability of great force, globalization has rendered imperialism impossible.

Thus rejection of the imperialism thesis does not mean that one should take up the integrationist alternative with its excessive stress on globalization as involving the displacement of particularistic national and/or local social relations by universalistic transnational social flows. This is because, in my view, globalization is best understood as an emergent property of the international system produced by the inability of states, corporations and cultural producers to solve their problems within the confines of existing national and international structures (Murphy 1994; Woodiwiss 2001: 176–194). Globalization, then, is an instance of what Marcel Mauss (1924) called a 'total social fact' in that it involves the fusion of the local, the national and the international with the result that there are occasions when developments along any of these dimensions of the social have consequences for the global that are normally beyond the capacity of national and international entities to control, no matter how powerful they may be.

When I say that the internal dynamics of a globalizing world are 'normally beyond the capacity of national and international entities to control', I do not mean that they are either necessarily globally controllable or inherently uncontrollable, but only that they cannot be controlled by the methods of geo-political 'business as usual' as exemplified by such pre-globalization strategies as are summarized by the term imperialism, whether of the go-it-alone or UN-mediated variety. Rather, I mean that they can only be controlled through being prepared to be engaged in unusual business, such as that Thomas Kuhn (1970) identifies as resulting from paradigm changes in the natural sciences and the consequent discovery of new entities, processes, relationships, and exemplary ways of working.

The relevance of all this to the sphere of human rights is that the paradigm that has guided our thoughts, actions and institution-building in the area no longer makes much sense. First, the pursuit of rights is leading to the multiplication of wrongs, witness the thousands of innocent civilian victims of the impetuous attacks on Serbia, Afganistan and Iraq that were launched in the name of the civil and political rights commonly summarized as 'freedom'. Second, recognition is being demanded for the fact that values other than those of individualism or indeed socialism may/should be the source of rights claims. These are the values of the non-West and most obviously of Asia; that is, the values associated with Islam, Confucianism, Buddhism, Hinduism and indeed both Catholic and Orthodox Christianity as well as Judaism and multifarious animisms.

In short, the current international human rights regime appears to be in a state of severe crisis: its effects are increasingly often the opposite of those intended; and the ethical assumptions upon which it is based appear to make little sense and offer less protection to the majority of the world's population. How then, and assuming of course that it is considered worth saving, might one go about saving international human rights discourse from itself? How, more practically, might we go about transforming it into a discourse consonent with the value complexity of an at least partially globalized world? We are a long way from finding the answers to these questions, but a start has been made thanks especially to the Asian-based critiques which point to social order, hierarchy, benevolence, duty, and loyalty as sources of virtue and therefore of rights and wrongs.

Some of these virtues, notably those validating social order and hierarchy, already inform international human rights discourse. Thus it is well established that rights should not endanger social order and the very idea of rights assumes, and to that degree validates, the existence of hierarchies that may result in abuse. However, the other and more positive non-Western values have no place in international human rights discourse. As a result no protection is available when states or superiors more generally fail to do their duty, act benevolently, or reward loyalty. The ultimate source of these absences from international human rights discourse is the deeply entrenched individualistic and liberal Western view that such behaviors were and are aspects of social relationships that were and are traditionalist and *therefore* inherently oppressive. However, the fact remains that the majority of the world's population depends upon the consistent enactment of such behaviors and the underlying vivacity of the values that inform them. Thus to exclude them from international human rights discourse is both to diminish the effectiveness of traditional means of social defense and deny to the global majority what little protection global institutions can provide. What is more, the baleful effects of these absences are particularly likely to be felt when the capitalism spawned in part by the same inividualism and liberalism arrives in the lands of the majority. Given, then, the irrelevance of international human rights discourse to the global majority, why bother with it at all, and why not simply return to traditionalist or so-called 'fundamentalist' moralities? This the question that I will now attempt to answer.

Human rights and the unacknowledged problem of social difference

Within the global context, then, a major cause of the irrelevance of human rights to the lives of the global majority is the absence from the discourse as it has developed of any acknowledgement of the pertinence of the social-structural differences exhibited by states save for their level of economic development. More specifically I would argue that the problem this absence creates may be broken down into three components. First, an artificial narrowing of the doctrine of justiciability (the doctrine that the only 'real' rights are those that are enforceable through the courts) which, as it is presently understood, privileges civil and political rights over social, economic and cultural ones. Second, an equally artificial narrowing of what might be termed 'allowable' social-structural differences to economic ones which, given that they rest on the developed/undeveloped distinction, imply an unacknowledged and largely Ameri-centric evolutionism that assumes that the present nature of the 'modern', American-led West defines the best or even the only possible future for the less developed world. Third, and relatedly, a serious failing – maybe wilful, maybe not – on the part of the representatives of some Western states in particular to understand the highly restricted nature of the entitlements that economic and social rights represent – not cake every day for all but a democratically and locally defined minimal share of whatever cake is going.

To develop the 'irrelevance' point, there is an irony inherent in the distinction between justiciable civil/political and the supposedly merely programmatic economic/social rights. And it is that, although the distinction was intended to help those in need, it in fact discriminates against them. Thus it was introduced, in what one must assume was good faith, so as not to impose too great an economic burden on developing societies and because economic/social rights are for some reason thought to be more expensive to implement than civil and political ones, which only require imposing buildings, well-found offices and princely salaries for politicians and legal personnel for their implementation. Such reasoning is, however, profoundly mistaken since and to repeat, as Thomas Marshall (1949) made clear so long ago and indeed the Economic, Social and Cultural Rights Committee has more recently attested in one of its 'general comments' (Alston 1992: 495), the discourse of what Marshall termed social citizenship rights is concerned with procedurally establishing equality of status with regard to certain minimum material conditions rather than the equalization of material conditions that many of the proponents of the narrow reading of justiciability seem to fear. Moreover, the International Covenant on Economic Social and Cultural Rights (ICESRC) Article 2 only requires States Parties to deploy 'the maximum available resources' (emphasis added). Thus to say that even such a minimal and cheaply deliverable entitlement as a right to 'adequate housing', for example, is not justiciable cannot mean that it could not in principle be pursued through the courts since all such a possibility would require would be appropriately drafted legislation, for which many models exist in the statute books and administrative regulations of the more developed societies. Rather, what it does mean is that there is no international legal requirement for the existence of such legislation. One result is that any response to need is therefore left to the discretion of governments and their calculations of political advantage without any danger that a court might make an order that, for example, ultimately required them to forego some of their expensive, state-provided cars in favor of sheets of corrugated-iron roofing to be distributed among those in need. Another result is that, since Article 1 of the ICESCR defines resources to include those made available 'through international assistance and co-operation, especially economic and technical', there is also no possibility that the richer countries could be legally held to account with respect to the level of assistance they provide.

Tragically, the distinction therefore catches many millions of people in the less developed countries in a vicious double bind. This double bind arises for the following reasons. First, because of the artificial narrowing of what is considered to be justiciable many are currently deprived of legal remedies with respect to violations of certain civil and political as well as economic, social and cultural rights. Second, the coverage of human rights discourse is now so broad and its requirements so institutionally specific, in many ways quite properly, and, less justifiably, so Western-inspired that it reaches deep into the inner recesses of social structures where the social routines pertaining to human rights are not simply interconnected with many others but depend upon them for their functioning (see Zhang Yimou's film *Qui Ju*). Thus, because of the discourse's implicit evolutionism, the only way in which, to use Jeffrey Harrod's (1987) term, the 'unprotected' will gain full access to their rights is when the societies in which they live reach Western levels of development. However, it cannot be assumed, as the concept of programmatic rights implicitly suggests, that in time and as they develop all of them will or should converge on the kind of 'modern' society that the specification of the object of application instances, namely one combining liberal democracy, a capitalist economy, a supposedly 'open' or meritocratic class structure, and an individualistic value system (Woodiwiss 2001: ch. 4). This is for two main reasons: 1) the operation of the global economic system is as likely to prevent development in some societies as it is to encourage it; 2) the environing social relations are often culturally specific, very different from those associated with the supposed 'modern' archetype, and presumably protected by both the right to self-determination as developed in the UN's 1970 Declaration on Friendly Relations and, by implication at least, the much more recent acknowledgement of indigenous rights.

In sum, the double-bind that many people in less developed societies find themselves in thanks to the narrow construction of justiciability is as follows: first, they are currently denied economic and social rights that according to international law are or could be theirs; second, they will only be able to enjoy them in the future if they sacrifice much that they value in their cultures and the quality of their social relations; that is, if they sacrifice much of what is often misleadingly termed their 'social capital' (Putnam *et al.* 1993, 2000, and for a critique see Chatterjee 1998). Thus, if they make such sacrifices it may well be that their lives will become less secure thanks to the breaking of many of the social ties upon which they currently depend to protect themselves from the arbitrariness of the powerful and the vagaries of fate (on the general point see Taylor 1999, and for a detailed and insightful discussion of some attempts to re-invent 'traditional' protections under such headings as 'restorative justice', see Broadhurst 1999).

Translation and the articulation of social difference within human rights discourse

In my view what needs to happen if we are to be able to ameliorate the situation is that a way must be found both to insist on the equal necessity of all rights and to allow the pertinent UN institutions to engage in a very limited process of sociologically informed conceptual translation or substitution between the two sets of rights. I use the qualifier 'limited' in connection with the translatability for which I will argue for two reasons. First, legally, no human right may replace any other, given the indivisibility of the two sets of rights and the presence of articles in each set that prohibit the use of any right to justify the violation of any other. Second, socially, no such replacement has been demanded by any influential state or even body of opinion; that is, even when one looks at the most forceful Southern critiques, notably that produced by certain 'conservative' Asian governments, with only slightly more care than usual what one discovers is that, although there is a great deal of criticism of Western hypocrisy in the application of human rights standards and a more general suspicion of the West's intentions in applying them, there is no overall intellectual rejection of human rights nor even of civil and political rights (Langlois 2001). Thus, with respect to civil and political rights, there are no principled rejections of the protections provided in relation to the physical integrity of individuals, the legal process, nor even the idea that such rights should be equally available irrespective of religion or gender, although among some Islamic writers, for example, there are disagreements concerning the nature of 'cruel and unusual punishments', and resistances to allowing believers the freedom to give up their faith and women to choose their husbands. Nor is there any intellectual rejection of the right to political participation. Rather, the principal concern of Asian governmental critics relates to the freedoms of speech and association that the West and in particular the US tends to see as most fundamental, and which the US also tends to see as validating a more diffuse 'market populism' (Frank 2000). The Asian governmental concern is not so much that these liberties might degenerate into license, although there is an element of this, but that their untrammelled expression might lead to breakdowns in social order and therefore interruptions in the development process. In sum, absolute substitutability is neither possible nor necessary. However, this need not mean that the rigorous observance of one set of rights could not lead to one or more articles in the other set entering a state of abeyance and thus being subject to reactivation only if such rigorous observance is not maintained.

Although some Western governments understandably may have been reacting more to the actual human rights records of certain of the Asian governments involved rather than to their philosophical positions, there is nevertheless something surprising and indeed hypocritical about the Western expressions of horror at Asian concerns. For Western countries too have not only hesitated in giving full support for freedom of speech but have indeed imposed restrictions and not just under the exceptional conditions specified in the United Nations Civil and Political Covenant. Thus, for example, Holocaust denial is prohibited in some Western countries and there are limitations on hate speech and pornography in many others, certain religions do not enjoy the same liberties as others, especially if they have been designated as cults or 'fundamentalist', and labor's freedom of association has been subject to extensive and widespread limitations. More disturbingly, the British and American governments have also shown themselves willing to compromise even that most basic of civil and political rights represented by the writ of *habeus corpus*, in the context of the current, so-called War on Terrorism (Dworkin 2002).

There is much more that could be said about each of these sets of limitations – for example, it is very difficult for any Western nation to make claims about its support for freedom of expression once one thinks in the broader terms represented by the concepts of freedom of information and freedom of communication (Hamelink 1994), since both in the West itself and globally the means of information and communication are largely in a few corporate hands. In this text though I wish to make my point by restricting myself to some of the issues surrounding labor's freedom of association.

Thus the limited translation I will focus on involves the civil and political right to freedom of association, on the one hand, and a range of economic and social rights, on the other, since such a translation seems critical with respect to the local as well as global acceptability of Asian and indeed many Southern social differences. Although the extent of the translatability I advocate is very limited, it would nevertheless help to resolve a major global difficulty. This is the current impossibility of agreement concerning the most obvious measure that could be taken to civilize the globalization process, namely the addition of a 'social clause' to the protocols of the World Trade Organization (WTO). This is because the current draft, sponsored by the West, comprises a list of core labor standards that, because of their stress on freedom of association, would exclude most of even the best-governed states in Asia and the South more generally (for a detailed discussion of this problem and a possible way of resolving it, see Woodiwiss 2003: ch. 5).

Breaking open the 'human rights box'

For all these reasons, the current status of human rights discourse as a source of support for the world's weak and meek is not high (Odinkalu 2000). The reasons for this low status have been succinctly and graphically put by Joanne Bauer using a recently fashionable American vernacular idiom:

> The human rights box is a set of historical and social circumstances that enables the human rights framework to gain currency among elites while limiting advances, and even creating setbacks among the general population. Metaphorically, the box contains a universe of options and opportunities for the few while sealing off the vast majority.
>
> (Bauer 2000)

In my view and indeed Bauer's, what gives structure to this box is the aforementioned privileging of civil and political over economic and social rights. This, at any rate is the aspect of the box that I intend to focus on in this attempt to break it open by reflecting on, to use one of Chatterjee's titles, 'Community in the East'.

The essential preparatory step to be taken if the box is to be broken open by allowing translation between the two covenants, or so it seems to me, is that human rights should be de-sacralized. This is because they are currently most often spoken of as if they were transcendent ethical principles. They are not. Of course they were inspired by one such principle, the inherent dignity of humankind. However, as is evident from even the most cursory consideration of the content of the pertinent texts, they do not themselves restate this principle. Instead, their relationship to it is one of means to an end, albeit means that, rather confusingly, should be accorded the same status as principles. However, the latter change in their honorific status does not change their logical status. It merely reflects the melancholy fact that, to quote the Universal Declaration of Human Rights, the end in question – 'recognition of the inherent dignity . . . of all members of the human family' – is not an exhalted one. This is because it is protective rather than aspirational in nature. As such it testifies to humankind's capacity for evil (cf. Badiou 2001), whether it be the physical torture or the overworking of others, rather than humanity's potential for good. This, as I intend to demonstrate below is an intellectually liberatory realization in that it provides the key with which the human rights box might be social scientifically unlocked.

Put in the briefest possible way, the reason why human rights are so often mistaken for ends is because of the larger social context in which they developed. That is, neither the end of protecting human dignity nor they as particular means were derived from a single set of ethical principles but from at least two. One was the liberalism that informed the enumeration of civil and political rights and the other was the socialism which played the same role in relation to economic and social rights. The strongest proponent of the former was the US while that of the latter was the Soviet Union. Thus human rights became simply one more arena of a super-power conflict that was justified on ethical grounds. The result was an at least implicit expectation that the eventual victor might insist that its set of protective ethical principles should displace those of its defeated adversary. In the event, some spokespeople for the victorious power have gone much further and claimed that their victory vindicates not simply the protective aspect of their ideology but its aspirational aspect too.

I have elsewhere (Woodiwiss 2003: ch. 2) presented much evidence for the operation of this conflictual structural logic with respect to the development of international human rights discourse. However, in fact and fortunately, the victory of the US over the Soviet Union in the Cold War has not been accompanied by any such ethical triumph even though it has been accompanied by a good deal of ethical triumphalism. This is because the former Soviet Union was not the only sponsor of the social and economic rights it championed. They were also strongly supported many of the US' allies in Western Europe and, more recently, Asia. In other words, social and economic rights are gradually being re-confirmed as what they always were despite the obfuscations consequent on the exigencies arising from the Cold War, namely practical means to a protective ethical end that can be very variously defined.

Two things make this realization intellectually and indeed ethically liberatory when it is developed in a sociological context. First, it provides a way of moving beyond what has become one of the principal obstacles to creative thought in the human rights area, namely that represented by the now very ideological debate between universalism and relativism. Fundamentally, this possibility arises because of the necessarily concrete way in which rights as means are and indeed have to be socially specified. Such concreteness makes any claim to or insistence upon their universality in precisely the same form everywhere inherently more difficult and therefore less compelling ethically than would be the case if abstract principles were involved. Thus human rights as means, even especially valued means, may be regarded as much more malleable and even as mutually substitutable than when they are regarded as principles defining ends. The point being that their purpose is not to insist on the organization or re-organization of social life around one or other set of aspirational principles, but rather to assure certain very basic conditions of human being (the freedoms from torture, hunger, or overwork, for example) and pertinent forms of human action (freedom of speech, association, and collective bargaining, for example) in very different social contexts; that is, my argument will not be the one most often heard in Asia, namely that economic and social rights should take priority over civil and political rights, but rather that we should be able to find ways in which a very limited number of each type of right can be translated into the terms of the other. Second, it means both that human rights discourse may be freed from the burden of specifying the good for the world, and, as importantly, that the pursuit and definition of the good may continue as an open-ended and universal activity rather than one monopolized by those countries and ideologies that are presently powerful – surely humanity is still capable of aspiring to more than freedom from mutual abuse?

Liberal social science and the recognition of community in the East

I have explained at length elsewhere (Woodiwiss 1998) how I think the challenge posed by 'Asian Values' might be understood and responded to sociologically. That response was long on substantive analysis, stressing as it did the necessity of escaping from essentialist and stereotypical representations of Asian societies and embracing instead a conception of such societies as varyingly hybridized cousins of rather than others to similarly hybridized and varying 'Western' societies. It was, however, rather short on theoretical argumentation and it is this aspect that I would like to develop in this chapter by enriching my earlier argument with borrowings from two additional sources, namely the works of John Rawls and Partha Chatterjee – not as strange a pair of bedfellows as might at first appear, or so I hope to show.

How, then, might reflecting on, to use one of Chatterjee's titles, 'Community in the East' aid us in prising open the human rights box? Essentially by helping us to realize that, contrary to the conventional wisdom, there is no necessary antipathy between Asian Values and respect for human rights since in fact Asian communitarian values may be seen to entail respect for human rights, provided only that the current, self-appointed and most often liberalistic guardians of the human rights temple can be brought to share this realization. What, then, are the required circumstances? By what means might the guardians be brought to realize this relation?

With a pleasant and encouraging irony, these two questions may be answered together since the best guides as to the circumstances under which Asian communitarian values may be seen to entail respect for human rights seem to me to have been provided by a number of liberal thinkers. Significantly though, the thinkers I have in mind – John Rawls, Max Weber and Wesley Hohfeld again – all operated at the limits of liberal common sense since each of them was ultimately prepared to allow the empirical rather than the ideological to be the final judge of theory, with the result that their ideas became usable within other analytical traditions.

In many ways the most surprising and, given the accusations of betrayal that greeted it, the bravest answer to the question as to how the human rights box might be prised open by considering 'Community in the East' is that produced by the man whom many consider to be the high priest of contemporary liberalism, John Rawls, in his book *The Law of the Peoples* (1999). What caused him to challenge the limits of liberal common sense was a combination of the logic of toleration, the resilient diversity of the global polity and the need to avoid war. For Rawls, the combined effect of these three elements produces the recognition of the possible global legitimacy of a variety of familialism or what he terms 'decent hierarchical societies'. To be globally legitimate, such a society would have to exhibit the following five characteristics or qualifications to its hierarchical character.

1 It should be internationally pacific.
2 It should be governed on the basis of a legal system premised upon a minimal set of what Rawls regards as the only truly universalizable human rights: freedom from slavery; liberty of conscience, and the prohibition of genocide.
3 Respect for these rights should be enforced by imposing legally enforceable duties or obligations on the population, especially its most powerful members.
4 Those who administer such a non-liberal legal system should do so in good faith in that they are genuinely committed to the underlying

communitarian values and not simply using them as a figleaf to hide any kind of self-serving authoritarianism.

5 The polity should include some sort of 'consultative mechanism' that need not be democratic but which should nevertheless allow genuine communication between the powerful and the less powerful.

Bold and brave though Rawls's suggestion undoubtedly is, in my view, it unnecessarily limits the range of truly universalizable human rights and, relatedly, begs at least three questions that require answering if sharing his tolerance is not to result in merely sharing some wishful thinking. These questions are: Why should one expect a rule of law of any kind to be present in the sort of familialist or communitarian societies he has in mind, let alone a rule of law premised on even a selection of human rights? Why should one expect any mechanism of consultation to be present, let alone one that gives a voice to the less powerful? Finally, can a system of enforcing respect for human rights based on duties and obligations really be regarded as legally equivalent to one based on liberties and freedoms?

As a sociologist rather than a political theorist, Weber subjected the conceptual side of his liberalistically inspired thought to a necessarily more rigorous process of empirical testing than did Rawls. Indeed, induction from observations played an important role in the construction of his ideal types. For this reason, one of Weber's ideal types is of particular pertinence to answering the first two of Rawls's begged questions. This is the ideal type of that Weber calls patriarchalism but that we more often refer to today as familialism. Its pertinence arises because it was inducted on the basis of studies of the great familialist ethical systems, namely Judaism, Catholic Christianity, Islam, and Confucianism.

For Weber, patriarchalism was the elementary form of traditional authority and is defined as follows:

> [It] is the situation where, within a group (household) which is usually organised on both an economic and kinship basis, a particular individual governs who is designated by a definite rule of inheritance. *The decisive characteristic ... is the belief of the members that domination, even though it is an inherent traditional right of the master, must definitely be exercized as a joint right in the interests of all members and is thus not freely appropriated by the incumbent.* In order that this shall be maintained, it is crucial that in both cases there is a complete absence of a personal (patrimonial) staff. Hence the master is still largely dependent upon the willingness of the members to comply with his orders since he has no machinery to enforce them. Therefore the members are not yet really subjects.
>
> (Weber 1968: 231, emphasis added)

For Weber, then, patriarchalism was a strictly hierarchical political structure justified by a familialist discourse and resting on an economy and a wider set of social relations structured in large part by kinship. Clearly, given the nature of contemporary state and economic forms, patriarchalism no longer has a political or economic referent outside of some relatively self-subsistent indigenous communities. However, it seems to me that the *belief* which is the decisive characteristic, does still have a referent. Patriarchalism today signifies a familialist discourse of rule that, regardless of institutional context, both assumes the naturalness of inequalities in the social relations between people and justifies these by reference to the respect due to a benevolent father or father-figure who nonetheless does not 'freely appropriate' all power to himself but exercises a joint right.

However, for this to be a legitimate discourse of rule today and given the displacement of kinship relations by the development of the massively powerful elaboration of the idea of a 'personal (patrimonial) staff' represented by the state and the arrival of the capitalist economy, the question that obviously arises is: 'How is the "decisive characteristic", namely the "belief of members that domination [is] exercized as a joint right" to be sustained?' Well, the means of sustaining this belief that were discovered, tried and tested in Western Europe in the course of the same displacements of kinship by the rise of the state and capitalism were twofold and have yet to be improved upon. They were the rule of law, which prevents power being 'freely appropriated by the incumbent', and representative democracy, which ensures that the compliance of the ruled is more or less freely given. In other words, nothing can take the place of the rule of law, representative democracy, and therefore the rights that underpin them, even in societies that wish to preserve a familialist discourse of rule. And this is why there is no need to restrict the number of truly universalizable human rights in the way that Rawls does.

The answer to the first two of Rawls's begged questions that I derive from Weber are that, given the arrival of the state and capitalism, the rule of law and representative democracy have to be present if familialist regimes are to be regarded as legitimate in their own, let alone, Western terms. Thus whereas Rawls uses the term 'decent' to refer to what he considers to be a legitimate form of Asian communitarianism, I use the more specific but within its sphere of pertinence much more demanding phrase enforceable benevolence' (Woodiwiss 1998: 3–4). The latter refers to a mode of governance where, while social relations remain distinctly hierarchical, the content of benevolence is democratically decided and its delivery legally and ultimately popularly enforced. The point here is that the social embeddedness of a human rights regime constructed on such a familialist basis should mean that such a regime could prove to be more effective in familialist societies in Asia and elsewhere than one premissed on the individualistic or even social-democratic means of qualifying inequality that Westerners have resort to. This is because it would work with the grain of the culture rather than against it. And what this means is that subordinates are placed in the position of asking superordinates to live up to their own values rather than, if subordinates were having to insist on their liberties, demanding that they be given something that they had never had and which can be therefore readily branded as an alien cultural intrusion.

I now wish to turn to the issue of how the difference nevertheless still represented by all forms of familialism may be accommodated within the discourse of human rights and therefore to the third of Rawls's begged questions: 'Can a system of enforcing respect for human rights based on duties and obligations really be regarded as legally equivalent to one based on liberties and freedoms?' At this point the thinker I wish to invoke (again) is Hohfeld since what distinguished him from many of today's liberal thinkers was that he paid close attention to the actual language of the constitutional and legal texts within which rights are defined which is a sort of empiricism. More specifically, it is his disaggregation of the rights concept that makes it possible to see that duties and obligations in the form of powers and claims ceded may be seen as the equivalents of liberties and freedoms in their social consequences. This is also the idea that creates the possibility of translation and the articulation of social difference within human rights discourse. But why should one think that it is likely to be effective as part of strategy for empowering the weak and the meek? Elsewhere (Woodiwiss 2003: ch. 3) I have indicated that evidence for the effectiveness of this analysis may be derived from the historical and contemporary experience of Western Europe. To summarize, with respect to labor rights, only the US has a labor rights system whose critical premise is a liberty, while there are not only wholly justiciable but also, in their contexts, far more effective systems that have been democratically approved and rest on 'liberties' translated into economic and social rights and delivered on the basis of either powers (Australia and France) or claims (Sweden). Moreover, reflecting the nature of the different forms of rights as diverse means of achieving overlapping ends, the process of translation I am arguing for is already well established politically and juridicially with respect to labor rights. Thus, despite their often constitutionally guaranteed freedom of association, unions have often felt able to accept qualifications to their independence. These often include the virtually universal requirement that they should register with a state agency which is very often empowered both to require that their constitutions contain certain basic elements and to exercise an oversight over their internal affairs and so ensure that the constitution is observed. And also the many laws that restrict the organizational, tactical and even strategic and political options available to unions. In other words, even Western unions have accepted many qualifications to their independence *vis-à-vis* the state. They have also, in some instances and more controversially, accepted qualifications to their independence of employers. Here I am thinking of the many types of joint consultation arrangements, as exemplified by many Western European cases as well as the Australian one.

What, of course, has allowed trade unions to accept these qualifications to their independence and indeed freedom of association is not only the confidence imparted by participation in a wider set of democratic institutions but also the fact that these qualifications have had a positive side in the form of some bargained compensation for this acceptance. Typically this compensation has taken the translated form of other legally enforceable 'powers' or 'claims' including a wide array of statutory contractual terms plus welfare entitlements of many and various kinds. Likewise in Pacific Asia, although freedom of association as well as the freedoms to organize and bargain have in many instances been greatly restricted, many compensations have been achieved through translation, at least where democracy and the rule of law have been in place. In Japan these take the form of the Labor Standards Law and a legally developed right to 'lifetime employment'. In Hong Kong and Singapore, they take the form of very good individual contracts of employment that incorporate many elements derived from the more protective International Labour Organisation (ILO) Conventions and, especially in the case of Singapore, very substantial citizenship rights with respect to housing and education.

Instead of further rehearsing this evidence here, I will now answer the question concerning the effectiveness of such translation as a means of empowerment abstractly by deploying an argument I have derived from Chatterjee's (1998) work. Although what I shall take from Chatterjee's work is abstract, I should point out that his original argument was also empirically produced: it arose out of his still ongoing radical rethinking of the history of the 'modern state' in India. The central point made in the course of this rethinking was that, as in the West but probably to an even greater degree, neither the colonial state nor its post-colonial successor has ruled in the way that liberal political theory suggested that it should – that is, by recognizing individuals as sovereign powers and therefore the creators of a civil society which ultimately controls the state and with which it has to deal as the ultimate source of state sovereignty. Instead Chatterjee reworks the insights summarized in Gramsci's concept of 'hegemony', and also contained in Michel Foucault's reflections on liberal governance and the concept of 'governmentality' (Burchell and Miler 1991) to argue that the state has actually ruled on the basis of its own presumed sovereignty. And it has done so in India not by constituting individuals as autonomous subjects as in the West but constituting them as members of what are often termed 'communities' such as castes, tribes or ethnic groups for its own governmental purposes, whether these be matters of economics, public order, health, education or whatever.

His point is not so much that state discourse about communities is phoney, although it often is, but that, phoney or not, it is how the state actually relates to its citizens and therefore represents, wholly unintentionally, the provision of a means through which the population may in time be able to transform itself into a new form of sovereign citizenry. That is, the way to democratize the state and civilize capital is not so much through painstakingly trying to create a civil society that might anyway be illusory but, instead, for individuals and groups to return the interest and attention of the state wherever and whenever it takes an interest in them. This is a thought that clearly has wide and counter-intuitive implications for the West too in that (contra much Western communitarian theory – for example Puttnam 2000) it suggests that the alleged decline in the vibrancy of civil society is more likely to be caused by the social *retreat* of the state rather than its activism. Obviously enough, the more immediate point I wish to take from all this is that where, as in much of Asia and the South more generally, governmentalities produce civil societies rather than vice versa, not only are states, almost by definition, better able to cede 'claims' and 'powers' than respect 'liberties' and 'immunities', but also when pressured they can actually deliver, as the postwar histories of Japan, Hong Kong and Singapore all attest. Thus the answer to the question why one might think that making the two human rights covenants translatable into each other's terms might provide an effective means of protecting the weak and the meek is that this is what is suggested by both the *modus operandi* and the histories of both Western European and post-colonial states.

To summarize, the bare bones of my argument for a paradigm shift in the ways in which we think and act in relation to human rights are as follows. First, there is the point derived from the work of Rawls and Weber that there are other ways of living the dignified life that human rights are supposed to secure than those premised on personal autonomy, individualism and self-reliance. In other words, one may be a respected member of not just the political and economic hierarchies validated in the West but also of the culturally and/or religiously validated hierarchies of the lands of the majority. Second, there is the point taken from Hohfeld that 'real' or justiciable rights may be constructed as claims and/or powers *vis-à-vis* the powerful as well as asserted as liberties. Third, there is the point derived from Gramsci, Foucault and Chatterjee that, especially where democracy and the rule of law are present, a reversible set of governmentalities rather that a largely mythic civil society represents the most effective way of exercising constraints on states and other superordinates. In brief, any value may be the source of a right, and any right may be constructed so as to make it legally and politically enforceable.

On this basis, then, it is possible to hope that we may be approaching the discovery of a strategy for overcoming the current crisis in the human rights sphere brought about by the tension between a discourse produced in a world of empires that is now being used in a partly globalized and, I hope, post-imperial world. Such a strategy would have to include:

- *recognizing* that the present array of human rights is only a selection from a far wider array of possibilities;
- *facilitating* this recognition by giving equal status to economic, social and cultural rights as compared to civil and political rights;
- *further facilitating* the practical acknowledgement of such recognition by allowing states to translate some specified liberties among those represented by civil and political rights into economic and social claims and/or powers, if and only if, this was likely to result in increased protection for their citizens;
- *finding* room in the array of human rights for claims to dutiful and benevolent treatment where other forms of rights protection are unavailable.

Thus my suggestion is that the lesson to be learnt from reflecting on 'community in the East' is not that the current privileging of civil and political over economic and social rights should be reversed but rather that valued aspects of Eastern difference and indeed communitarian approaches more generally may be preserved through allowing the limited mutual translatability of the two covenants. The principal advantage of embracing the idea of translation, then, is that it provides an internationally legitimate means with which to recognize and reconcile cultural differences.

Conclusion

The most general argument of this chapter has been that, if human rights are seen not as grand statements of human aspiration but instead as comprising an instrumentarium with which people may protect themselves against abuse, a way may be found of breaking out of the 'human rights box' that currently so limits their utility. Of course the general idea of human rights has a particular genealogy, but the result of acknowledging this should be the eschewal of claims to ideological or civilizational privilege rather than their amplification. Thus, while it is clear that the general idea may be traced back from the grand, eighteenth-century European and American declarations, through William Blackstone's 'Commentaries on the Laws of England', to the Magna Carta of 1215 and even the Ancient Greek and Roman Republics, this knowledge should be used critically and for reconstructive purposes. It should not be used as a justification for self-congratulation and an excuse for locking the box, as is the case with the current form of the doctrine of 'justiciability'.

This is for at least three reasons. First, as Marx made so clear in his 1843 text *On the Jewish Question*, and as the necessity of struggles on the part of multiple social movements have subsequently confirmed, the rights most often associated with this genealogy may also be seen as a way of ideologically and legally entrenching an egotistical individualism that may exclude the possibility of addressing the problems posed by inequalities of various kinds. Second, when knowledge of this genealogy is used to interrogate contemporary international human rights discourse, it becomes clear that the so-called Western tradition of rights thinking has been disproportionally influential given that the purpose of the international discourse is the protection of all the world's peoples relative to the actual dangers they face rather than simply those faced by the population of the West. Third, those who deploy knowledge of this genealogy for celebratory purposes display a breathtaking degree of sociological naivety. That is, they do not see that precisely because of the specificity of this genealogy the effectivity of the protections afforded by the rights involved is critically dependent on their imbrication with certain social-structural and institutional forms. Thus there is a tendency for them to think of these rights, once they have been proclaimed, as either self-enforcing or as automatically enforced by whatever institutions exist. The particular difficulty this creates is that, while many in the West are often very quick to condemn failing states, they are also very slow to criticize themselves for either setting inappropriate and therefore ineffective standards or failing to provide the resources necessary to meet whatever standards they insist upon.

The reconstructive lesson derived from this critique is that, provided international human rights discourse is freed from ethical imperialism, it is indeed capable of providing the basis for a universally usable defence against abuse. This is not simply because its sources of inspiration were anyway broader than those summarised as liberalism and extended to the tradition represented by Marx and various egalitarian social movements. Nor is it simply because, when compared with the liberal record, this tradition may be shown to have provided at least an equally effective basis for the protection of labor. More profoundly, it is because the new paradigm that emerges from this critique opens international human rights discourse to a wealth of locally and diversely generated insights as to how the abuse of human frailty might be reduced. In other words, it suggests a way in which the discourse may be saved from its possible fate as a figleaf which excuses abusers of their responsibilities and instead ensures that it becomes a more truly universal means by which they may be held to account.

There is, however, at least one major problem with my argument which even I, as its doting author, can see. This is the danger that translation could also be the occasion for regression, most obviously as regards gender relations. As one example among many others, this particular danger arises because the UN treaties are all much more insistent on gender equality than are the prevailing discourses on gender relations in many States Parties.

However, this is a difference that illustrates both the success of Western nations in obtaining UN assent to their understanding of what is right, and the difficulties of legislating for very disparate societies in that what is obviously right in some societies is not so obviously right in others. It is also a difference and a problem that requires me to elaborate a little on the procedural aspect of the translation work that I advocate. As I presently conceive it, translation would be a formal procedure additional but akin to the current arrangements pertaining to treaty reservations. That is, a formal, public and reasoned notification of an intention to translate would have to be lodged with the pertinent UN committee which would assess and comment upon it in the light of both its own understandings of what the relevant treaty requires and those set before it by other expert and interested parties. As a result not only would the international community know what was at stake and so be able to decide whether or not to accept the translation, but so too would the population of the State Party making the notification who should of course be able to make a political issue of it if they wish. In this way, then, the possibility of regression should be obviated although the result might often be an agreement to disagree, the refusal of the UN to sanction a particular translation, and severe doubts about whether or not a particular treaty article was being enforced. However, the resulting aporia and doubts are inevitable given the intrinsic difficulties of the human rights project, and the great advantage over the present situation would be that the problems the project faces would be made visible as opposed to remaining the sources of distrust that they are currently.

References

Alston, P. (1992) *The UN and Human Rights: A Critical Appraisal.* Oxford University Press: Oxford.

An-Na'im, A.A. (1990) *Toward an Islamic Reformation: Civil Liberties, Human Rights and International Law.* Syracuse University Press: Syracuse.

An-Na'im, A.A. (ed.) (1992) *Human Rights in Cross-Cultural Perspectives: A Quest for Consensus.* University of Pennsylvania Press: Philadelphia.

Badiou, A. (2001) *Ethics: An Essay on the Understanding of Evil.* Verso: London.

Bauer, J. (2000) 'Human Rights for All? The Problem of the Human Rights Box', in *Human Rights Dialogue*, Series 2, no. 1, pp. 1–3.

Bauer, J. and Bell, D. (eds) (1999) *The East Asian Challenge for Human Rights.* Cambridge University Press: Cambridge.

Berlin, I. (1969) *Four Essays on Liberty.* Oxford University Press: Oxford.

Broadhurst, R. (ed.) (1999) 'Crime and Indigenous Justice', Special Issue of *Australia and New Zealand Journal of Criminology*, (32)1.

Burchell, G. and Miler, P. (eds) (1991) *The Foucault Effect: Studies in Governmentality.* Harvester Wheatsheaf: London.

Chatterjee, P. (1998) 'Community in the East', *Economic and Political Weekly*, Feb. 7, pp. 277–282.

Dworkin, R. (2002) 'The Threat to Patriotism', *New York Review of Books*, 28.

Frank, T. (2000) *One Market under God: Extreme Capitalism, Market Populism and the End of Economic Democracy*. Doubleday: New York

Hamelink, C. (1994) *The Politics of World Communication: a Human Rights Perspective*. Sage: London.

Harrod, J. (1987) *Power, Production and the Unprotected Worker*. Columbia University Press: New York.

Hohfeld, W. (1919) *Fundamental Legal Conceptions as Applied to Judicial Reasoning, and Other Legal Essays*. Yale University Press: New Haven.

Huntington, S.P. (1997) *The Clash of Civilisations*. Simon and Schuster: New York.

Kent, A. (1993) *Between Freedom and Subsistence: China and Human Rights*. Oxford University Press: Hong Kong.

Koh, T. and Linden, M. van der (eds) (2000) *Labour Relations in Asia and Europe*. Asia-Europe Foundation: Singapore.

Kuhn, T. (1970) *The Structure of Scientific Revolutions*. University of Chicago Press: Chicago.

Langlois, A. (2001) *The Politics of Justice and Human Rights: Southeast Asia and Universalist Theory*. Cambridge University Press: Cambridge.

Linden, M. van der and Price, R. (eds) (1999) *The Rise and Development of Collective Labour Law*. Peter Lang: Berne.

Marshall, T. H. (1949) 'Citizenship and Social Class', in Turner and Hamilton (1994) *Citizenship: Critical Concepts*. Routledge: London,

Mauss, M. (1924) *The Gift: Form and Reason for Exchange in Archaic Societies*. Reprinted 1990 by Routledge: London.

Murphy C. N. (1994) *International Organisation and Industrial Change*. Polity: Cambridge.

Odinkalu, C.A. (2000) 'Why More Africans Don't Use Human Rights Language?', *Human Rights Dialogue*, Series 2, no. 1, pp. 3–4.

Putnam, R., Leonardi, R., and Nanetti, R. (1993) *Making Democracy Work: Civic Traditions in Modern Italy*. Princeton University Press: Princeton.

Puttnam, R. (2000) *Bowling Alone: the Collapse and Revival of American Community*. Simon and Shuster: New York

Rawls, J. (1999) *The Law of the Peoples*. Harvard University Press: Cambridge, Mass.

Shue, H. (1980) *Basic Rights: Subsistence, Affluence, and US Foreign Policy*. Princeton University Press: Princeton.

Taylor, C. (1999) 'Conditions of an Unforced Consensus on Human Rights', in Bauer and Bell (1999) *The East Asian Challenge for Human Rights*. Cambridge University Press: Cambridge.

Turner, B. and Hamilton, (eds) (1994) *Citizenship: Critical Concepts*. Routledge: London.

Weber, M. (1968) *Economy and Society*, 2 vols, University of California Press: Berkeley.

Wilson, R. (ed.) (1996) *Human Rights, Culture and Context*. Pluto: London.

Woodiwiss, A (2003) *Making Human Rights Work Globally*. The Glasshouse Press: London.

Woodiwiss, A. (1998) *Globalization, Human Rights and Labour Law in Pacific Asia*. Cambridge University Press: Cambridge.

Woodiwiss, A. (2001) *The Visual in Social Theory*. Athlone: London.

Note

1 Although the argument outlined here first saw the light of day at the conference from whence the present volume derives, a book length version has since been published (Woodiwiss 2003). Accordingly, I am happy to be able acknowledge the permission of The Glasshouse Press to reproduce sections of the published text in this development of the argument.

INDEX

For Product Safety Concerns and Information please contact our EU representative GPSR@taylorandfrancis.com
Taylor & Francis Verlag GmbH, Kaufingerstraße 24, 80331 München, Germany

www.ingramcontent.com/pod-product-compliance
Lightning Source LLC
Chambersburg PA
CBHW050709280326
41926CB00088B/2894

* 9 7 8 0 4 1 5 4 8 0 3 0 7 *